WELCOME TO BANGKOK
KRUNGTHEP

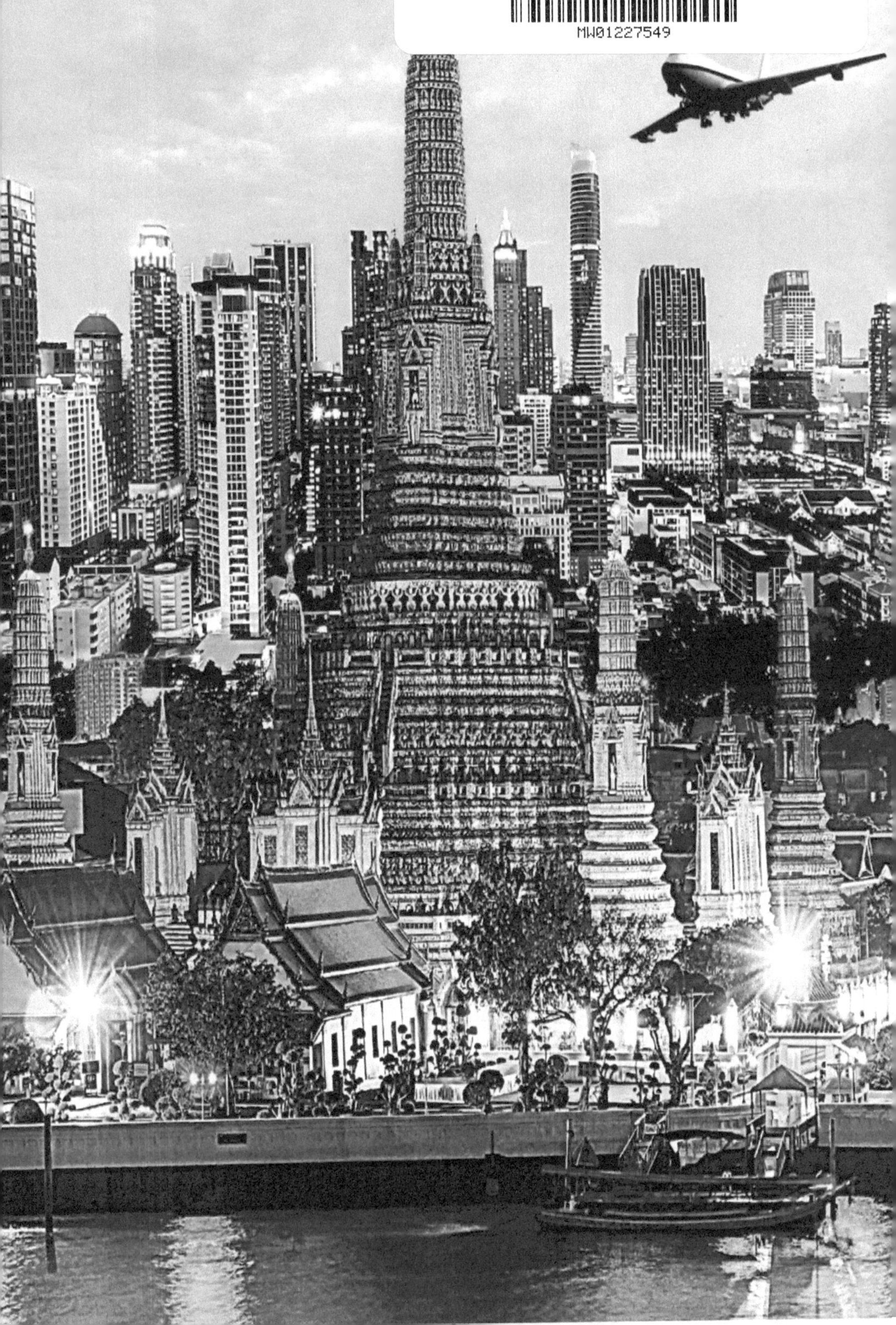

To my parents,

for always loving and supporting me.
I can't express how much my parents mean to me
and it seems that I have lost my best friends
when they passed away. I only can focus the
mind to wish them luck and happiness
for whatever they reborn,
that's all the best thing I can do.

Love you with all my heart.

The content and recommendations presented are not intended to be a substitute for a reader's tour program. The authors, photographs, or participants in this book disclaim any liabilities or loss in the content of places and advice herein.

Tourist Guide License No. 11-76006

"I will never forget my exciting experience in Bangkok. *At that time, I was only 10 years old. A country girl like me who was used to a small house with natural surroundings in the countryside with my parents came to the capital with the idea that Bangkok was like a paradise on earth and made me felt that I was a little angel there. The bad day in my life was when I got lost with my sister in the unfamiliar capital city. My sister supposed to take me a tour to the school she attended and the place she stayed (in a dorm) nearby. In the past, there were not many public buses, we had to scramble up that day (as usual during the working days), she took me on a very busy bus, imagine that the bus at that time was very crowded. My sister let me get on the front door but she had to get on the bus at the back door. We kept looking at each other all the time while standing far enough apart. But from the chaos of the people who went up and down; after that I didn't even see her in the bus. I wasn't aware of where she got out of the bus. I was terrified, but decided to hurriedly get off the bus at the coming stop and walked back in the direction the bus had come. It was a lonely sidewalk in the heat. On the side of a dusty road in the afternoon, seeing no one or even a house, my little heart trembled and my throat was dry, no money no cell phone or even public phones, It's the moment I heard the old Thai song; (the negative lyric with sadness) my mom usually sang along the radio, in my brain during trembling walking; 'Don't go to Bangkok, trust me, stay with tigers, it's safer than in Bangkok.'*

I started to panic and fear began to capture my little heart….

TABLE OF CONTENTS

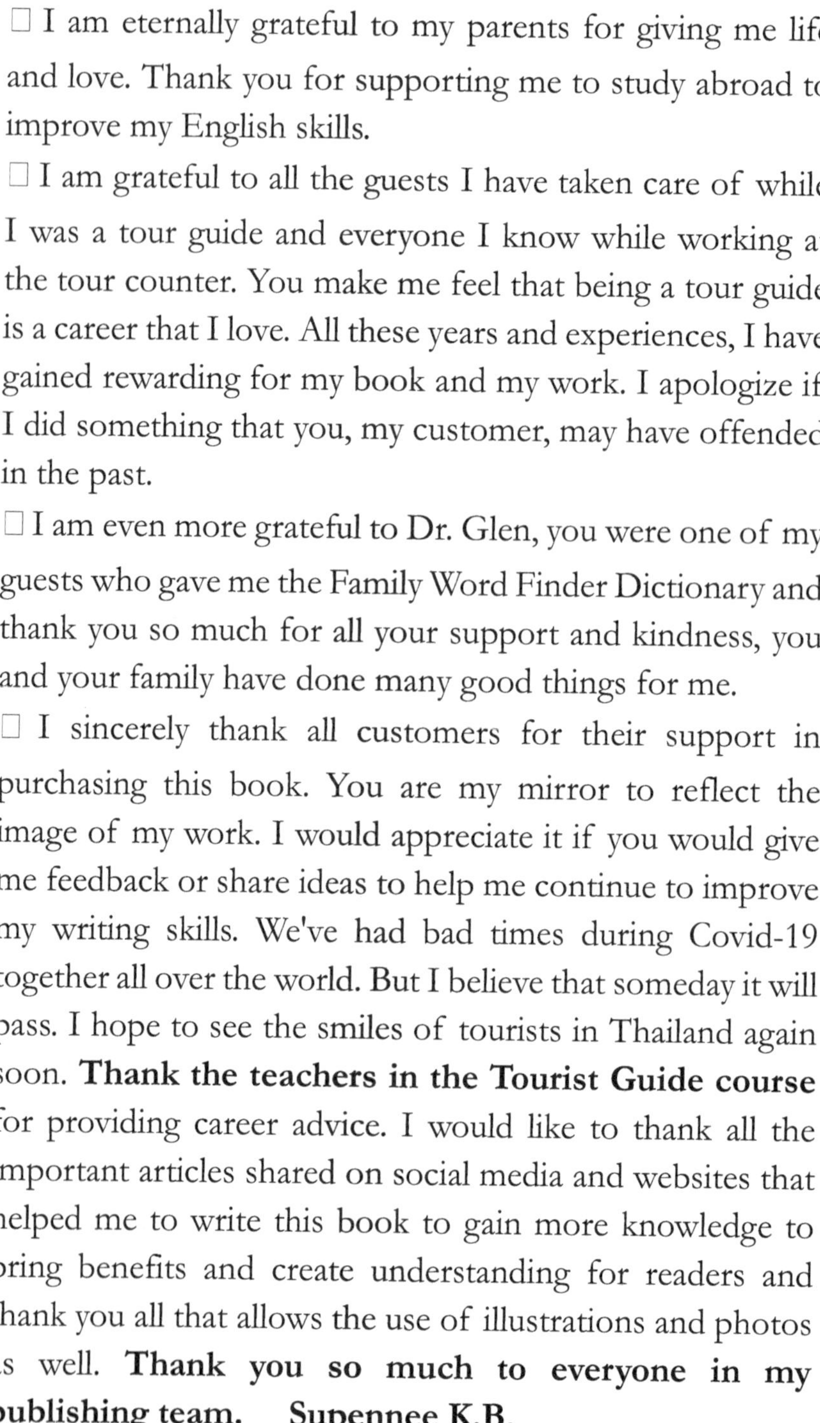

ACKNOWLEDGEMENT

□ I am eternally grateful to my parents for giving me life and love. Thank you for supporting me to study abroad to improve my English skills.

□ I am grateful to all the guests I have taken care of while I was a tour guide and everyone I know while working at the tour counter. You make me feel that being a tour guide is a career that I love. All these years and experiences, I have gained rewarding for my book and my work. I apologize if I did something that you, my customer, may have offended in the past.

□ I am even more grateful to Dr. Glen, you were one of my guests who gave me the Family Word Finder Dictionary and thank you so much for all your support and kindness, you and your family have done many good things for me.

□ I sincerely thank all customers for their support in purchasing this book. You are my mirror to reflect the image of my work. I would appreciate it if you would give me feedback or share ideas to help me continue to improve my writing skills. We've had bad times during Covid-19 together all over the world. But I believe that someday it will pass. I hope to see the smiles of tourists in Thailand again soon. **Thank the teachers in the Tourist Guide course** for providing career advice. I would like to thank all the important articles shared on social media and websites that helped me to write this book to gain more knowledge to bring benefits and create understanding for readers and thank you all that allows the use of illustrations and photos as well. **Thank you so much to everyone in my publishing team. Supennee K.B.**

Before I take you to see the details of Bangkok tours, I would like to introduce the historical background of Thailand to give you a better overview of the country in a nutshell. You will undoubtedly understand the way of life and be able to be a part of Thailand, no matter where you travel Bangkok and other provinces.

BRIEFLY HISTORICAL BACKGROUND OF THAILAND

AREA AND REGIONS

Thailand is officially known as **Kingdom of Thailand**. It is a nation-state located at the center of Indochinese Peninsula in Southeast Asia, formerly known as **"Siam"**, the government announced its official name change to Thailand since 1939. The evidence of inhabitants in Thailand was since 20,000 BC. **Tai** or **Thai** people began to migrate to this area in the 11th century and settled many of kingdoms; such as Sukhothai, Lanna, and Ayutthaya Kingdoms. Therefore; the historians started the Thai history from Sukhothai Kingdom, then Ayutthaya Kingdom, Thonburi Kingdom, and Rattanakosin Kingdom till nowadays.

Sukhothai Period (about 1249-1464); established by Por Khun Sri Intarathit; his son named Por Khun Ramkhamhaeng the Great who initiated the first Thai alphabet and made the kingdom was tremendously prosperous during his reign. There were 8 kings ruled the kingdom for about 215 years then become as a personal union with Ayutthaya Kingdom later. The stones with the inscriptions of the Thai alphabets during his period were kept at Bangkok National Museum.

Ayutthaya Period (about 1350-1767); Ayutthaya Kingdom was able to annex Sukhothai as part of it. The first loss of the city to Burma was in 1569 but King Naresuan the Great could fight against the Burmese Army and declared the independence for Ayutthaya in 1584. The kingdom was utterly different in the reign of King Narai the Great; when the foreigners came in the country for trade with the Siamese and the kingdom was vastly expanded by the king. Ayutthaya was attacked and destroyed and lost to the Burmese Army again in 1767, the second loss during the war with Burmese. There were 33 kings ruled Ayutthaya Kingdom for 417 years.

Thonburi Period (about 1767-1782); King Taksin the Great; who declared the independence for Ayutthaya Kingdom and established Thonburi; the eastern side of the Chao Phraya Riverbank; opposite to Bangkok City, to be the new capital within his period for 15 years. He's the only king of Thonburi Kingdom.

Rattanakosin Period (1782-1932 for absolute monarchy and become constitutional monarchy since 1932 in the reign of King Rama VII till at the present); King Phra Phuttha Yodfa Chulaloke the Great or called as King Rama I who was the first king of Chakri Dynasty (the present dynasty) established Bangkok to be the capital of Siam in 1782. King Chulalongkorn the Great or Somdej Phra Piya Maharaj or King Rama V; he was one of the beloved kings who led Siam to be modernized. He was the king who ordered the abolition of slavery and commoners in Siam and initiated the development to the country such as administrative system of provinces, establishment of railways, water supply, electric supply, postal and telegraphy, canals for water-transportation, and etc. King Bhumibol Adulyadet the Great or titled King Rama IX; has been the Thai's beloved king since his reign until now, he created many projects in nationwide; all the projects have been called as The Royal Initiative for Sustainable Benefits, for enhancing the quality of people's living. He was the longest-reigning king in Thailand and Southeast Asia for 70 years and 126 days (1946-2016).

King Bhumibol was called the father or "Por Luang" of all Thai people from his kindness and mercy to everyone in all regions. He has been acclaimed in Thailand for his contributions to the "Sufficient Economy" Philosophy. Kofi Annan, United Nations Secretary-General awarded King Rama IX the highest achievement award in human development.

Although His Majesty the king Bhumibol has already passed away, all of His Royal Projects has been inherited, maintained and developed by his son; the present king or **King Vachiralongkorn** or titled King Rama X, to sustainable benefits for his people to a better quality of lives all over Thailand. His Majesty King Phra Wachiraklao Chao Yuhua or King Vachiralongkorn; was born on 28 July 1952, is the current King of Thailand who is the 10th monarch of the Chakri dynasty. He is the only son of King Bhumibol Adulyadej the Great (Rama IX) and Queen Sirikit, he was appointed as the Crown Prince in 1972 when he was 20.

When King Rama IX died on October 13, 2016, he was expected to ascend the throne immediately but delayed because he wanted to give people time to mourn his father. He accepted the throne on December 1, 2016 and organized a funeral of His Majesty King Bhumibol Adulyadej on October 26, 2017. His coronation ceremony was held on May 4-6, 2019 but the Thai government has counted his reign as far back as his father's death. King Vachiralongkorn became the oldest of the Thai monarch to ascend to the throne.

Thailand is the 50th largest in the world with an area of 513,120 square kilometers (198,120 sq. mile) and the 20th largest population in the world; approximately 70 million. Thailand has a diverse landscape. The country is organized into the 77 provinces include **Bangkok**; the capital city. There are six geographical regions in Thailand; the Central, the North, the East, the West, the South, and the Northeast regions.

THE NAMES OF PROVINCES IN EACH REGION.

CENTRAL REGION: The **central region** is a floodplain. **The Chao Phraya River** is the largest river in the country, formed by the Ping and the Nan rivers that converge at Pak Nam Pho in Nakhonsawan Province making the central region the most fertile region and is regarded as one of the world's most important rice-growing areas. The names of provinces are **Bangkok, Nonthaburi, Pathum Thani, Nakhon Pathom, Samut Prakan, Samut Sakhon, Samut Songkram, Phra Nakhon Si Ayutthaya**, Ang Thong, Singburi, Chainat, Lopburi, Saraburi, Suphanburi, Nakhon Nayok, Nakhon Sawan, Uthai Thani**, Sukhothai,** Phitsanulok, Phichhit, **Kam Phaeng Phet,** Phetchabun.

WEST REGION: The **western region** of Thailand is the valleys and mountain ranges that lie from the western part of the north which border Myanmar and adjacent to the east coast of the Gulf of Thailand. The provinces along the west side of Thailand are **Tak, Kanchanaburi**, **Ratchaburi, Phetchaburi and Prachub Khiri Khun.**

EAST REGION: The **eastern region** is covered with short mountain ranges and adjacent to the east coast of the Gulf of Thailand and the provinces on the east side of Thailand are Chachoengsao, Chanthaburi, **Chonburi,** Prachinburi, Rayong, Sa Kaew and **Trat.**

NORTH REGION: The **northern region** is a complex high mountain area, where the highest point in Thailand is Doi Inthanon at 2,565 meters above sea level and is also covered by forests which are extremely important watersheds of the country. The provinces are **Chiang Mai,** Lamphun, Lampang, **Chiang Rai**, Phayao, **Mae Hong Sorn**, Nan, Phrae, and Uttaradit.

SOUTH REGION: The **southern region** of Thailand is part of the Malay Peninsula flanked by the sea on both sides. The narrowest point is at the Kra Isthmus and expands into the Malay Peninsula. Sonkhla Lake is the largest lake in Thailand, located in the southern region. The provinces in the southern part are Chumphon, Ranong, Nakhon Si Thammarat, **Surat Thani, Trang, Phuket,** Narathiwat. Pattani, Phatthalung, Songkhla, Yala, Satun, **Phang Nga and Krabi.**

NORTHEAST REGION: The **northeastern region** is the area of the plateau; mainly is at Nakhonratchasima Province. The names of provinces are Amnart Charoen, Bueng Kan, Buriram, Chaiyaphum, Loei, Mukdaharn, Khon Kaen, **Udonthani,** Mahasarakham, Kalasin, Nakhon Phanom, **Nakhon Ratcha Si Ma**, Nong Bua Lumpu, **Nong Khai**, Roi Et, Sakhon Nakhon, Si Saketh, **Surin**, **Ubon Ratchathani**, Yasothon.

Our language is the Thai language.

สวัสดีค่ะ ยินดีต้อนรับทุกท่านสู่ประเทศไทยค่ะ

Hello. Welcome everyone to Thailand.

Thai language firstly appeared in 1283 by King Ramkhamhaeng the Great. It was appeared nationwide and used in official work on March 31, 1933 and in 1942, the Office of the Royal Thai Academy was established for reforming the Thai language. Right now, The Thai language has 44 alphabets and 21 vowels with 5 tone marks for strokes. Each tone of Thai pronunciation refers to an exact word.

WEATHER

The weather in Thailand is tropical and hot; there are mainly two seasons in nationwide, the Monsoon season (June-October) and the dry season (November-May). The temperature is average about 22-35 Celsius. 71-95 F

Winter in Thailand

Provinces with cold climates include Nan, Chiang Rai, Phayao, Mae Hong Son and the highlands with mountainous areas known as "doi" especially; everywhere in the north and northeast where temperatures are 0-10 degrees Celsius. In November-February is ideal for a camping trip in the forest for the most Thai people. You can also note that the names of attractions for winter adventures often begin with “Phu” or “Doi”, which means “mountain” or high hill. The popular places for tourists to travel to experience the cool weather are Doi Inthanon, Phu Chi Fa, Phu Lanka, Phu Soi Dao, Doi Pui, Phu Kradueng, and etc.

POLITICS AND GOVERNMENT

Thailand has a democratic regime with the king is as head of state which is a constitutional monarchy and parliamentary democracy. The present king is King Vajiralongkorn (King Rama 10th of Chakri Dynasty) The head of government and the leader of the cabinet is the prime minister.

PUBLIC HEALTH SYSTEM

Thailand has a good **Public Health System**. We have lots of modern hospitals and medical clinics with high technology situated in all major provinces each region. Drug stores with registered pharmacists are found easily in Thailand for common diseases.

COVID-19 SITUATION AND PREVENTION

The latest update for Thailand Pass is good news; Thailand Pass will be canceled; effective from July 1, 2022 onwards. But travelers will still need to show proof of either vaccine certificate or Covid Free-Test results. The ATK tests will be checked by airline staff at check-in for departure and on arrival in Thailand. People in Thailand and travelers are advised to strictly follow the standard of prevention such as wearing a mask in public, hands hygiene by washing hands with soap and or using hand sanitizer and keep a physical distance by arranging seats with distance between one another in public transport, restaurants, coffee shops, theaters, etc.) Hand sanitizers/Gel alcohol are found everywhere.

Between July 2021 and mid-March 2022, after the government eased restrictions, 86 filmmakers from 33 nations came to Thailand. Foreign filmmakers choose Thailand to shoot 196 movies. (revealed by the Ministry of Tourism and Sports)

The recommendations for wearing masks in Thailand on June 17. 2022 were: Wearing the mask is required inside any building unless you are in a restaurant or coffee shop, fitness center, singing in Karaoke clubs, but after activities; you have to wear mask on again. Another is at the crowded areas like public transports, markets, and concert place etc. The other is the request to those who were infected from the Covid-19 before should wear masks during speaking or stay the same area with others.

INTERNET

There are major internet companies are available at the airport such as; True, AIS, DETAC. Since we are encountering "The New Normal" Era; work from home or during vacation somewhere are lifestyles happened nowadays, so the internet is available everywhere. The Ministry of Tourism and Sports and together with the Tourism Authority of Thailand supposed to launch a project called "Workation Paradise Throuout Thailand" to provide new opportunities for hotel industry by upgrading its services for more choices to the guests who would like to combine work and travel together.

THAI CURRENCY

Our currency is called **Baht.** The banknotes are 1000, 500, 100, 50, and 20 Baht. The coin notes are 10, 5, 2, 1 Baht and the small ones are 50 and 25 Satangs. (100 Satangs equal 1 Baht)

ECONOMY

Thailand is classified as a newly industrialized economy; manufacturing, agriculture, and tourism are leading sectors of the economy.

Thailand is the world's largest producer and exporter of rubber, accounting for 40 percent of the world's natural rubber. Other high-value crops are sugar-cane, cassava, chicken, pork, mango, mangosteen, guava, pineapple, tropical fruits, shrimps, corn and soybeans. Thailand is also known as the world's major food producer and is the 5th largest food exporter in the world besides; Thailand is the largest dairy producer and exporter in Asian countries. The automobile industry in Thailand is the largest in Southeast Asia and the ninth largest in the world.

Thailand has many natural attractions such as national parks, mountains, forests, beaches and places full of history. There is an ancient civilization with architecture and antiques that are unique in art of different eras in every province across the country. Thailand is the **"Land of Smiles"** or recognized as **"Yim Siam"** from people around the world. It has been ranked as one of the best destinations in the world, making tourism to be one of the leading sectors of the Thai economy.

THE CULTURAL AND NATURAL WORLD HERITAGE SITES BY UNESCO

Thailand is ranked the 7th richest country in cultural heritage in 2021; according to a survey of global marketing communications firms and The Wharton School at the University of Pennsylvania, USA.

It was reported that the U.S. News & World Report website announced the list of rankings. It was named the **2021 "richest country in the world's cultural heritage,"** in collaboration with BAV Group; a global marketing communications agency, and The Wharton School at the University of Pennsylvania, USA, which surveyed more than 17,000 people from 4 regions.

The issue of considering the ranking of countries with rich cultural heritage includes the way to access to culture with a rich history, great food, a wealth of historical and geographical attractions, the top 10 "richest countries in the world in cultural heritage" for 2021 are firstly Spain, then Italy, Greece, France, Mexico, India, **Thailand,** Egypt, Turkey, and Japan.

There are six cultural and natural world heritage sites by UNESCO in Thailand.

- ❖ **Ayutthaya Historical Park; was declared a cultural world heritage site in 1991 of a true national Thai Art,** located at the center of Ayutthaya Province, 75 Kilometers from Bangkok. The sites include Wat Ratchaburana, Wat Mahathat, Wat Phra Srisanpetch, Wat Phra Ram, and The Hall of Phra Monkol Borpit.
- ❖ **Sukhothai Historical Park was** declared a cultural world heritage site in 1991. The areas are part of the Historic Town of Sukhothai and Associated Historic Towns. The site also includes the associated historical parks in Kham-Phaeng-Phet province and the Sri Satchanalai District of Sukhothai. Sukhothai Historical Park is in Sukhothai Province; the northern region, nearby the center of town, away from Bangkok about 440 kilometers, and the other is in Kampaeng Peth is the nearby province to the south of Sukhothai.
- ❖ **Thungyai-Huai Kha Khaeng Wildlife Sanctuary coupled with Thung Yai Naresuan Wildlife sanctuary was declared** a natural world heritage site in 1991. The total land is about 1,536,296.29 acres, homes of a large number of wild animals and plants; like all other sites in the mainland of Southeast Asia.

The two sanctuaries are located in Uthaithani, Tak, and Kanchanaburi Provinces. Buses for all provinces and plane for Tak.

- **Ban Chiang Archaeological Site was declared a cultural world heritage site in 1992 according to its ancient red pottery** which describes the site of the unique cultural tradition of living and civilization of about 5000 years ago. The site is in Udorn-Thani Province; located in the northeastern region or called "Isan" for Thai; the distance is about 650 km from Bangkok. There are flights to go to Udonthani.

  You can travel to Udonthani by public buses at the Northern Bus Terminal at Mo Chit; ride the Skytrain from the airport to Mo Chit Station and catch a taxi there or get the train to this province from Bang Sue Grand Station.

  Udonthani is one of the provinces, close to the Nongkai province; the border of Laos, where you can start exploring Isan Provinces from here easily. It's a large town with many attractions. Don't miss to admire the beautiful pagoda at Wat Pah Ban Thad; the famous temple since Luang Ta Phra Maha Bua was alive (1913-2011); he's the former abbot who's a leader of many of "Phra Pah" or "Forest Monks" to access to the Buddha's Teaching from his Concentration Learning for Mindfulness and become worshipped among not only; the monks but also the people in Thailand and others. He started the help Thai Nation Project; a charitable effort dedicated to helping the Thai economy and brought tons of gold to the Treasury.

- **Dong Pha-Yayen-Khao Yai Forest Complex** was declared a natural world heritage site in 2005; with the areas of Dong Phraya Yen and its group; namely, Khao Yai, Thap Lan, Pang Sida, Ta Phraya National Parks, and Dong Yai Wildlife Sanctuary.

The total lands are 6,155 Square Kilometers which covers the 6 provinces; Nakorn-Ratchasima, Saraburi, Nakornnayok, Prachinburi, Sa Keaw, and Buriram Provinces. It has been called "The East Forest of Thailand". **Khao Yai; a famous and popular attraction among tourists, is** the first National Park of Thailand situated in Nakorn- Ratchasima province where are homes of wild elephants; which are seen along the road. **Ride to Khao Yai for an hour by motorway.**

❖ **Khaeng Krachan National Park;** the largest national park in Thailand was recently named a UNESCO World Heritage Site on July 26, 2021. It consists of rainforest on the eastern slope of The Tanasserim Mountain Range; the borderline between Thailand and Myanmar, with the highest peak of 1,513 meters above medium sea level, with many wildlife and rare plants, found here. The climate is dramatically humid with heavy rains. The tourist attractions are open only during August-October in the areas of Khao Phanoen Thung and Ban Krang. Kaeng Krachan is one of the popular destinations for adventurers for camping and Butterfly lovers. One of the amazing Thailand Tours is to see a swarm of butterflies all over the land in April here. When you go to Hua Hin or Cha Am Beach, you will pass by Khaeng Krachan National Park. **You can reach Thailand's six cultural and natural World Heritage sites at UNESCO World Heritage Convention from Bangkok conveniently.**

NEIGHBORING COUNTRIES

Thailand **borders** Myanmar in the north and the west, Laos in the north and the northeast, Cambodia in the east, the southeast, and the Gulf of Thailand and Malaysia in the south. There is The Andaman Sea on the western side.

Once you are in Thailand, you may add our neighbored countries to your lists so you can make your vacation more valuable in one time traveling to Southeast Asia.

Laos is connected to the north and northeast of Thailand. You can go by public buses from the northeastern Terminal in Bangkok, trains, and by direct flights to Vientiane or Luang Phrabang (for 1 hour). You can also drive the car thereby crossing the borders. There are many boundary posts in many provinces such as Nan, Uttaradit, Phayao, Chiang Rai, Loei, Nong Kai, Nakhon Phanom, Bueng Kan, Mukda Harn, and Ubon Ratchathani.

- ✓ **Vietnam**, you can travel from Laos easily by bus or travel by plane from the two airports in Bangkok.
- ✓ **Cambodia**; there are boundary posts in Si Saketh, Surin, Sa Kaew, Chanthaburi, and Trat Provinces. You can ride public buses or vans from Bangkok to reach the checkpoints or get a direct flight there.
- ✓ **Myanmar**; there are boundary posts in Chiang Rai, Chiang Mai, Mae Hong Sorn, Tak, Kanchanaburi, Prachub Khiri Khun, and Ranong Provinces where you can reach them by local buses, taxi, and direct flights from Bangkok, but traveling by plane from Bangkok to Myanmar is more convenient.
- ✓ **Malaysia**; there are boundary posts in Yala, Satoon, Songkla, and Narathiwas Provinces. You can go from Bangkok by bus, train, and car to cross the border.

Some of the countries are not connected to Thai borders but it's easy for you to catch the planes from Bangkok for a short visit like in **Hong Kong, Singapore, and Indonesia.**

RELIGION

Buddhism is our main religion (95% of the population). Others are Islam, Christianity, Hinduism, and others. There are about 40,000 temples and monasteries in Thailand. The temples are called **"Wat"** and followed by its name; most of the temples are full of ancient architectures and sculptures. Not only temples you can visit but some of them have museums to tell about historical backgrounds for the provinces you go. Thailand is also full of many suitable temples and Centers of Meditation Practices which are popular among Buddhist foreigners from all over the world to stay ordained and learning mindfulness during their vacation. You have to contact the temple you would like to be ordained and follow the monk disciplines in Thailand.

THAI FOOD

Thai food is always Rice and chilli; which are the most important ingredients. Other ingredients are basicly include garlic, lime juice and fish sauce. Thai food is mainly served with rice (steam rice or sticky rice) and side dish. The most famous dish in Thailand since the ancient time is called **"Namprik Platoo"** or a kind of steam mackerel fish mixed with chili paste, along with a side dish like steam vegetable and fresh tropical vegetable supplied as a set. Most of the Thai curry contain coconut milk and fresh turmeric, similar to Indian food, Malaysia and Indonesia. Many of the Thai dishes are also originally Chinese dishes (many Chinese people in Thailand) such as congee, steamed buns, rice vermicelli and pork leg with rice, soy bean paste, soy sauce and tofu dish.

Thai food is eaten with a variety of dipping sauces and condiments such as chili fish sauce, chili powder, chicken sauce, chili sauce, and sides. One of the foreign chefs said that Thai food is not simple but more emphasized in arranging incompatible parts to create a well-rounded meal.

Thailand is also acknowledged as "The Kitchen of the World". All regional Thai-style food has a variety of flavors and quite unique recipes. The mixture of all ingredients makes the taste mellow and perfect in all dishes. Thai food menus can be divided into 4 major regions; the North, the Central, the Northeast, and the South. The food cooked has its own uniqueness; depends on the geography, climate, and food sources of each region. Anyway, the Thai culture of cooking food is accepted by people all over the world, in terms of deliciousness, beauty, and delicate showing the uniqueness of Thailand. The food menus I would like to recommend for you to taste are all our favorite menus.

Tom-yum Koong (Shrimp Spicy Soup with mixed herbal plants, fresh chili, seasoning with lime juice, and fish sauce) it's good when it's served right away after cooking and it's perfect with steam jasmine rice.

Pad Thai (Fried Rice Noodle and shrimps or prawns mixed with a special sauce which tastes sweet and sour; (the sauce made from tamarind juice and brown sugar seasoning with fish sauce or salt) served with bean sprouts and chives. Real Pad Thai comes only with eggs, sliced tofu, and dry tiny shrimps. **Pad Kra-prow; a** hot and spicy fried meat with herbal basil leaves), this is a Thai popular dish or a portion of fast food to be made fast for making you feel appetized; we order this on top of rice and a fried egg which is good enough for one meal. It costs about 50 Bahts from street food or a small restaurant or food court inside the department stores. **Curry; is** a kind of spicy soup from coconut milk mixed with green or red chili paste added to some vegetables and meat. It's super delicious from chili paste made with great finesse by the cook and fresh coconut milk cooked for a good curry.

Massaman Curry; its taste is noticed as sweet curry from the mixed spicy chili paste and peanuts for the curry sauce. It's cooked with meat, potatoes, onions, and tomatoes. This dish is similar to Indian food but tastier and spicier to be a typical Thai-style dish. It's mostly popular among tourists.

Panang Curry; is different from Pad Panang, its milder chili pastes mixed with coconut milk cooked with meat and basil leaves. **Pad Panang;** Red Chili paste stir-fried with meat and sometimes mixed with vegetables.

Larb is the local northeastern and northern dishes. It's the mixture of ground meat and herbal plants including chili powder for a spicy taste; the differences between these dishes of the two regions are the tastes and some herbal ingredients to make their smells easily noticed. Larb becomes the signature dish for anyone who goes within those regions.

Must try **Som-Tum or Papaya salad;** it's a hot and spicy pepper with fresh garlic pounded with raw and crispy chopped papaya, dry tiny shrimps, peanuts, lime juice, and tomatoes added. It's good to eat with fried or grilled chicken and sticky rice. **Yum** is a kind of Thai salad but the mixtures are hot peppers, vegetables, and grilled meat. (Spicy taste is recommended.)

Fried or Steamed fish/meat/seafood with spicy chili sauce or sweet and sour sauce. It's a seafood dish that you can find in many restaurants.

- **Rice / Egg Noodles or Plain Rice soup**; a bowl of noodles is called "Guay Tiew" and a bowl of rice is called "Kow Thom"; both of them can be mixed with meatballs or sliced/ground meats in soup and spring onion. Noodle is a light meal and helps you get rid of hungry very well, but rice soup is normally for breakfast or late dinner. Find them everywhere and most are popular Street food.
- **Fried Rice** with /without meat is popular for a fast meal or "made to order" cooked by the vendors' nearby streets and restaurants. Most of the fried rice is ordered with shrimp or crab meat. If you don't know what you want, start with fried rice.

- ❖ **Stir-Fried meat or without meat;** is "made to order" cooked by vendors, for people who are selective for the meal; for example, some are Vegan, some don't eat beef, some don't eat some kinds of vegetables, etc. We call this kind of restaurant or street vendor "Arhan Tham Sung"; it's nice because it's just cooked in front of us.
- ❖ **Moo Krata/ Suki/;** the hot pot for grilling or cooking by you in a restaurant; served with raw meat, vegetables, and unique sauces. It's popular among the family and a group of friends, by sit around the stove and enjoys cooking together.
- ❖ **Khow Kaeng** is a meal easy, fast, and saves money for a rush hour during working days; there are many small restaurants or vendors with trolleys full of ready-made food and rice to help rush people for a fast meal or take away.

What is your favorite Thai Food?

❖ **Thai Desserts; fruits and flour are the** most of the ingredients of Thai desserts included with coconut meat, juice, and milk and sugar, the pandan leaf; the green leaf shrub used for a beautiful and sweet smell for Thai dessert.

According to CNN Report; there are some of Thai desserts; namely **mango with sticky rice** and Thab **Tim Krob**, are praised to be the world's 50 most famous desserts. Mango; with many types of them, is a popular fruit in Thailand during the hot season. The mango served with sticky rice is a ripe mango; yellow color skin, taste sweet and eat with the sticky rice which top with coconut milk (awesome taste, you must try), sometimes it's served with mango-ice-cream. Thab Tim Krob; is a piece of water chestnuts coated in tapioca flour in small cubes, when it's served, the cubes will be put in local syrup and fresh coconut milk and some ice put on top. It tastes sweet, crunchy and cool to make you feel fresh and energetic during the hot day. There are hundreds of desserts in Thailand waiting for you to try. Basically, the Thai desserts have coconut milk and palm **sugar or sugarcane for their main ingredients with coconut meat, banana, taro, chestnut, beans, pumpkin, eggs, sticky rice, herbal plants, etc; some is formed as cake and some is liquid form served as a hot dish but some is mixed with ice for eating in the summertime.**

Besides; the restaurants and street food, all kinds of Thai food can easily be found in many places you are:

- ❖ **Food courts and Food Plaza** inside the shopping malls or department stores have many good menus for you to try. You can find a variety of street food to try at the Food Court of Suwannaphum Airport on the 1st Floor as well.
- ❖ **Buffet** at some hotels; many hotels provide Buffet Breakfast, Lunch, and Dinner with a variety of International food at affordable prices. It's a choice for having meals at a nice and cozy place.
- ❖ **Superstores, the local markets, and grocery stores; that** provide raw food and things you need for daily uses, are found almost everywhere. There is nice food packed for ready-to-eat and it's OK. **7/11 or other convenient stores** are everywhere for serving you ready-made Thai food all the time.
- ❖ **Petrol Station;** nowadays, the new popular place for eating is at a gas-station anywhere you meet. I love it **because it's easy to park and many kinds of food to eat.**

FRUITS IN THAILAND

Must try Durian! There are many typical **Thai fruits** known all over the world like; Mango (Please try ripe mango with sticky rice), Durian, Rambutan, Longan, Pineapple, Orange, Banana, Lychee, Papaya, Dragon fruit, Grape, Mangosteen, Watermelon, Guava, Tamarind, Jackfruit, Pomegranate, Strawberry, Avocado, Custard Apple, etc.

You can find many nice fruits in superstores and in a local market. Try to eat the fruits in season.

Fruits in Nov-Jan; grape, ripe papaya, rose apple, guava, pine apple, sugar cane, jujube, water melon, and sapodilla.

Fruits in Feb-May; tamarind, grape, watermelon, banana, jackfruit, mango, durian, lychee, and rambutan.

Fruits in Jun-Oct; mangosteen, ripe papaya, bananas, Thai melon, longan, pomelo, orange, guava, and custard apple.

Talat Or Tor Kor is recommended for a high quality of fruits; it's nearby Jatujak Market where there is plenty of fruits and delicious meal at the food plaza. (It's not so far from the airports, BTS: stop at Mo Chit Station and walk about 10 mins. Or ride MRT: stop at Kham Phaeng Petch Station is direct to the market.

THAI FESTIVALS

The famous festivals nationwide are **Songkran Day Festival and Loy Krathong Day**; Songkran Day is the grand festival of Thailand with the public holidays are in between 13th-15th April, is recognized as the Thai New Year Celebration which may last up to 10 days. The other is Loy Krathong Day Festival; on Full Moon Day in November during high tide.

You can check the events when you reach the hotel for the present events or if you suppose to visit Thailand for big events, please also check the specific events that may be performed within the hotel. I would like to suggest you look around the areas of the hotel you book. The big events are usually planned and announced in every province like Songkran Day and Loy Krathong Day.

Most festivals are performed inside the temples but some of them are with parades in the center of town and some are performed at some public areas like markets, malls, shrines, and many hotels located nearby the river; usually have celebrations for the events at the hotel; especially, Loy Krathong Day, etc.

Several festivals are related to Buddhism and traditions of the old town sites and dated according to the Full Moon Day of the Buddhist Lunar Calendar, so the dates are not fixed. Kathin Tradition is one of the most popular for Thai Buddhists; the tradition is to offer the monk robe to a temple where lack of robes and to create harmony among the people who comes from different places to join this ritual after the Lent Day. It's only a month period for Kathin Festival and quite important for the Thai Buddhists and monks all over the country.

SONGKRAN FESTIVAL

This is **"The Water Festival"** in the country. The people use water and a nice fragrant powder to greet each other at New Year Celebration. The meaning of water festival is "Fresh and clean"; for welcoming good things to life, washing away the sufferings, anxiety, and distress.

The tradition has been held since the ancient time with the belief that if we pay respects by pouring the water upon the Buddha statues and the statues of the important Monks, bath the parents; or the elderly in the family, the monks in the temples nearby homes; we will be blessed for being lucky and happy. We sometimes only pour on their hands but bathing parents have been a long-standing tradition in Songkran Day. One of Songkran's traditions is creating Sand Pagoda; it is an old tradition during Songkran Day and found only in Thailand and Laos nowadays; from a Buddhist belief since ancient times; to pay respect to Buddha and to express apology for taking the soil on the feet (by walking in temple's area) from the temple.

The fun time of the Water Festival among the young children is by shooting or splashing water in the streets with plastic guns. **Khaosan Road and Silom Road** are the most popular places in Bangkok. Chiang Mai is a popular province in Thailand and most tourists think of this festival whenever they are in Thailand. **April** is the beginning of the hot season in Thailand and people enjoy this Water Festival very much. Parties are everywhere during this long vacation the hottest time of the year**. Each region has its own culture** of Songkran Day Festival; but with the same belief among Thai, it's the Family Day, the day people await Songkran Day to have a chance to be back to hometowns to meet parents and all members of their family. Not only to enjoy each other but also can make merits by offerings and set free animals during the long holiday together at least once a year. There are several incidents during Songkran Day Festival you should be careful: Traffic jams are along the roads to all regions and cause many accidents. Many hotels in the tourist areas are fully booked. Many famous restaurants are crowded with customers. Most tickets for all kinds of transportation are fully booked and drunkards are around the town because everyone stops working and enjoys their parties. You have to be careful during participation in the events. Be careful of the dirty water thrown or any perfumed powder and the lewd men who tried to find a chance to touch female's body.

Loy Kra-Thong Day Festival is famous for fireworks and riverboat parties during the high tide on Full Moon Day in November; after Buddhist Lent Day one month.

"Kra-thong" is blooming lotus-shaped baskets made from banana leaves decorated with flowers and lighted candles with incent sticks for paying respect to The Goddess of the Rivers. It's the belief that if we ask for forgiveness from the Goddess of Rivers; to forgive us the bad things we have done like, throwing things into the rivers and canals anywhere before, we will get a good wish come to life. The glittering of plenty Krathongs floating along the waterways of the Chao Phraya River in Bangkok gives a picturesque view and an amazing night by the river all over the riverbank areas. Don't miss to join the event on the riverboat; you can book the Dinner Cruise Tour for enjoying Loy Krathong Festival from the Tour Service or the River City Pier.The grand Loy Krathong Festival is well known as **Yi Peng or the Lantern Festival in Chiang Mai at Ping River**. Several lanterns are released into the sky, it's nice to see but you have to be careful of the fire lanterns; some of them dropped on the market and caused the damage before.

One of the big events is on **Chinese New Year Day** at Yaowaraj. Thais of Chinese descent will observe the tradition **for 3 days**, which are pay day, worship day and travel day. **The Pay day** is the day before the end of the year. It is the day when Thai people of Chinese descent must go to buy food, fruit and various offerings before the shops closed for a long vacation. **The worship day** is; in the early morning to pay homage to various gods, the offering is Three meats are pork, duck, chicken, or add fish liver as five meats liquor, tea and paper money. In the late morning, pay respect to the ancestors, parents, relatives who have passed away for an expression of gratitude according to Chinese traditions. The offerings consisted of sweet and savory dishes (mostly made according to what the deceased liked), as well as the burning of paper money, paper clothes to dedicate to the deceased and it is considered the time when the family can be gathered as much as possible, will exchange red envelops of money after eating together. In the afternoon, worship for the spirits of the deceased brothers and sisters. The offerings will be khanom khong, candle candy, taro with sugar, silver and gold paper along with firecrackers to ward off evil and for good luck.

The day of travel is the New Year's Day. It is the first day of the first month of the Chinese New Year. Nowadays; the Chinese will hold an ancient custom of worship and blessings from elders and loved ones by bringing golden oranges to give for the reason in representing the sign of happiness or fortune, it is a day in which the Chinese are considered auspicious and refrain from committing sins, no debt collection, don't touch the broom, and will dress in new clothes to go out for blessings and relaxing outside their homes. Long weekends make the roads empty.!

The Candle Festival is one of the famous festivals in Ubon Ratchathani Province in the northeast region; called "Isan" by locals. It's one of the tourist attractions for Thai and foreigners. The tradition of Candle Parades happens during The Buddhist Lent Day every year; it's a day after Full Moon Day on the 8th Month of the Buddhist Lunar Calendar.

Many big candles are carved into different images related to Buddhism with the decorations and performed by the people or the groups of communities and agencies of the province. It's fantastic to see all the beautifully carved candle parades in the street during The Candle Parade Contest at the center of Ubon Ratcha Thani Town. **Must see! You can go to Isan by local buses at the Northern Bus Terminal at Morchit near Jatujak Park. Domestic flights are available every day to Isan provinces.**

The other one of famous festival in the Isan Region is called the **"Bunk Fai Phaya Nak"** Festival on the day when Buddhist Lent Day ends. People go to Nong Kai Province for watching this strange phenomenon. They are natural phenomena of lights overspread from Mae Khong River to the sky and it's believed by worshippers that; the lights come from Phaya Nak; a mystical serpent in the river during paying homage to Buddha's Relic. The river is always crowded with their hope to see those Phaya Nak show the lights above the water to the sky, some shout and cheer with joy and the people seem to be very excited to see these mysterious serpents in the sky.

MORE OF INTERESTING FESTIVALS

- The Vegetarian Festival in Phuket
- Phi Ta Khon or the Ghost Festival in Loie
- The Buffet Monkey Festival in Lopburi
- The Umbrella Festival in Chiang Mai
- The Elephant Festival in Surin
- The Chinese New Year Festival at Yaovaraj Road in Bangkok
- Phu Khao Thong Festival at Wat Saket etc.

TRANSPORTS

Skytrain (BTS) and Underground (MRT); are the mass Rapid Transit Networks in **Bangkok** and Continuing Areas. It is a rail transport system in urban areas in Bangkok and its vicinities. It was opened for the first time in 1999. Currently; there are total of 8 lines, 137 stations, a distance of over 210.25 kilometers. The additional lines and included with extension lines are in progress for about 124 kilometers long with 103 stations. Besides; in the future, the Airport Rail Link will have the connecting lines for Don Muang, Phayathai, Lad Krabang and U Tapao; it's under the process and may be finished by 2027, will pass by 5 provinces; Bangkok, Samutprakan, Cha Choeng Sao, Chonburi, and Rayong. *****From **Suwannaphum International airport;** you can start your trip on your own easily. We have **taximeters and public buses** on the 1st Floor, **car hire** on the 2nd Floor, **BTS** or Airport Link at the Basement Floor (you can connect MRT or subways by this Airport Link Skytrain) to downtown conveniently.If you prefer more comfortable and save time for traveling to your hotel, then choose **Tour Services and AOT on the 2nd Floor** for going to your hotel; by showing your destination and checking the prices at their counters, this is the best way for guarantee you to go to the right place you book, especially; when you are the first time in Thailand. **Some hotels have multiple branches and have the same name.** Therefore, you should show your address to the driver before leaving the airport in order not to waste time and expenses, because perhaps you will be lost most of the day until you find your own place to stay. The traffic sometimes is so bad that you might get bored of Bangkok.

Domestic flights are affordable prices and convenient to all regions of Bangkok. There are 2 airports; Suwannaphum Airport; the international airport and Don Muang Airport for mostly domestic and neighboring countries like Laos, Vietnam, Cambodia, and Myanmar.

Tuk-Tuk or "Sam-raw" is good for the short trip only. Please always ask the price before riding and don't let him wait for you. They are not tourist guides so please consider when they offer you too cheap a tour you are interested.

Taxi Meter; please choose the new car and photo the registered no. inside the car, make sure you have the address of your destination to show to them. Many of taxi drivers came from upcountry and may get lost, I have to tell some of them the direction as usual for saving money.

Ferry Boats, River Boats, shuttle boats, and Express Boats are available for avoiding traffic on the road but don't ride the crowded boats, especially in rush hours. A boat tour along Klong San Saep Canal gives you a nice view of Thai living along the canals and many of beautiful temples located along the canal's sides. The boat transport is a choice when you want to travel faster; if you are close to a pier in Bangkok.

Local trains to other provinces are available at the main railway station; it's at **Bang Sue Grand Station; the state Railway of Thailand for inter-city and commuter rail which is located** near Chatuchak Park. You can still book a train at Hua Lum Phong Station; the former state railway, and other stations you are near also.

Song Thaew Pick-up; this transport is modified from pick-up truck by having 2 rows of passenger-seats at the back; one can sit with the driver. It's mostly found in upcountry provinces. You can say the address you want to go to the driver before getting in. It cost about 20 Bahts or more (depend on the price of petrol which increased) for going around the town. You can still see some of them along the suburbs of Bangkok.

Sam Lor; the tricycly where you can go maximum 2 persons only. Sam Lor is still found in some provinces for a short distance.

Motorcycle-Taxi; is tremendously popular among Thai in Bangkok because it's faster than riding a public bus especially; during rush hour, it can go through the narrow sub-lanes along the alleys in downtown of Bangkok. Ask for a helmet if you need to ride.

PRODUCTS AND SOUVENIRS

The top 10 products for exporting in Thailand are automobiles, computers, rubber, plastic, chemical, steel, rubber products, jewelry, and machines.The popular souvenirs most tourists shop is jewelry, Thai silk, hand-made products, dried fruits, and some herbal products.Thailand's gem and jewelry ranked as the country's fifth largest export (about 3.62%); as the report of Jan-Aug 2021, it grew by 27.6%. The jewelry in Thailand is well known for beautiful design and clarity of stones besides; the workmanship in jewelry is widely appreciated and recognized by global market.

According to the emphasis for research and development by the public sector which is known as GIT Standard or Gem and Jewelry Institute of Thailand, to ensure the products bought for creating the consumer's confidence and satisfaction in the quality of the products. The famous stones are ruby and sapphire which found a lot in Thailand. The famous high-quality jewelry is from reliable stores with a product guaranteed. They are popular gifts for tourists because of the designs and neat workmanship in both cheap and expensive ones. The famous gemstones are **Rubies and Sapphires in Thailand**. Chan-tha-Buri Province is famous for precious stone mines, but the central market is in Bangkok. **Thai silk** is a unique hand weaving that is known for its patterns and colors. When worn, it is elegant and unique, no matter what kind of clothing it is designed to be for both women and men.**If you would like to see a variety of handmade products, there is an exhibition of Regional Thai Products at Muangthong Impact Exhibition Center which is announced on their website. You can admire a very beautiful Thai design in textiles at the Queen Sirikit Museum of Textile in The Grand Palace. It is where Her Majesty the Queen (in the reign of King Rama IX) initiated to promote and support the Thai handicrafts in Thai silk and cotton and made it well-known worldwide.

THE NATIONAL PARKS

The idea of establishing a national park in Thailand was initiated after World War II. Due to the rapid population growth rate caused the need for cultivation area to be increased. The result from the need for lands, therefore the forests were damaged and transformed the areas into fields. Besides; along with the advancement in material and technology, modern weapons were used to devastating hunting wildlife. The number of wild animals were decreased rapidly, some of wild animals have gone extinct. Finally, the government realized that the country should protect natural resources; especially forests and wildlife were important.

Therefore; the idea of establishing an arboretum, forest park and national park were discussed and designating **Phu Kradueng Forest** in Loei Province as the first forest park in the year 1943. The management of the forest park was suspended during the World War II. In 1959, the government that time ordered the Ministry of Agriculture and the Ministry of Interior to jointly determine the forest area for the establishment of a national park again. Later on, the results of the meeting of the committee determined that 14 forest areas were selected to be established as a national park, including **Doi Suthep Forest, Doi Inthanon Forest, Doi Khun Tan Forest, Lan Sang Forest, Nam Nao Forest, Thung Salaeng Luang Forest, Phu Kradueng Forest, Phu Phan Forest, and Phu Phan Forest. Khao Yai, Khao Sa Bap Forest, Khao Khitchakut Forest Slob Mountain Forest Sam Roi Yot Forest and Khao Luang Forest.** In 1961, there was a royal decree that various areas become a national park with Khao Yai being the first national park of Thailand in 1962.

At the present, Thailand has about 155 national parks (the total is included with the ones in the process of establishing) in about 48 provinces which are rich forests and wildlife. There are varieties of jungle activities; like, trekking, hiking, nature trails, camping, fresh water rapids rafting, zip line, jumping, camping in many national parks in every province. There are about 1,200 places like bungalows and camps for your accommodation in the parks of Thailand.

You should get details from the National Parks Office from their websites for accommodations or can find hotels near the park for adventure, please also check the weather and activities the park allows tourists that time.

BEACHES AND SEA SHORE

Thailand's territorial waters have more than 900 islands distributed in 19 provinces; the biggest island is Phuket, then Samui, Chang, Talutau, Pha Ngan and Kood Islands respectively. The province which has the most islands is **Phan-gna** Province, with 155 islands, then **Krabi** Province, with 154 islands and **Suratthani** Province, with 108 islands. There are about 521 beaches distributed in 21 provinces; about 360 beaches of the Gulf of Thailand and 161 beaches of Andaman Sea.

There are 29 popular islands in this book for you to explore. You will enjoy many water activities such as scuba diving, snorkeling, skiing, surfing, swimming, nature trails, and etc. These beautiful islands will make your dream destination more perfect and memorable on your long holiday.

WELCOME
to Bangkok

BANGKOK

Bangkok is the capital and most populous city of Thailand. It is the center of government, education, transportation, finance, banking, commerce, communication and prosperity of the country. It is located on the Chao Phraya River Delta. The Chao Phraya River which is the main river of Thailand flows through and divides the city into 2 banks; namely Phra Nakhon (Bangkok) and Thonburi. Bangkok has a total area of 1,568,737 square kilometers. It has a registered population of over 10 million people.

The actual name of Bangkok is listed in Guinness World Records as the world's longest place name at 168 letters;

"Krungthepmahanakorn Amornrattanakosin Mahintharayutthaya Mahadilokphop Nopparat Ratchathani Bureerom Udomratchanivwate Mahasathan Amornpiman Ourtan Satith Sakkathatiya Wisanu Khamprasit".

The meaning of the name is; the vast city of the Gods, Prosperity, Blessings from many sacred Buddha statues like The Emerald Buddha, with nine Gems and great beautiful Palaces. It's a heavenly deity that is the residence of the kings who incarnated down which were bestowed by the sacred God; names Thao Sakka Devaraj. It is where God Vishnu (God of Architecture) has created.

The Thai call Bangkok **"Krungthep Mahanakorn"** for the official use and call Krungthep in general. It's not noticed by locals for the real long names until Assanee and Vassan; the Thai popular rock-star artists, who made the names as a beautiful song, and that's the time people seem to recognize this long name of Bangkok.

Bang-Korg or Bangkok was the name called since the Ayutthaya period but it was found in the western documents appeared in many words like Bancoc, Bancok, Banckok, Banckock, Bangok, Bancocq, etc. According to the shreds of evidence; The word "Bangkok" was written by the French Patriarch in the documents sent to Paris and King Rama IV took this word used for calling the capital city in the official documents sent to the Westerners and the name of Bangkok was officially used since that time.

Bangkok or "Krungthep Mahanakorn" or "The City of Angels" was established as the capital of Thailand in **1782** during the reign of King Rama I of the Chakri Dynasty; the current reigning dynasty of the Thailand Kingdom or Rattanakosin Era. The names of kings belonged to Chakri Dynasty and the period of reign is as follow:

1. King Rama I or Phrabat Somdet Phra Phuttha Yod Fah Chullaloke Maharaj. (1782-1809)
2. King Rama II or Phrabat Somdet Phra Phuttha Lert Lah Napalai. (1809-1824)
3. King Rama III or Phrabat Somdet Phra Nang Klao Chao Yu Hua. (1824-1851)
4. King Rama IV or Phrabat Somdet Phra Chom Klao Chao Yu Hua. (1851-1868)
5. King Rama V or Phrabat Somddet Phra Chulachom Klao Chao Yu Hua. (1868-1910)
6. King Rama VI or Phrabat Somdet Phra Mongkut Klao Chao Yu Huaa. (1910-1925)
7. King Rama VII or Phrabat Somdet Phra Pok Klao Chao Yu Hua. (1925-1935)
8. King Rama VIII or Phrabat Somdet Phra Maha Ananda Mahidol. (1935-1946)
9. King Rama IX or Phrabat Somdet Phra Boromchanakathibet Maha Bhumibol Adulyadej Maharaj. (1946-2016)
10. **King Rama X or Phrabat Somdet Phra Maha Vajiralongkorn Phra Vajira Klao Chao Yu Hua is the present king. He was crowned at the Phaisan Thaksin Hall on May 4, 2019.**

On the sixth of April every year is observed as the Chakri Memorial Day. The Thai commemorate the virtues of the Chakri Dynasty Kings who ruled Thailand with peace, happiness, and fertility since 1782. **Prasart Phra Thep Bidon; a royal Castle** at Wat Phra Kaew, is enshrined the statues of the 9 reigns as a memorial and Thai people will come to worship here on April 6 every year. Tourists can visit the inside.

Bangkok is the 11th most skyscraper city in the world in 2020. Various shopping centers or cultural landmarks such as the Grand Palace, and many old temples are in Bangkok; about 500 temples in this capital city. **Siam Square, Khao San Road and night entertainment areas** attract many foreign tourists.

Besides; Bangkok has more than what the big and modern city looks like, you can still find the old styles of buildings and houses which are full of history where you can still vaguely recall being stayed or living in the past. Many important events and places occurred here because of the relevant places located in Bangkok. It is also the main center for all kinds of business and traveling to all regions conveniently by all kinds of transportation. You can unknowingly reach the provinces adjacent to Bangkok that have been incorporated into the metropolitan area. There is no doubt that you will have a variety of attractions when you are in Bangkok.

THE BANGKOK METROPOLITAN REGION

The city's urban sprawl reaches into parts of the six other provinces in form Bangkok Metropolitan Region making Bangkok an extremely primate city. The six provinces border Bangkok; namely starting from the north, **Pathumthani, Nonthaburi, Cha Choeng Sao, Samutprakan, Samutsakon, and Nakhonpathom.** With the exception of **Chachoengsao** (I also add Chachoengsao for your information; next to Chonburi), these provinces and Bangkok formed The Bangkok Metropolitan Region.

Whenever you visit Bangkok, you will have a chance to look around at other provinces nearby conveniently by public buses, sky trains, subways, cars, taxis, and tuk-tuk to explore the variety of things, local living, and places within Bangkok and its neighbors together.

Suwannaphum Airport is located in Samutprakan, the province where is called "Paknam" or the mouth of The Chao Phraya River which flows to the Gulf of Thailand. The old airport located in Bangkok is Don Muang Airport; the airport for domestic and available only on some routes to other countries. Both of the airports are not so far from each other. **The shuttle buses between the two airports are free**; you only show the flight ticket. Please check the flight time before catching the shuttle buses because it's quite a long ride and sometimes wait too long. If you prefer going fast; a taxi is recommended. I don't recommend sky trains or shuttle buses if you have less than 2 hours before the next flight.

"***My first time in Bangkok was in 1968 when I was young.*** *I never knew that Bangkok what did it looked like but always heard my parents' era hits on the radio and was able to sing along and there were many songs about Bangkok, some was negative poems but some song was beautiful; paint Bangkok liked a paradise, I kept this beautiful picture in my mind and dreamed of seeing Bangkok one day. When my father took my sister to study in Bangkok, I thought my dreams were about to come true. I remembered how excited I was when my father allowed me to visit my sister for a summer vacation in Bangkok and had a plan to take us to various places there.*

When I entered Bangkok that time, I felt a little upset with the dusty roads and smoke from all transports everywhere especially when I entered the downtown of the city, I was amazed by the buildings and the streets which full of almost all of kinds of automobiles, I started choking on car smoke and was uncomfortable with the heat and dusty environment. The house we stayed (my father's friend's house) was woefully small and smelt bad. (I thought about the bad smell of a dirty canals nearby) Suddenly, I thought of my hometown and my mom.

I will never forget my exciting experience in Bangkok.

At that time, I was only 10 years old. A country girl like me who was used to a small house with natural surroundings in the countryside with my parents came to the capital with the idea that Bangkok was like a paradise on earth and made me felt that I was a little angel there. The bad day in my life was when I got lost with my sister in the unfamiliar capital city. My sister supposed to take me a tour to the school she attended and the place she stayed (in a dorm) nearby. In the past, there were not many public buses, we had to scramble up that day (as usual during the working days), she took me on a very busy bus, imagine that the bus at that time was very crowded. My sister let me get on the front door but she had to get on the bus at the back door. We kept looking at each other all the time while standing far enough apart. But from the chaos of the people who went up and down; after that I didn't even see her in the bus. I wasn't aware of where she got out of the bus. I was terrified, but decided to hurriedly get off the bus at the coming stop and walked back in the direction the bus had come. It was a lonely sidewalk in the heat. On the side of a dusty road in the afternoon, seeing no one or even a house, my little heart trembled and my throat was dry, no money no cell phone or even public phones, it's the moment I heard the old Thai song. **It was the** *the negative lyric with sadness, my mom usually sang along the radio, in my brain during trembling walking;*

'Don't go to Bangkok, trust me, stay with tigers, it's safer than in Bangkok.'

I started to panic and fear began to capture my little heart, but never cried. I didn't know how to find my father and sister; no money, no cell phones or even public phones. I walked like a blind girl but never stopped. "I have realized now that the extreme fear makes people fight for survive; like it happened to me that time when my fear went to the extreme, it gave me the light shone in my head, I took a deep breath and stopped walking for a while at a bus-stop and thought about where my sister and I had to go, suddenly, I walked faster along the road; from bus stop to bus stop until some houses by street appeared at the opposite side. I crossed the road there with hope. The dark clouds were gone when I saw the sign of my sister's school where the dormitory she stayed was at the same area. Yes! We supposed to come over here. Although I didn't see my sister or my dad yet but I felt safe when I met someone who seemed to be my sister's classmate whose house located within this lane and she took care of me well until I met my sister and my dad in the late afternoon finally. This experience was dramatically worse than a nightmare; my father punished my sister for negligence in caring for me who's still a little girl because I might be kidnapped into slavery. Gangsters abducting children for slave labor were a frequent headline back then that I never really knew.

My dad then was my first tour guide in Bangkok since I came back to go to school again when I reached thirteen years old, but we came to live in Nonthaburi area because it's cheaper than in Bangkok. He took me tour around Bangkok and explained the roads and places I should come or avoid, I was unmistakable learner and I got used to more places in Bangkok, Nonthaburi and Samutprakan by roaming around during weekend and school long holidays with my friends. I would like to tell you that almost half of the population of Bangkok come from upcountry to find work and do business which many people are struggling to make a living. One of the key things is to be proficient in where and how to get to a place. There's no doubt if some of the taxi drivers you ride does not know where your hotel locates although he uses the navigator from cell phones therefore; you will pay more when he gets lost. When I was sixteen years old, I moved to Bangkok for the high school (pre-university) located near the Siam Square and stayed at the hostel at Ratchaprasong Intersection; the center of Bangkok, for many years before going to study in the Philippines. I was an expert amateur guide for my friends who visited Bangkok whenever my friends and relatives from other provinces visited our family. My favorite hobby I usually did was riding the public buses to see Bangkok included with the neighbor provinces every weekend, I thought that it's a good way to learn direction for many locations. I love my career when I started working as a tourist guide and I chose to be a driver for my clients as well.

For almost 50 years I have lived in Bangkok. I can say that Bangkok is the most wonderful city for me. **It's a city full of flavor** *to life such as; beautiful, ancient, smiles and laughter, quiet corners, noisy and crowded, modern high-rise buildings, slums, garbage dumps, clogged pipes, flooding, marathon traffic jams, pickpockets, delicious Street-food, a pleasant coffee shop, flea markets, the view of beautiful Chao Phraya River, the shadow of Krung Thonburi, and etc.* **Wow!**

I have tried to find in other provinces before but I feel like I've never been anywhere like Bangkok. Bangkok has everything I like. I love Bangkok and the Thonburi side and of course I will never get lost again! ***Tour with me and you will understand why Bangkok is one of the world's most popular tourist destinations!***

WHY BANGKOK IS YOUR DESTINATION?

BECAUSE BANGKOK IS ONE OF THE MOST EXCITING CITIES IN THE WORLD! It's among the world's top tourist destinations and has been named the world's most visited city consistently in several international rankings. The reasons Bangkok becomes a popular destination among the most tourists will give you the ideas for your plan, how you will arrange your trip, where you should go when you should come here, what your vacation will be and whom you will be with! **The top things you should know about Bangkok:**

1. **Bangkok is the first step to Thailand.** It's the best place in Thailand where you can settle and plan the trip yourself before deciding what to do the next steps. You need to look around Bangkok at least 2-3 days before going to other places. Getting to know Bangkok It will make you feel more familiar with Thailand when traveling upcountry.
2. **Bangkok is full of warm hospitality and smile.** When you enter Thailand at the airport, you will undoubtedly get a smile from the Thai you meet. You will surely get a warm welcome from the staff of the hotel with a **"Wai"** which is a sign of respect and ready to help. Giving a "Wai" in general; is by connecting your palms together between your chests and lowering your head until the nose touches the index fingers. There are some forms of "Wai" like paying respect to others, especially the elderly people who sit; we sit on the floor in a position of squatting and wai.

Wai for Buddha Statue or monk is by kneeling on the floor or sitting on the legs and wai. But for paying homage to Buddha image or monks we usually **"Krab";** by pressing the thumbs between the eyebrows and bending down the head (it's like a child-pose in yoga) with the palms on the floor three times. Krab three times is the way to respect Buddha, His Teaching, and His disciples who is Buddhist monk, can do to the sacred pagoda enshrined the Buddha's relic. Wai comes by saying **"Sawasdee Ka"** while men say **"Sawasdee Krub"** for hello, good morning, etc.

Ka and Krub are suffixes added during speaking for showing politeness. **"Kob Khun"** means "Thank You" We smile at each other even though we don't know each other before and give a Wai to others for thanking or asking for help. Smiling always comes along with Wai every time.

The favorite words you may hear in Thai: "Sawasdee" means good morning, afternoon, evening, hello, hi, and goodbye. **"Kin Kow Rue Yang?"** means "Did you have breakfast? Or Lunch? Or "Dinner". Kin means Eat, Kow means Rice, Rue Yang means Did you? We usually call Kow for the meals; but if you would like to mention "Breakfast", you can say "Kow Chow", "Lunch" is "Kow Klang Wan" and "Dinner" is "Kow Yen". Chow is morning, Klang wan is noontime and Yen is evening. **"Pai Nai"** means "Where are you going? "**Kor Toad**" means; when you do mistakes; like saying sorry, excuse, or apologize to someone, but can also say during someone's speech or have a conversation, or asking for help from others you don't know. "**Mai Pen Rai**" means "Never mind", "It's O.K" "**Mai Mee Pan-ha**" means "No problem", or "No worry" Don't forget to add "Ka" and "Krub" for women and men and smile!

3. Bangkok is affordable in all things you need.

Compared to other Asian countries of the same status, Bangkok is best known and popular for cheap and good food, transport, consumer goods, and accommodation.

You can find food on the street or even in some restaurants; like 50 Bahts a meal, stay in a guest house for 200 Bahts and ride a public bus from the airport to Khaosan Road for about 60 Bahts. For example; you can survive about 25 US dollars per day for necessary factors in Bangkok, You can get a portion of nice food from street vendors nearby your hotel, or at a international fast food, grocery stores, superstores, and 7/11 which are found everywhere for your fast meal and some personal items for your daily uses.

- **International Food is** found in many places; like restaurants, hotels, or some department stores with food courts, community malls, or neighborhoods of tourist areas.
- **Many Coffee shops and Café** have snacks and food to eat for your convenience when you also want a cup of brew coffee in one place.
- **Gas Station** is also a place where you can see a convenient stores and bathrooms. You can get some food, coffee and others you may need.

The accommodations in Bangkok are priced from their grade and location (see details in location) but it's still particularly cheap such as; hotels (started from 500 Bahts), guesthouses (started from 150 Bahts), homestays, condos, apartments, hostels, houses for rent, and resorts.

If you prefer elegant and luxury hotels, they are mostly available everywhere in Bangkok, especially by the riverbank and the center of downtown.

The good locations which are convenient and comfortable such as; **Silom Rd., Sukhumvit Soi 1-101, Khaosan Road, Siam Square, Yaowaraj, Riverside areas, Nearby airports, Nearby Democracy monument, Nearby Victory monument, Nearby Skytrain stations along Phahonyothin Road, Soi Aree, Saphan Kwai areas, Bang Sue, Jatujak and Ratchada Road. The suburban areas of Bangkok** are also nice to stay as long as there are Skytrain stations (BTS and MRT) like staying at the areas of **Ladprow, Ramindra, Rangsit, Chaeng Watthana, Rama II, Petchakasem, and Bangkok-Nonthaburi Roads.**

Nowadays, the transports are extremely convenient from the rapid transportation network of rails. Almost everywhere in Bangkok location have Sky trains and Undergrounds so tourists can choose many nice hotels with low prices along with the suburb. **The fares for transport** are cheap for both public transport and taxi-meter. You can start your trip from the airports by Skytrain, taxi, car rent, buses, vans and T**our service**. Learning how to travel in Thailand is by getting a tour; especially you are the first-time traveler, because you will feel more comfortable and worth for your time. In my view, it's the best way to get to know the city fast if you have had a professional tourist guide going with you. I really recommend if you are a first-time traveler in Thailand. Traveling in the low season (May-Sept) will save your money indeed for both accommodation and transport. If you love the rainfalls and are not crowded then choose the low season to economize your expenses in everything in Bangkok.

4. **Bangkok is the center for easy and convenient traveling around by a variety of good systems and modern Transport.** All kinds of transport are in Bangkok: **Sky trains and Undergrounds** can make you feel easy by dropping anywhere you want rapidly**, buses** give you a local experience, **tuk-tuk** makes you feel different, **taxi meters** sometimes can take you to the wrong place or getting lost but it's still OK to save your time, **trains** help you to have a nice trip to upcountry for changing climate, **planes** make you feel relaxed when you want to go far away provinces within an hour **and fun walk** along footpaths to indulge the atmosphere of the local livings and street food!

5. **Bangkok has both mirrors of modernization and rural locations.** Bangkok's global ranking the sixth in 2021 as a convention city of the International Convention Destination Competitive Index compiled by Australia-based convention and meetings industry consultancy Gaining Edge. The city is ranked in terms of its infrastructure, accessibility, logistics, professional community, destination appeal, and cost to meeting planners and organizers. Thonburi side is where you can still see the old style of living in Bangkok like some wooden houses along the riverbanks located near the tall buildings of 5-star hotels, and luxury condominiums.

Most of the residences in Bangkok come along with flea markets-places and temples, it's where you will see people wear local clothes; like old-fashioned robes wrapped around, the people bath in the canal in front of their homes, and see some merchants with the old style of carrying poles for selling kinds of stuff walking along the dense buildings in Bangkok and cried out for their goods. Most of the old restaurants have wooden cabinets with glass to give a clear view of the fresh food they have prepared to make customers confident in various ingredients in cooking.

6. Bangkok is full of delicious street food.

It makes you have a good appetite anytime you see or just smell it from the street you pass. The food cost you with reasonable prices and you can find something to eat 24 hours in Thailand. You must try noodle soup, Pad Thai, fresh-made Rice with ordered recipes you wish, grilled pork and chicken sticks, meatballs, etc. The famous street food is at Yaowaraj Road, Dinso Road, the Giant Swing areas, nearby the riverbanks, Silom Road, Sukhumvit Road, Kasetsart University Skytrain Station, Tha Wang Lang areas, Tha Phra Chan areas, Or Tor Kor Market, Onnuch BTS station, Asoke Station, Nonthaburi, Nearby Wat Saketh, Banglumpoo Market near Khaosan Road, etc.

7. **Bangkok is Safe for living and roaming around.**

If you choose a hotel in a city center surrounded by a lot of residential properties, you will feel that it is not scary, because it's like you're in one of your homes. Please avoid places that are rarely visited. You may have to look at the **locations** I wrote in the upcoming chapter.

Don't choose the hotel because it's too cheap as it might waste your travel time. Don't trust the taxi driver if he offers you a hotel. When someone persuades you to go along, you must first hesitate. The easiest way is to find a place near the BTS station or popular areas in downtown Bangkok. You may pay a little more but you can save on traveling time instead, and because you will be able to travel with no limit. Remember where you are staying, what Sky train station is nearby, or such as a building or sign. Try to use public transport such as trains, buses, ferry boats, songthaews (public pickups) or by foot. Join a tour with a tour guide if it's your first time and remember the places you went. It's the best way to access into the city well from a licensed guide and I think this is the best way to help you learn about the locals and quickly learn how to get around on your own. Everywhere in the world there are good people and bad people, if you run into problems, you can go to tourist police points all over the city. Generally speaking, I think we have to always be aware of the people and the environment wherever we go, untrustworthy in order to take care of yourself, from the beginning abroad and use discretion before paying every time, whether online or offline, during the journey. **When booking your accommodation online, always make sure that the booking date matches the date you booked.**

Anyway, most of the Thai characteristics are friendly and helpful people and this is one of the charms of Thailand that you want to visit more than once.

8. **Bangkok is close to Khao Yai National Park with many homes of wildlife and adventurous places that keep you excited from many activities.** It takes about **one hour and a half** to reach this popular park. Many tourists want to come to Khao Yai for seeing some wild elephants along the roads! Before going to Khao Yai National Park, you should get details from the National Parks Office on their websites for accommodations or find hotels near the park, checking the weather and activities the park allows tourists at that time. Khao Yai can be a one-day trip for sightseeing from the airport by starting early in the morning and come back in the evening.
9. **You can go to the beaches for one day trip from Bangkok.** You can ride from Bangkok for one to two hours to reach the ocean; resort towns, snorkel, dive, and lie down by the beaches; see details in Pattaya City, some islands in Sattaheep, or visit the old resort town at Cha-am and Hua Hin by bus or taxi. Samutprakan locates at the mouth of The Chao Phraya River which flows to the Gulf of Thailand; where you can see the nice seagulls by the shore and have a nice Thai seafood here; you can get there by Skytrain. Please see all details of **the popular 29 islands** in this book for more exploration where you can reach a beautiful beach easily from Bangkok anytime.

10. **Bangkok is the first step to the unique Thai architecture and history.** There are about 500 temples located in Bangkok and the well-known ones in the world are in Bangkok such as; Wat Phra Kaew, Wat Pho, and Wat Arun.
11. **Location of the Grand Palace; The landmark of Thailand is in Bangkok.** Please see all details about the Grand Palace; a wonderful place that you should add to your first Thailand tour list.
12. **Bangkok National Museum is tremendously popular for visiting nowadays.** It is the first national museum in Thailand. located in Phra Nakhon District, in Bangkok. It's the areas of the Bowon Sathan Mongkhon Palace or The Front Palace which was the palace area of Somdej Phra Bowon Ratchachao since the reign of King Rama I. The location is Sanam Luang Ground in the west and facing the Volunteer Monument and is beside the current National Theater. **Inside the museum** consists of various royal residences, including the Siwamokkhaphiman Throne Hall, Phutthaisawan Throne Hall, Isara Winitchai Throne Hall, Wiman Village, Isarat Rajanusorn Throne Hall Museum Building, and Mahasurasinghanat Building.

The museum was originally located in the Grand Palace at the Concorde Tower (The Sahathai Samakhom pavilion at present) which is called "Museum" or "Museum of the Concorde Tower", with the opening ceremony on September 19, 1874. Later on, His Majesty King Chulalongkorn (King Rama V) moved the museum for exhibition of ancient items into some parts of the Front Palace area which was empty when the position of the Front Palace was already cancelled that time.

In the reign of King Prajadhipok (King Rama VII), the whole area of this royal palace of the Front Palace were transformed into a museum and the Phra Vajirayan Library were established as Museum for Bangkok in 1926. Within the areas of the museum, there are exhibits about Thai national history; the History of Art and Archeology in Thailand, Fine arts and ethnography including various temporary exhibitions. Bangkok National Museum is the museum with the largest number of visitors in Thailand, there were approximately 710,007 Visitors from its record in 2012. **I recommend t**he Bangkok museums, it's a place for helping you to get more details about Thailand's history. **You can visit here when you visit** the Grand Palace.

13. Bangkok has pleasant weather all year round.

Bangkok has a tropical savanna climate like most of Thailand regions. It's influenced by South Asian Monsoon but it has three seasons; hot, rainy and cool with average of 22-35 Celsius; the hottest month is in April, the monsoon season is about May-Oct. Bangkok is always still a good time for visiting all year round; you will find it's cheaper during the rainy season than the hot season with a pleasant climate!

14. Bangkok never sleeps!

Everywhere you go or walk by the streets, you see a market or vendors selling goods like; fresh food, fruits, clothes, second-hand products, used cars, electrical appliances, antiques, Buddha statues, religious supplies, gold and jewelry, street food vendors, furniture, etc. Flea markets for food and goods are found both day and night.

Food vendors at night markets or as locals call "Talat Tho Lung"; which means "Markets till morning" are Thai favorites. This kind of market is very popular among Thai people because some of them work late at night and many people who enjoy nightlife love here after parties. The market is full of delicious food and some market has souvenirs for selling to tourists. One of the reasons to go night markets is because it's not hot at night so the people feel relaxed and more comfortable than in the daytime.

15. You can enjoy many big events and exhibitions in Bangkok all year round at **The Impact Exhibition Center, The Sirikit Convention Center, BITEC Bangna, Siam Paragon Hall** and many exhibitions for seasonal product sales at a large mall in Bangkok. We are well known for OTOP Exhibition; it's meant One Tambon-One Product; Tambon means sub-district, where the locals produce their home products for their communities.

**The big event of many exhibitions is performed at Impact Exhibition Center (the place is not so far from the airports); for OTOP products every year. The huge exhibition halls are where you can enjoy shopping from all regions in Thailand together with cultural shows.

You will enjoy the atmosphere of each region created at OTOP and get to know all kinds of Thai food from the regional Thai food fair.

Normally the fair at Muang Thong happens in November-February. Don't miss it if you are in Bangkok! It's nice to walk around the air-con market areas from 10 am- 22.00 pm. The favorite among Thai is all regional food sections where you can eat and take away. You can taste the food from every province in one place. There are hotels near Impact Exhibition Center and you can check for big events here like, Motor Expo for all automobiles displayed and sales, books, travel, Money Expo, Big Sales, the special royal projects exhibitions, and etc. If you have a long holiday in Thailand, please try once for the special events here. Some of the main events and exhibitions are performed at **the Royal Paragon Hall, Siam Paragon Bangkok.** If you are near this area (Siam Skytrain Station), you can check if there is an interesting exhibition.

16. **Bangkok is home to large shopping malls.** You can find them in all districts; for central districts at Siam Skytrain Station, Ratchaprasong intersection, Sukhumvit Lines, Victory Monument, Ladprow Intersection. Please see all details in Large Shopping Malls in Bangkok.
17. **Bangkok has many kinds of Entertainment and Amusement Parks for family tourists.** The popular fun parks in Bangkok and nearby are Siam Park near the airport, Dream World near Rangsit, Safari World at Ramindra Road Soi 109, and Ocean World at Siam Paragon at BTS Siam Station.
18. **Bangkok has a good Public Health System and is full of well-known hospitals**. You can find lots of modern hospitals and medical clinics with high technology all over Bangkok. The drug stores are easily found everywhere in Bangkok.

19. **Bangkok is tremendously cosmopolitan and international.** There are many global foods, stores, product chains, and imported goods from all over the world in Bangkok. The area between Sukhumvit Soi 1 and Soi 63 is popular as residential area for western expatriates. Many Janpanese are mostly in Sukhumvit Soi 21 or Asoke intersection and Soi Thong Lo or Sukhumvit Soi 55 where you can find Janpanese products, Sukhumvit Soi 15 and 39 are Indian expatriates and the Sukhumvit Soi 12 has a Korean Town for variety of Korean shops and restaurants.
20. **Bangkok Nightlife is amazing;** the nightlife at Soi Cowboy (between Sukhumvit Soi 21-23), Nana Entertainment (Sukhumvit Soi4), and Patpong Street are known all over the world as the red-light districts. (See details in another chapter) No more boring life when the night comes as you can enjoy the rooftop bar, Pubs, and nightclubs in 50 districts of Bangkok, enough to keep you entertained at night in any area.

21. **Bangkok is named "Venice of The East".** Bangkok is situated in the Chao Phraya River Delta in Thailand's Central plain with several canals make it's known as "Venice of the East". There are almost 2,000 Klongs or canals all over the city. Many floating markets are almost seen everywhere you are near the rivers or canals. Don't miss a boat tour and cruising along the Chao Phraya River for exploring canals in Thonburi side which offer the view of old wooden houses and typical Thai living along the canals. Ride a speedboat through a narrow lane of the orchid farm will give you a wonderful travel experience. As I always take guests off the beaten path for exciting and rewarding trips for my travelers.

**The original Floating Market that still keep old styles of living by canals is at Dam Noen Saduak District in Ratchaburi Province (Please see all details in the coming chapter); where you can see vendors on a small boat or "Sampan" Boat, carrying their fruits and food along the canals to the center of the market. It's only about 120 kilometers from Bangkok and you can do within one day. I recommend joining the tour group or private tour with a tourist guide. Some of the floating markets are in Bangkok such as Taling Chan, Klong Lat Mayom, Kwan-Riem, Wat Saphan, Bueng Phraya, Bang Nam Phueng (Samutprakan), Don Wai (Nakonpathom), Wat Thakian (Nonthaburi), Tha Kha and Amphawa (Samutsongkram), and there are many floating markets are made to simulate the atmosphere of the original one and also are popular among tourists in Bangkok and nearby towns.

22. **Massage in Bangkok is fantastic.** Wat Pho is one of the popular places for traditional Thai Massage. Many massage-shops with certified massagers where you can trust are all around Bangkok.
23. **Bike Touring around Bangkok is fun.** If you prefer to ride bicycle, I recommend you to join with the bike-tour with leader who takes you around. I don't recommend you to ride motorbike or bicycle in Bangkok or any busy traffic provinces, it's very dangerous to do that. Don't trust on the traffic lights or "Stop" sign; whenever you suppose to cross a street anywhere in Thailand, be sure that all the cars stop or it's safe to walk across.
24. **Express way networks for easy traveling;** Bangkok has many express way networks for rapid traveling. When you ride taximeter, you should ask the driver to go by express way by adding a little bit more payment for toll.
25. **Wonderful China Town in Yaowaraj;** the Yaowaraj Road is full of fun with old architectural buildings built in the Thai-Chinese style and is densed with all kinds of markets for goods and delicious street food. You can go by MRT and drop at Wat Mungkorn Station Exit 1 near Wat Leng Nuei Yee; the old temple of China Town.

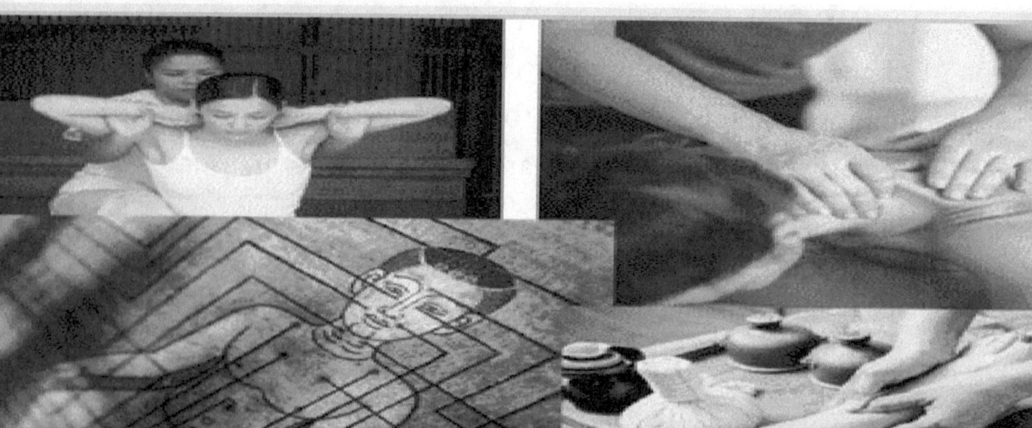

26. **Wonderful Indian Food at Indian Market Town;** it's called Pahurat.
27. **Bangkok is the center of fashion.** You don't have to bring your own clothes when you are in Bangkok because you can find shops for clothes by street, shops and department stores with cheap and good quality.
28. **Numerous retail outlets and many hotels in Bangkok;** see along Sukhumvit Road, Phahonyothin Road, Ratchadapisek, Silom, Ratchaprarop, and etc.
29. **Bangkok has the largest mall of Southeast Asia at Icon Siam.** BTS Skytrain is at **Jaroennakon Station exit 2-3** or shuttle boats available at Sathon Pier for going to Icon Siam.
30. **Large wholesale market at Bo Bae Market and Pratunam will make you never tired of shopping.** The markets seem to be well-known for those foreign and Thai merchants who want to buy clothes for selling.
31. **Khaosan Road;** the heaven for backpackers from all over the world is in Bangkok where you can experience the guest houses and the fun night entertainment.
32. **Jatuchak, the largest Weekend Market is situated in Bangkok and best known all over the world.**
33. **Modern Theaters and movie houses you must try once in Bangkok.**
34. **Bangkok has several parks and green zones for your lungs**; Lumpini Park, Suan Luang Rama IX Park, Chatujak Park, Queen Sirikij Park, Suan Benjakiti Park, Suan Wajirabenjathat, Chao Phraya Sky Park and some of the parks of Bangkok's neighbor. (see details of the parks in Bangkok)

PLAN FOR YOUR TRIP

Before you choose a place, you want to visit, you have to check the length of time you can have, for example like hours or days. I wish you could do a tour somewhere even for few hours in Bangkok. Don't just sit and wait at the airport, **but if you have less than 7 hours for transit in Thailand, please do not go out of the airport.** You can enjoy the coffee shops, Thai restaurants, or traditional Thai massage where most of them are on the 3rd or B Floor at the airport.

If you have one in mind, please see details if it is appropriate for your time. It's better to just pick one place and see everything in the area than to look around by getting in and out of the car to go to many places in a short time. Bangkok traffic is unpredictable in some places and if you're traveling by train, it takes time too. Please make sure you don't miss your flight. The guided tours I mentioned here are all worth a visit, even if you only see one.

Transit Passengers from 7 hours or more:
You will have 5 hours for a tour because you need about 2 hours for document procedure for the departure point. I recommend you to visit a place nearby the Suwannaphum airport like, the **Samut Prakan** areas (see its detail) or travel by sky train **to Phayathai Station** and connect sky train to **Siam** Station for shopping and enjoy the downtown It takes about 2 hours for traveling back and forth, then you have three hours for walking around the malls. You can get a car hire at the tour counter for a temple and city tour in Bangkok such as; **The Marble temple or Wat Pho** if you are the first-time visitor for the fast visiting and photo-taking, the direction for the two temples are more convenient from the airport. Please choose one place you really love to see and stay there to admire the uniqueness of the architecture and local living nearby as much as you can have time to do. **If it's on Sunday; The Grand Palace is the best choice for about half-day tour (4-5 hours).** I love to recommend you to go to The Grand Palace because it's the landmark in Thailand and a good location to admire the view of The Chao Phraya River. You can also see more places within this area and nearby places like **Wat Phra Kaew Tunnel and the Reclining Buddha at Wat Pho. Please keep in mind that you may need 2 hours or more at the Grand Palace and if possible; you can enter Wat Pho behind the Grand Palace for the Reclining Buddha only.** ***The temples are mostly opened early in the morning and closed about between 17.00-18.00 pm and the Grand Palace time is at 8.30 -15.30. The palace and/or Wat Phra Kaew may be closed during the royal ceremony.

Please also check if the palace is open to the public on the day you want to visit. Anyway, Wat Pho is nearby and can be a substitute place if you miss the Grand Palace.

The other choice for the Saturday-Sunday is by going to **Jatujak Market**. Get the airport link to Phayathai station and connect the sky train to Mo Chid Station. Please always be aware of the time you have, because it is a large market with thousands of shops where you can easily forget your departure time. Set the alarm clock when you are here!

There are also some nearby **hotels to the airport for a temporary** stay, if you're tired from the long flight the hotel normally charges for 6 hours included with transport for pick-up and drop.

You can check at the tour counter for the hotel rates before booking online. The hotel inside the airport's area is the Novotel Hotel; a 4-star hotel which is located at the back of the airport where you can walk from the basement floor. The hotel has a counter service at the airport; you can check at the Tour Service Counters.

One full day in Thailand

Each tour option recommended here is appropriated for exactly one day in Bangkok; for example, you have like from early morning till dawn and fly at night (10.00pm)

- ✓ Must see; **The Grand Palace and Wat Pho then a market place.**
- ✓ One whole day for **Ayutthaya Cruise Tour**. (the tour started about 7.00 am- 18.00 pm) or have a car hired for Ayutthaya (see the details in it)
- ✓ **The riverboat trip** for The Grand Palace, Wat Pho, Wat Arun, and Wat Rakang and walk around both sides of the riverbanks and have a good time for Thai food at the piers.
- ✓ One day tour to **Damnoensaduak Floating Market; when you can s**tart the trip from the airport about 6.00 am and visit Nakhon Pathom or Kanchanaburi for the Bridge over the River Kwai. You can have time for shopping in Bangkok if your flight is late at night.
- ✓ **The temples and the city tour**; Wat Trimit, Wat Pho, and the Marble Temple and look around the city.

- ✓ **Ride the riverboat at Sathorn Pier** for river view and see the local living and visit the temples and the places on the river bank, like hop on-off.

- ✓ **The Ancient City and Crocodile Farm, the Erawan museum** and **Wat Asokaram** in Samutprakan.
- ✓ In case you would like to visit the beach, you should start the trip early in the morning and go to the **Pattaya City, you can** enjoy the beach activities and visit **The Sanctuary of Truth** and a temple there.

You can choose to stay overnight in Pattaya City instead of Bangkok if you have the flight the next day. Pattaya seems to be an easy traveling from the Suwannaphum Airport; the traveling time is about one-and-a-half-hour ride there from the airport.

- ✓ **The whole day trip for Kanchanaburi province (see its detail)** for the bridge over the River Kwai and others in one day.
- ✓ **Hua Hin is fun if you have** one night and one day in Thailand, for example you arrive Thailand in the afternoon and have one whole day free for relaxing at Hua Hin and have the flight early in the morning (next day). It takes 3-4 hours ride between the airport to Hua Hin but the night market and attractions there are nice for visiting. Please always make sure you have already checked in for your departure flight so you can save your time, you can have a handbag with you, don't take big luggage; you can leave the luggage with the left-luggage room at the airport.
- ✓ Please carry your important documents with you, like your passport and enough money. The Left-Luggage Room is available on the second floor of the Suwannaphum Airport.

- ✓ **Suphanburi** province is also close to Bangkok where you can admire some old temples and a large aquarium at **Bueng Chavak**, and I think you need a car hire to do the trip in one day.
- ✓ One day and one night during the cool season; **Nov-Mar** is also good to adventure at **Khao Yai where you can** relax in the natural surroundings and admiring some temples there. (Don't go in the rainy season; Jun-Sep) It takes one and a half hours for a ride there.
- ✓ **Lopburi** is also a good choice for sightseeing on one day trip by catching a train from Bangsue Grand Station or Hua Lumphong Station to Lopburi province to admire the old town close to Bangkok.
- ✓ **Ride the Skytrain from the airport to explore downtown by hoping on-off; by Sukhumvit route till Keha station in Samutprakan, Phahonyothin route till Rangsit station or Nonthaburi route for Ko Kret. (see detail of Nonthaburi)**
- ✓ **Please try the traditional Thai Massage if you have time.**

- ✓ **3-4 days in Thailand:**
- ✓ Two days for exploring Bangkok **Metropolitan Region (see their detail**) plus one night at Pattaya beach or Kanchanaburi or Ayuttaya.
- ✓ **Explore the Grand Palace and temples in Bangkok**; Wat Trimit, Wat Pho, The Marble Temple, Wat Saketh, Wat Ratchanadda, Wat Intraviharn, Wat Suthat, etc. plus one-two night in Pattaya City.
- ✓ **Fly to Phuket Island** and one day in Bangkok for The Grand Palace and places nearby.
- ✓ **Fly to Samui Island** and one day in Bangkok for The Grand Palace and places nearby.
- ✓ Enjoy Bangkok, Damnoen Saduak, Ayutthaya, and Kanchanaburi. **Fly to Chiang Mai or Chiangrai** and one night in Bangkok for a half-day tour to The Grand Palace.

✓ 5-7 days or more in Thailand

Must stay in Bangkok for a couple of days for The Grand Palace, the temples, local market, nightlife and some of amusement parks and ride sky train all over Bangkok included with the top attractions nearby Bangkok like, the Damnoensaduak Floating market, The Historical Park and temples in Ayutthaya and Kanchanaburi. The rest of your vacation you can set the plan for enjoying at the beach somewhere (see 29 islands and Chonburi detail) or trekking in the northern province or exploring the northeastern region to the provinces close to neighbor countries for the diversity of attractions and make the most of your Southeast Asia Tours; I recommend:

- Hua Hin, Pattaya City, Koh Chang in Trat, Sattaheep or Pattaya in Chonburi.
- **Explore islands**, like Phuket, Samui, Pha-gnan, Phan-gna, and other islands nearby. (For Andaman Sea; Oct-Dec, and Jan-Apr for the Gulf of Thailand)
- Explore the rural areas and the cultural world heritage by UNESCO at **Sukhothai and Kam Phaeng Phet** before going to Chiang Mai.
- **Enjoy the north** at Chiang Mai / Chiangrai and Mae Hong Sorn and Nan.
- **Udonthani for Ban Chiang and enjoy Mae Khong River at Nongkai.**
- **Nakonratchasima or Korat etc.**

BANGKOK AND BANGKOK METROPOLITAN REGION

Bangkok is a popular city for both Thai and foreign tourists because there are many attractions that are easily accessible.

With more than 200 years of Bangkok being the capital city, it has a rich history and culture to be discovered from many temples, palaces, museums, street food, cheap accommodations, parks, and other places that make every day full of fun by taking buses, trains, boats, taxis, and many tour-services. The Thai Pavilion at the World Expo 2020 in Dubai is ranked as one of the most popular in the mobility zone from its charm of unique design and the interesting Thai products.

When you arrive at the airport, please check if you have a transfer from the hotel you booked and look for the sign of your names; normally the hotel representatives will have the hotel name on the sign shown, it may be at the exit no.4-5. If you would like to tour by yourself, **PLEASE CHECK THE TABLE OF CONTENT AGAIN FOR THE PLACES YOU WOULD LIKE TO GO OR IF EVERYTHING IS IN YOUR PLAN THEN REFRESH YOURSELF AND GO.**

Please dress modestly when you would like to visit any temples. I recommend the ladies should have "a robe wrapping around" in your bag during your trip so whenever you want to enter the temple you can use it. However; The Grand Palace does not allow dresses or clothing that are sleeveless or skirts; above the knees, and men wearing shorts with slippers enter the area. There are cheap clothes for sale nearby, you can have it as a souvenir from Thailand!

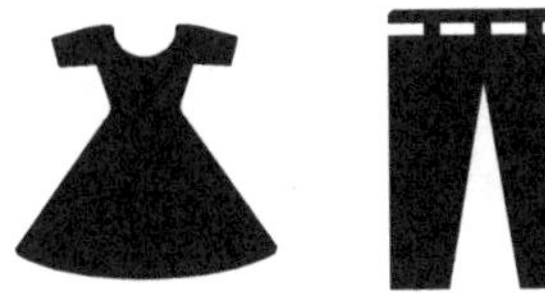

THE GRAND PALACE/ WAT PHRA KAEW

The must-visit for Thailand is **The Grand Palace and the Emerald Buddha Temple; the landmark of Thailand. It's** the most fabulous place you should not miss! You can come to the Grand Palace by MRT by going to **Sanamchai Station**. (airport link -Makkasan-MRT Petchaburi -Snamchai) If you would like to go faster, please get a taxi so you can also have time to visit Wat Pho, Wat Arun and enjoy looking around the Chao Phraya Riverbank for admiring more attractions.

The Grand Palace; was established in 1782 in the reign of King Rama I, situated in Bangkok; the capital city since that time. The reason for choosing this capital because Thonburi; the former capital, was not suitable; with the river passing through the center of the city, would be easily attacked. The other reason was; Thonburi Palace had two temples on each side, so the palace was located within a limited area. King Rama I then ordered to establish the new palace in Bangkok; on the east bank of the Chao Phraya River, the main river of Thailand. **King Rama I or Phra Phutthayotfa Chulalok Maharaj** was born in 1737 and died in 1809, was the founder of Rattanakosin Kingdom (1782-1932) and the first monarch of **Chakri Dynasty of Siam** (called for Thailand that time). He ascended the throne in 1782-1809. His Majesty the king had a very important royal duties during his reign; from his skill, strength and effective command of combat; especially the war with Burma, to protect the country from invasion of enemy; it was victorious every time during his reign. In the reign of King Rama VII, the monument of King Rama I; was ordered to be built for honoring Phra Phutthayotfa Chulalok Maharaj as the first king of Chakri Dynasty during the 150th year Anniversary Celebration of Bangkok, was situated near the Phra Phutthayotfa Bridge or Memorial Bridge. The statue was made of bronze in sitting position with 4.6-meter-high from the base and 2.3 meter wide. **April 6th** is the day for remembering his grace; the present king and queen go for putting wreaths and flowers and also people join this occasion. The Palace was original divided into three parts; the outer, middle, and inner wall.

The fortifications of the grand palace and the royal temple were installed with 12 gates and 17 ramparts.

Nowadays, the Grand Palace is opened for public for two parts; the temple of The Emerald Buddha or **Wat Phra Kaew** and within the center wall palace areas. Please dress modestly and try to see all buildings opened for public as much as you can, some of the hall is opened only for some important occasions. If you visit here without a guide, you should get information from the officer there about the special events.

WAT PHRA KAEW

Wat Phra Kaew or The Temple of Emerald Buddha was established in 1782, in outer wall of the palace. The tradition of the temple built inside the palace were done since Sukhothai Period such as Wat Mahathart in Sukhothai Palace and Wat Phra Si Sanpeth in Ayutthaya Palace. The temples built inside the palaces were different from other temples in general seen because there's no monk stay in these temples. The temples situated in the palaces were built only for the king and queen and the royal family to perform religious rituals and ceremonies but it's open for public and sometimes allowed the people to participate in special events during Buddha's Day as well.

STEPS FOR ADMIRING WAT PHRA KAEW

THE HERMIT SCULPTURE

The hermit's name was **Mor Chiwaka**; the personal physician of Lord Buddha. His statue was built during King Rama III period and situated here for commemorating of the Thai Traditional Medicine; the statue made of bronze with a mortar for crushing the herbal medicine placed in front of the hermit for the people whose belief about making a medicine in front of statue enhanced their medicinal properties.

PHRA RABIENG OR THE BALCONY

The balcony was rebuilt and renovated by each reign. It was constructed to hold all the buildings in the temple separated from the palace. There are beautiful mural paintings of Ramayana Epic drawn and painted along the wall.

THE MURAL PAINTINGS OF RAMAYANA EPIC. Ramayana Epic was an ancient epic of India; telling about the war between King Rama and Tossakanth. The paintings consist of 178 sections which were painted on the wall since King Rama I period, the whole painting have been renovated many times to maintain the beauty of the Thai arts. Please start the Wat Phra Kaew Tour by walking along the mural paintings and at the same time you are able to see other places and surroundings outside the balcony before getting inside the main hall at the middle of the temple.

YAK GUARDIANS: The Yak Statues or the demon figure come from a character in the Ramayana Epic; there are six pairs built as the guards of each gate. The statues were decorated with colorful Chinese porcelains and all built in the reign of King Rama III.

SALA LAI: Sala Rai was built in the reign of King Rama I. It is a pavilion without walls, located around the ordination hall, total 12 pavilions are identical in shape size and height It is a pavilion with a Thai-style roof covered with colored glazed clay tiles. The gable is an image of the goddess gilded with gold on a white glass floor decorated with blue bouquet, rooster leaves, swan's tail and startled Naga, the floor is made into 2 levels, covered with marble. It is used for students to pray during the Buddhist Lent season which has been continued to nowadays.

THE GOLDEN PAGODA OR PHRA SIRATANA CHEDI: You can walk to the top of the pagoda site to admire a huge golden pagoda which was built in the reign of King Rama IV, about in 1855 for enshrining the Relics of Buddha. It was in Bell-Shape or Ceylonese Style; with 40-meter-tall, made of brick and mortar decorated with golden mosaics throughout the pagoda. There are 4 entrances to get inside the Phra Chedi (Pagoda) which is a round hall with the walls that are plastered with white paint on it, hanged with a white tiered to the small pagoda of Buddha's Relic situated in the middle of the room. The small Chedi which enshrined is a pagoda engraved with all black lacquer.

PHRA MONDOP OR SCRIPTURE HALL: Phra Mondop is situated at the middle between the golden pagoda and Prasat Phra thep bidon. The building was built in the reign of King Rama I for housing Buddhist Scripture. The Mondop Hall is a seven-storied castle roof, the exterior walls are decorated with gilded bas-reliefs decorated with mirrors depicting Thep Phanom (the angel in the "wai" position) within the rectangular frame. The 4 doors of this Mondop are pearl-patterned doors.

The base part of Phra Mondop is tiered where the upper floor depicts an angel sitting between the arches. The bottom part is Garuda images and Ghartha people sitting alternatingly. The interior is enshrined with the Tripitaka Cabinet (Buddha's Scripture) decorated with pearls. The floor is woven with wire mats made of silver.

PRASAT PHRA THEP BIDON OR THE ROYAL PANTHEON

Prasat Phra Thep Bidon was original named "Phuttha Prang Prasat", built in the reign of King Rama IV in 1855 for the purpose of keeping the Emerald Buddha inside, but the castle was too narrow for performing the religious rituals. Therefore; in 1903; in the reign of King Rama VI, the castle was repaired and changed the name to be Prasat Phra Thep Bidon and the king ordered to bring the five king statues kept inside this hall and commanded to be a tradition to pay homage to the statues every year on April 6 which he designated as the Chukkree Day since 1918.

It's the only castle in the temple, built in Chaturamuk pattern; means solid with four faces or tetrahedron, the top is Prang shape (the Khamer art that looks like corn shape) with the crown and glazed tiles decorated.

At the present; **the nine Chukkree dynasty former kings' statues** kept here and the hall is opened to the public on April 6th every year included with the days announced by the Royal Office during special occasions. When you are at Wat Phra Kaew, you will notice when it's crowded around the hall if it's opened.

PHRA BUSSABOK: Phra Bussabok is a small open structure used in Thai culture as a throne for enshrinement of Buddha images and the sacred objects. It's normally a square-based with rich decorations; it's quite similar to Mondop hall but smaller size. You will see Bussabok sculptures put at the four corners with elephant statues as the decorations around the Scripture Hall.

PHRA SUWAN CHEDI: The two pagodas built by King Rama I, made it dedicated to his parents, having the same size and height. Each pagoda was decorated with twenty wooden recessed corners covered with copper sheets and applied a lacquer and gilded gold over all the whole pagoda. The base of the pagoda is an octagon lined with marble above its base, with a sculpture of yaks or giants and monkeys total of 20 figures, all the figures' faces and dresses and body colors were typical of the Ramayana Mural Painting along the wall.

BELFRY or The Bell Tower: In the ancient time, people did not have clocks so the bell rung from the temple usually early in the morning for chanting and about 11.00 am for telling monks to have the last meal of the day; some of the temple strikes the bell for calling monks and people who stay for observing precepts that time to sweep and clean the road and the area of the temple in the afternoon. The people knew the time by hearing the bell rung since the olden days. The bell tower is counted as one of the compositions of a temple. The bell tower in Wat Phra Kaew is situated at the south of the ordination hall, was originally built since King Rama I period but it was rebuilt in typical Thai art decorated with Chinese porcelains in the reign of King Rama IV. Currently, it was renovated in the reign of King Rama 9th for the celebration of 60th Anniversary of His reign in 2006. **The bell in Wat Phra Kaew will be strike only on the special occasions; one of them is the day of the appointment of the new Patriarch and the number of times for striking the bell will be equal to the new Patriarch Number.**

MODEL OF ANGOR WAT: The historical background of this Angor Wat Model happened in the reign of King Rama IV during the time where some of the Cambodia's provinces belonged to Siam. The king commanded his people to explore this stone-castles for demolishing in order to be reproduced in Bangkok, so the people had a chance to admire the beautiful and amazing architectures of Khamer arts which were made of large stones. During the survey, the king's people found that all of the castles were too huge to be demolished; besides, they told the king that all of the castles were built for thousand years by ancient people and all made of huge stones which was hard to be moved to Bangkok, it should be remained at the same old place. Therefore, the king commanded them to make a model of Angor Wat from the picture taken and kept in Wat Phra Kaew. The model is now situated near Prasat Phra Thep Bidon and the golden pagoda. It's a miracle in ability of those Thai artists who conveyed the wonders of the world virtual reality with such details.

PHRA ASADHA MAHA CHEDI: The Eight Prang Towers are standing on the east of the temple. There were no evidences when these stupas built; the six of them built at outer wall and the other two were at inner wall of the temple. Prang is called for stupa or sometimes chedi or pagoda which is for keeping the ashes of the nobles and well-respected people. If the pagoda-shape is like corn shape; it's recognized as Cambodian style of stupa or known as "Prang". The Prangs were renovated during King Rama VII and King Rama IX periods for maintaining the original beautiful arts and architectures.

HOR PHRA OR BUDDHA STATUES HALL: There are many pavilions and halls being as Hor Phra around the areas such as; **Hor Phra Montien Tham,** is a Thai-style building, single-storey brick and mortar in rectangular shape, with a veranda around it and a double stacked roof, located at the northeast of the temple, built like Viharn hall for keeping the Buddha's Scripture, **Hor Phra Nak**; located at the northwest of the ordination hall is for keeping the Buddha statues.

PHRA VIHARN YOD: The structure of the building is beautiful in the form of Thai crown decorated with Chinese porcelain. It was originally built in the reign of King Rama I for keeping King Uthong's Statue. (King Uthong was the first king of Ayutthaya Capital Period.) King Rama III ordered to demolish the original hall which looked very old and built the new one into the spire-roof building decorated with Chinese porcelains and this Viharn hall was repaired again in the reign of King Rama V. This Viharn situated on your left-hand side when you stand in front of the main hall (at the worshipping area).

THE ORDINATION HALL OR PHRA UBOSOTH OR THE CHAPEL OF THE EMERALD BUDDHA: The large building at the middle of the temple is the ordination hall; the main hall where the Emerald Buddha is situated. You are not allowed to use cameras inside the hall and please kindly sit on the floor. (Please don't point the feet to the direction of Buddha) When you get inside the chapel, please find a place to sit (on the floor), try to find the front place facing the Buddha image. Photo is not allowed but you can take the picture outside the chapel. **Sitting in the Great Hall** in front of the Emerald Buddha and look around the room to admire the beauty of the mural paintings and various Buddha images for getting away from the heat outside. **May you meditate to take a break for a while, it will give you a surprising boost in mental energy, please try it!**

THE EMERALD BUDDHA OR PHRA KAEW MORAKOT

The statue of the Emerald Buddha is covered by the costumes that is changed three times a year of each season as a tradition done from the past; summer, rainy season and winter, by the present king that time. According to legend, the "Emerald Buddha" is worshiped and preferred by many great kings in historical evidence.

The full name of The Emerald Buddha is **called "Phra Phuttha Maha Manee Rattana Patimakon" or "Phra Kaew Morakot"**, built in the art of Chiangsaen which is the Lanna Art in the north of Thailand, in the attitude of meditation. The statue was made of jade (Nephrite) which is the green color like the emerald stone color. From the historical evidences; the statue was original found inside a pagoda of a temple in Chiangrai province in 1434, which was covered with lacquer plaster and gilded with gold, the pagoda covered the Buddha Statue was ruined by lightning and the mortar around the nose area was cracked down; appearing the green like-emerald hidden inside. The king of Chiang Mai requested for placing Phra Kaew Morakot in Chiang Mai for being as a sacred Buddha in the city but the event was a big surprise.

When the elephant carried the statue of the emerald Buddha refused to head to Chiang Mai but turned to Lampang direction instead, due to the situation; the king then ordered to place the Phra Kaew Morakot in Wat Phra Kaew Don Tao in Lampang province.

But later on, the Buddha Statue was finally placed in Chiang Mai in the reign of **King Somdej Phra Setthathiraj**; the great king of Lan Chang Kingdom; where Luang Phra Bang was the capital, who also came to ruled Lanna Kingdom; where Chiang Mai was the capital.

Lanchang and Lanna Kingdoms were related to each other, therefore; **King Somdej Phra Setthathiraj** could take the statue of the Emerald Buddha and Phra Phutthasihing; which is one of the important Buddha statues situated in Nakonsithammarat now, to be placed at Vientian; the new capital at that time for being the sacred center and blessed for the city and people of the kingdom. The king of Chiang Mai requested to move the Emerald Buddha back to Chiang Mai to be the sacred sites for people, he received the only Phra Phutthasihing Buddha statue.

When Phra Chao Taksin Maharath the Great reigned and established Thonburi City (1767-1782) to be the capital of Siam, he brought Phra Kaew Morakot or The Emerald Buddha and **Phra Bang;** the standing Buddha made of bronze covered with gold which is now situated at Luang Phra Bang Museum, to be placed at Wat Arun or The Temple of Dawn until the end of his period. During King Rama I period, the king took the Buddha statue on the royal barge crossed the river to Bangkok and placed the Emerald Buddha inside the main hall till nowadays and King Rama I returned Phra Bang to Luang Phra Bang of Laos.

The costumes of the Emerald Buddha are made of precious stones and gold and changed by the king by regarding of the three seasons; the cold season is about in November, the hot season in March and the rainy season in July that are on about the Buddhist Lent Day. The days for changing are depend on the Lunar Calendar and done by the present king or member of royal family only. The costumes at the present was newly made and has been used since 1997.

The former costumes are now kept at the royal museum of Wat Phra Kaew. The costumes were made and used since King Rama I period and were repaired many times by The Treasury Department until they were finally hard to be fixed; due to the details of craftmanship since more than 200 years ago. There are beautiful mural paintings on the wall around the Emerald Buddha represents the Buddhist cosmology and the Enlightenment of Buddha.

Wat Phra Keaw or Wat Phra Sri Rattana Satsadaram was established within the area of the Grand Palace to serve as a venue for the royal merits, the royal various ceremonies include religious ceremonies. The position of the temple therefore was built in the outer court where people could come to worship the Emerald Buddha but unable to access the royal residence. The direction of facing the front entrance and the buildings are based on traditions by facing to the east and the Sanam Chai Road is as the entrance road to the front of the temple and also the position of the Emerald Buddha; the principal image, with the Buddha images facing east corresponding to the events in the past Buddha history during His Enlightenment and with the belief that the Emerald Buddha is sacred, protecting Bangkok from evil spirits from outside threats; by facing to the east which is the direction to the Ghost Gate or called as **Pratu Phi.** The Ghost Gate played an important role in the history of Rattanakosin in particular Bangkok when people died from epidemics such as cholera, massive bodies had to be transported through the Ghost Gate for funeral services at Wat Saket. Nowadays; Pratu Phi is an old commercial district of Bangkok where you can find delicious food and street food like Phad Thai.

The **Pratu Phi** is an area around the **Ong Ang Canal** Intersection of Mahachai Road and Bamrung Muang Road between Wat Thepthidaram and Wat Saket. The name Pratu Phi (Pratu means Door, Phi means Ghost) came from the gate which was the route for transporting bodies out of the city gates of Bangkok.

If you will notice around the temple areas, you will see many statues of half animal in human body put by the gate or the entrance to the hall, they are called **Himmapan animals**; the imaginery creature that some of the poets described living in the Himmapan Forest or Khao Krailas, a mysterious land appeared in the Tribhum Phra Ruang literature (the ancient Literature of Buddhism) and Ramayana with the characteristics of many animals coming together in one, they are classified into 3 types, namely bibath (two-legged), quadruped (four-legged) and fish. Himmapan animals created in the temple were cast in gold and adorned with glass, standing on a dark gray marble plinth. You should look around for more details within the temple areas, some of them has the sign for the names and then come to the palace side by walking to the bell tower and turn left here.

THE PALACE AREAS

The Grand palace and the temple of the Emerald Buddha were built since 1782; in the reign of King Phra Phuttha Yod Fa Chula Loke the Great, King Rama I. The location of the Grand Palace is facing to Sanam Luang at the north, Ministry of Defense at the east, Wat Pho at the south, and the Chao Phraya river at the west. The total areas are about 152 rai. **The palace is divided into 3 parts**; **the front part** covers inner wall as the Bureau of the royal Household and His Majesty's Secretariat with the Royal Guards, **the middle court** is the location of the castles or called as **Prasart Rajchamontien** which built in both Thai and western architecture used for coronation ceremony and other important ceremonies by the king; consists of the **Phra Maha Montien Group**, the **Phra Thinang Chakri Maha Prasart Group**, the **Phra Maha Prasart Group**, and **Suan Siwalai**, and **the inner court** at the south of the palace is the location of the pavilions and houses for queen, princess and the female civil servants, the men whose age more than 13 years old; but except the king, are not allowed entering the inner areas. We are admiring inside the middle court where gathering many beautiful castles.

The small gate passing to the palace after visiting the Emerald Buddha Temple is to PHRA MAHA MONTIEN GROUP; the grand residential areas:

1. **The Phra Maha Montien Group**

This Maha Montien Palace was built in the reign of King Rama I for his residence and performing the coronation ceremony. The palace has been the place used for coronation every reign continuously.

The group of Phra Maha Montien has the main castles such as **Phra Thinang Chakapat Piman Throne Hall**; the principal castle of the group which is the site for royal ceremonies of the country and was the permanent residents of King Rama I-III. The architectural buildings designed as the triplets, single-storey, made of brick raised on a high base, having the corridors connected one another. **Phra Thinang Phaisal Taksin Throne Hall** is a part of Phrathinang Chakapat Piman, is where Phra Siam Thevathirat Statue; a sacred image of the country is enshrined and has been the place for the coronation ceremony of the Kings of the Chakri Dynasty Since King Rama II onwards. The hall was originally the residence of King Rama I; where he resided and performed the royal duties on some occasions, His Highness had the royal family, senior civil servants, came to pay their respects to His Majesty the King and performed the royal merit within the palace till at the end of his reign.

Phra Thinning Amarin Winitchai Throne Hall is adjacent to Phra Thinang Phaisal Taksin at the north and it's **the first part of the** group buildings you meet, which was built in the reign of King Rama I in 1782, was used as the audience hall where the king met his officers and the ambassadors. The hall now is used for the state occasions such as; coronation ceremony, the king's birthday and other special occasions from the palace. The building is built in typical Thai style, base-raised with 21 meter-wide and 31.5meter-long, covered with the glazed tiled roof.

2. The Phra Thinang Chakri Maha Prasart Group.

The next buildings which are the middle of the areas you are is stunning with the mixture of Thai and western architecture which is called Phra Thinang Chakri Maha Prasart Throne Hall. The Chakri Maha Prasart Throne Halls **are the buildings** with three spires roof lied from the north to the south of the palace belonged to the middle court and the inner court, built in the reign of King Rama V in 1877.

The building of Phra Thinang Chakri Maha Prasart Throne Hall was constructed in mixed styles of European (Victorian) and Thai architecture built for the king's residence, they were 11 castles in the group but some of them were demolished because they were too old to be repaired, nowadays only 5 halls left and mainly used for the royal banquet's halls. Due to its distinctive architecture than other royal residences, The Chakri Maha Prasart Hall has now become one of the most important attractions of the Grand Palace.

3. **The Phra Maha Prasart Group**

The group of this castles consists of the halls for performing the royal ceremonies located at the middle court and the inner court areas, built in the reign of King Rama I. The important throne halls are **Phra Thinang Dusit Maha Prasart;** the beautiful building you are admiring next to the Chakrt Maha Prasart, Phra Thinang Phiman Rattaya, Phra Thinang Arporn Phimok Prasart and Phra Thinang Ratchakanyasapa.

DUSIT MAHA PRASART HALL; the hall has been admired for a great art masterpiece of Rattanakosin. It's the only hall in the grand palace built with authentic Thai architecture. It was built in the reign of King Rama I, with a very beautiful spired roof on the top. It's the last hall you see before you leave the palace. This hall was enshrined the body of His Majesty King Bhumibol; King Rama 9th about a year and we were allowed to come here for paying respect to his body during the funeral period in 2016-2017. At present, the hall is used for the royal merits and some other ceremonies performed by the king.

4. Suan Siwalai

Suan Siwalai is a garden inside the palace located on the east side; it was the location of the royal residence of King Mongkut (King Rama IV), where he lived till his death, the palace was too difficult to restore or repair so it's demolished in the reign of King Rama V. There are many throne halls located here.

The new "Umong Maharaj" or Wat Phra Kaew Tunnel is now opened for public. The gate in front of the palace is opposite to Silpakon University and Tha Chang Pier. You can admire decorations of interior with marble walls; the highlight here is museum zone for Rattanakosin Kingdom history exhibitions. The purpose of building this tunnel is not only for preventing accidents from crossing the road, but also to make all tourists feel very convenient with public wash rooms, a suitable place for meeting point and a cool place for relaxing and away from the heat outside a while after touring. You can also see the map of The Grand Palace on the wall of this tunnel. You can walk along the wall and ramparts of the Grand Palace to Wat Pho or passing through the alley near the Ministry of Defense and the City Pillar to Wat Ratchabopith, Wat Suthat and explore the Giant Swing areas.

WAT PHO

Wat Pho and the Grand Palace can be combined tour for one day trip, but if you don't have much time; you can have a quick look inside Wat Pho. I would like to recommend you to visit this temple after when you visit the Grand Palace because you can walk here (in case you have many days in Bangkok). The location of Wat Pho is on Sanamchai Road, close to BTS Sanamchai Station and The Grand Palace. If you are tired after The Grand Palace tour, you can ride Tuk Tuk from the palace to Wat Pho instead of walking, but if it's not too hot to walk, I think you can enjoy the atmosphere along the pathway to Wat Pho.

The full name of Wat Pho is called **"Wat Phra Chetupon Wimon Mung-kha-la-ram"** or known as The Temple of Reclining Buddha or Wat Pho. Wat Pho was the 24th most popular tourist destination in the world in 2006, with almost 9 million visiting that year. The temple was one of the oldest temples in Bangkok but the year of construction was unknown. It's where King Rama 1st rebuilt the temple complex sites to make it the royal temple. Wat Pho was renovated and expanded during King Rama III period. The temple was considered as the center for public education in Siam; from the evidences of the marble illustrations has been recognized by UNESCO in its Memory of the World Program, it was also the birth place of traditional Thai massage or as a school of Thai medicine which has been taught and practiced at the temple. **If you enter Wat Pho from its parking; you will see both sides of this temple; one for public and the other is for the monk residents. But if you enter at the Reclining Buddha Hall you should go into the hall before others. You can** see the statues of **Yak; Demon Guardian** statues at the entrance and see the statues of **Chinese Guardians** beside the gate to the Hall of Reclining Buddha. **Phra Maha Chedi (Pagoda) of the four kings**; King Rama 1st -4th, which built for worshipping to Buddha, are large pagodas located near the Reclining Buddha Hall surrounded by walls. The architecture around the arch was Thai- Chinese style. The pagodas are decorated with glazed tiles. There is a pair of Chinese stone dolls decorated on each door. Wat Pho has the most pagodas in Thailand.

There are **99 pagodas and** stupas in the temple area; the 71 small stupas around built in the reign of King Rama 3rd for containing the ashes of the royal family, The 20 pagoda along the cloister; 5 ones of each corner contain Buddha's Relic and the 4 Phra Maha Stupas; Prang style; like corn shape, are outside the ordination hall. You will see the statue **of hermits in 24** positions around in the temple areas; in fact, there were about 80 statues of hermits in different positions with descriptions of each position, but some of the statues were destroyed and stolen, then only 24 left.

The Illustrations in the medicine pavilion is located near the large pagodas and close to the gate to the Reclining Buddha Hall. **Wat Pho** is known as the birthplace of Traditional Thai Massage and houses of Thai Medicine. The marble illustrations and inscriptions placed in the pavilion for public instructions have been registered by **UNESCO in its Memory of the World Programme in 2008.**

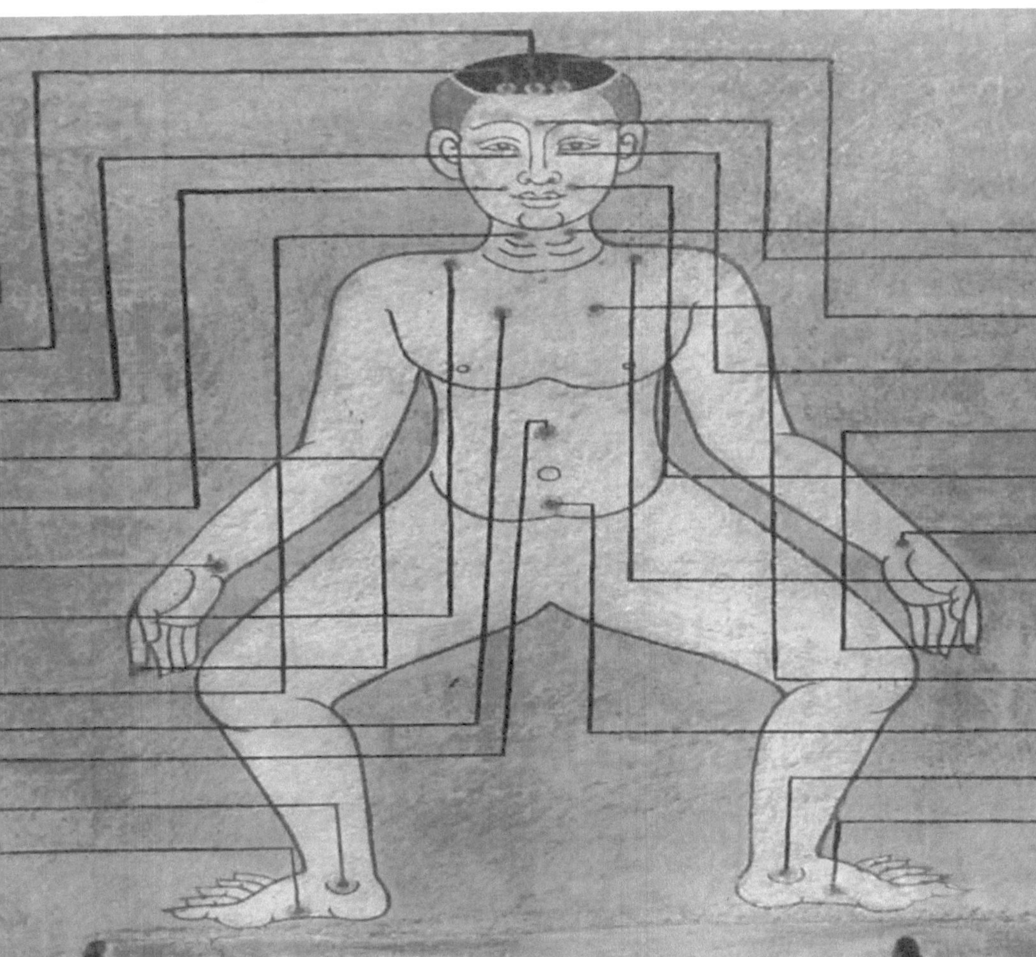

The temple still remains a center for tradition medicine. You can try Thai traditional massage or called as "Nuad" in Thai at the temple.

See the Hall of Reclining Buddha which is at the west of the temple near Chao Phraya River. The hall was built in the reign of King Rama III for covering the statue of the Reclining Buddha. The colorful mural painting inside the hall depicts about the outstanding Buddhists; for Phikkhu or monk, Phikkhunee means female-monk, Ubasoke(male) and Ubasika(female) for those who observe the Precepts in the temple; called as Athatakkha.

The beautiful Reclining Buddha was made of stucco cladded with gold sheets all over the statue; which is 46-meter-long and 15-meter-high, become the 3rd largest reclining Buddha in Thailand. Walk around inside the hall and admire this beautiful Reclining Buddha image. You can see the soles of the feet which are in laid with mother-of-pearl display 108 auspicious symbols of Buddha. **You will hear the sounds of coins** hitting the monks' bowl when you enter the hall. They are 108 bowls for people to drop the coins for donation; some people believe that they are offering to 108 monks.

When you leave the hall, you will see the beautiful huge pagodas or **Phra Maha Chedi** of the four kings. You can get inside this part to see details of Chinese porcelains decorated on the pagodas and see more of buildings in this area. **Before getting inside the Phra Mondop; you will see Yak or Demon Guardian of Wat Pho stand at the gate, the** Mondop building at Wat Pho is a Buddhist scripture hall with a square building and spire roof decorated with porcelains, there are three pavilions or Sala Rai near the Mondop. **Sala Kan Pa Riean**; the large hall nearby the Mondop, serves as a learning and meditation hall. Afterwards**, please go to the main hall** or the ordination hall areas. You can notice that many stupas situated around the areas of the temple.

The Ordination Hall is the main hall or the ordination hall for Buddhist rituals which normally enshrined the most sacred Buddha Statue of the temple which is called the principal Buddha image. The statue of the Principal Buddha in Wat Pho is named Phra Phuttha Theva Patimakon; which is 62 inches wide and 79 inches high, made of bronze and lacquered with gold and contained the ashes of King Rama I at the Buddha's base. See the **Phra Rabiang or double cloister** of this ordination hall which contains about 400 statues of Buddha in different positions, the statues were taken from the northern Thailand during in the reign of King Rama I. The cloister is intersected by four Viharns; contains the Standing Buddha statue from Ayutthaya at the east, the Seated Buddha sheltered by a naga (mystical serpent) is at the west with a small museum, the Buddha at the south which has five disciples seated for listening to Buddha's first sermon. The statues of Buddha at the south and the west were brought from Sukhothai by King Rama I and the Buddha put at the north was cast in the reign of King Rama I.

WAT RATCHABOPHIT

Wat Ratchabophit is located not so far from Wat Pho and The Grand Palace. If you walk along the alley where Ministry of Defense; the yellow building situated on the other side of the road where the Grand Palace is, you will discover one of the royal temples which was the last royal "Temple of King"; the king built according to the ancient royal tradition that the temples of the reign were built. The temple was where the two Popes; Pope John Paul II and Pope Francis came to visit the former Supreme Patriarch of Thailand in 1984 and 2019. Right now, it is the place where the present Supreme Patriarch of Thailand resides.

It was built in the reign of King Rama V in 1869 with unique layout; the Viharn and the ordination hall were joined by a circular courtyard, **a gilded Pagoda**; 43-meter-high covered with orange-colored tiles with a golden ball on the top, stood at the center. The beautiful **ordination hall** has 10 door panels and 28 window panels which were decorated with gilded black lacquer inside. The **entrance doors** were inlaid mother of pearl decorated. The interior was built in Italian architecture; inspired by King Rama V, during visiting Europe. The Principal Buddha Image is called **"Phra Phuttha Ankiros"** put on the marble base from Italy where enshrined the ashes of King Rama II, King Rama III, King Rama IV, King Rama V, Somdej Phra Sisuralai; King Rama III's mother, and Phra Ong Chao Lamom; King Rama III's daughter.

The **Drum Tower of the temple** was built with hexagonal spires decorated with Benjarong; it's a painted ceramic or called as Thai ceramics porcelain", its name means 5 colors but maybe more, in Naga and Erawan heads.

Wat Ratchabophit is the location of the Royal Cemetery. The cemetery contains monuments to members of the Thai Royal Family; especially related to King Chulalongkorn or King Rama V. The total royal monuments are 34 memorials.

THA MAHARAJ, THA CHANG AND THA PHRA CHAN PIERS NEAR THE GRAND PALACE

"Tha" comes from the word "Tha Rue" means "Pier" You should walk around along the river-bank and find something to drink and eat in a small restaurant at the old-style buildings nearby the temple. Many nice places at the piers like, Tha Maharai Pier and Tha Phra Chan Pier.

There are two piers close to The Grand Palace, **Tha Chang and Tha Maharaj** Piers. I always enjoy at Tha Maharaj Pier; which located next to Tha Chang Pier, take a break before moving further more places across the river.

If you walk along the road in front of the palace, there are interesting places you should see and visit such as; Wat Phra Kaew Tunnel, Sanam Luang Ground, the Bangkok City Pillar, Ministry of Defense, The Bangkok National Museum, Wat Mahathat and Thammasat University.

WAT MAHATHART

Visit **Wat Mahathart**; the center of the Buddhist Mahanikai School, it's originally built to house Buddha's Relic. The temple is opposite to Tha Maharaj Pier. We learned that the temple had many names before; it was called "Wat Salak" original built during Ayutthaya Period but when the temple was renovated in 1783, the name was changed to "Wat Nippanaram". Afterwards, King Rama I changed the temple's name to "Wat Phra Si Sanpetch" when he allowed the temple to be the place for "Sankhayana" or "Buddhist Council" and then changed to be the new name which was named after the temple's name in Ayutthaya; where enshrined Buddha's Relic, to be called "Wat Phra Si Rattanamahathart Raj Cha Vora Mahaviharn"; where the Buddha's Relic kept and the resident for the Patriarch of Siam. The temple was used for royal funeral and the nobles in the reign of King Rama V. It became the location of Pali College in 1889 and called as "Mahathart College" which was built for dedicating to his son; the Crown Prince who passed away.

In 1894, the new building of the temple was given the name by King Rama V as "Maha Chula longkon rajcha vithayalai" or "Buddhist University".

The construction was finished in the reign of King Rama VI who commanded for taking the former Crown Prince's money to donate for renovation of the temple and finally the present name "Wat Mahathart Yuwaraj Rangsalit" was given and it's local called as "Wat Mahathart" since that time. Walk along the pathways and see old shops for local food from street vendors and old style of herbs in skin balms and fragrant ointment. It's quite popular to shop those things here. **Thammasat University is** near Tha Phra Chan Pier; next from Tha Maharaj Pier. It's a state university, the 2nd oldest university since 1934.

You will discover **the market of the Thai Buddha amulets** for "votive tablet" or blessed statue of Buddha image at **Tha Phra-Chan Pier.** Buddha Amulets and sacred objects have been a belief tradition from worshippers who wished to have those objects for luck and safe from harm. Many of old consecrated sacred objects by the famous monks may be valued up to millions Bahts.

Enjoy the typical Thai restaurants of old time along the small lane nearby the riverside. Chan, one of my favorites is called "Café 79". Good food and good drink.

Stand on the ground of Sanam Luang; the large ground areas facing The Grand Palace, which is the historic center for the Royal Ceremonies. Nice location to take picture of The Grand Palace areas here.

When I was young, I came to see the Kite Flying Festival at Sanam Luang when trade winds flew. People brought their beautiful kites to flow in the sky.

Kite Flying was a traditional sport since Sukhothai Period (1238-1438) and has been very popular for Thai people. King Rama IV allowed people to play kite-flying at Sanam Luang or called as "Thung Phra Main". The event has been held during February-April for once a year together with many activities performed and exhibitions of Thai arts.

Sanam Luang Ground was the rice field in the ancient time. It's called "Thung Phra Main"; the site for royal for the cremation of kings and queens. King Rama V changed the name to "Sanam Luang". It has been used for the Royal Ploughing Ceremony since King Rama IV period and various ceremonies include the royal cremation of the former king and the royal family. Nowadays, it's listed as a historical site.

See **the Bangkok City Pillar Shrine** at the corner of street in front of the palace ground. The City Pillar Shrines or Lak Mueng is found every province in Thailand. Lak Mueng came from ancient traditions; Brahman's customs believed that it's the center of soul for citizens and needed to be respected to the guardian's spirit here.

See **the Bangkok National Museum (some more detail in Museums in Bangkok);** from Sanam Luang Ground, you can see the museum is situated by the street in front of Sanam Luang. This museum was established in 1874, the first museum in Thailand where located within the Palace of Front areas. You can see the **Memorial Monument of Thai Soldier-Volunteers with Allies** in World War I in 1914-1918.

The monument is situated in front of Bangkok National Museum, at the corner of Sanam Luang. The monument is built like pagoda shape, with arches on 4 sides decorated with marble. The front and the back of this monument engraved the reason for the declaration of war, volunteer recruiting, announcement of combat and the travel to the war. The other two sides are inscribed with the names of 19 soldiers who gave their lives with the date and places of their death. The remains of all dead soldiers were placed at the monument on September 24, 1919 in the reign of King Rama VI.

After enjoying the scenery of Sanam Luang, then continue to explore Ratchadamnoen Avenue or ride a ferry boat across the river at Tha Phra Chan near Thammasat University to **Tha Wang Lang Pier**; the west bank of The Chao Phraya River where located near Siriraj Hospital, one of the best medical centers in Thailand. **Siriraj Hospital is** one of the state hospitals in Thailand, it's the primary teaching hospital of the faculty of Medicine Siriraj Hospital of Mahidol University. The hospital was founded by King Rama V (King Chularongkorn) in 1888. It was the resident of King Bhumibol (Rama 9th) for treatment in between 2009-2013 and he died here in Oct13, 2016. You can visit museums inside the hospital which exhibits history of medicine in Thailand from traditional to modern medicine. Must try street food nearby the Tha Wang Lang Pier and enjoy walking along the food vendors. The location of Siriraj hospital is surrounded by many old buildings and much street food at the opposite side. You can explore the areas by walking through the small alleys through an old temple called Wat Rakang.

WAT RAKANG

Enjoy walking around and pass through a narrow lane which led to **Wat Rakhang Kositaram** or called as Wat Rakhang or "Wat Luang Por Tho".

The temple is one of the old temples of Ayutthaya Period. "Rakhang" means "Bell", so you can see a huge bell on the front ground of the temple. From the temple's historical background, an old bell was found in the temple ground during restoration in the reign of King Rama I. This bell was moved to Wat Phra Kaew and the king ordered to make 5 more bells for Wat Rakhang. At the **Wat Rakhang Pier** is situated a huge Monk Statue of Luang Por Toh; or Somdet Toh (1788-1872); he was one of the most famous and well respected monk in Thailand, his statues are seen nationwide in the temples and his amulets; which believed that the Buddha amulets are full of supernatural power, are sought among all worshippers. He was an abbot of Wat Rakhang during King Rama IV-V period. People come here for paying homage to his statue and have a chance for evening-chanting with the monks in the late afternoon at the ordination hall.

The ordination hall of Wat Rakang enshrined a beautiful principal Buddha or called as **"Luang Por Yim";** "Yim" means "Smile", the name of the Buddha came from when King Rama V visited the temple for religious ceremony and appreciated the statue and then he named the Buddha Statue as "Phra Yim Rub Fah"; means the principal Buddha smiles to everyone who enters the hall. The other beautiful unique architectures in Wat Rakang is **the Scripture Halls** situated near an old Phra Viharn Hall. This hall was the office hall of King Rama I during his serving in Thonburi Period and when he reigned as the king, he renovated the hall for offering to the temple as a Scripture Hall of the temple which is considered as one of the beautiful Tripitaka Hall. From Wat Rakang, you can ride a boat to Wat Arun and Wat Kalayanamit. There is a boat tour for 3 temples; Wat Rakang, Wat Arun and Wat Kalayanamit from the local taxi boats or you can get the riverboat passing by for dropping on-off the temples.

WAT KALAYANAMIT

Wat Kalayanamit is located next to Wat Rakang. It was built in the reign of King Rama III. You can come here from Pak Klong Talat Pier by ferry boat or come from Wat Arun. The temple is famous for the the principal Buddha image which built in "Pa Leh Lai" attitude and the mural painting of the ordination hall were described the picture of "Doctor Bradley" and his raft house.

"Phra Pang Pa Leh Lai" is the image of Buddha built in sitting position on a stone, the feet on the lotus, the right hand is turned upward on his right knee and the left hand is turned downward on his left knee, with an elephant statue kneeled down with a pail of water in its trunk and a monkey statue carried honeycomb for offering to the Buddha.

Doctor Bradley or Dan Beach Bradley was an American Protestant missionary who traveled to Siam in 1835 and lived until his death. He brought the first Thai-script printing press to Siam for publishing the first newspaper, performed the first surgery and introduced the western medicine and technology to Siam. He lived his life within Kudichin Community near the temple.

WAT ARUN OR THE TEMPLE OF DAWN

I usually ride a boat from Wat Rakhang to Wat Arun or **THE TEMPLE OF DAWN.** The temple looks so beautiful not only at dawn but also at night. If you join the dinner cruise tour, you will see the lights on the pagoda image with other small pagodas surrounded. It's a nice shot from the Chao Phraya River, the landmark of Thonburi.

Going to The Temple of Dawn can be done from Wat Pho or The Grand Palace by river boats from the 4 piers; Tha Tien, Tha Chang, Tha Maharaj and Tha Phra Chan, or ride MRT to Issaraphap Station exit 2 and walk for about 10 mins. **The Temple of Dawn** was an old temple since Ayutthaya Period. The former name is called Wat Chaeng; "Chaeng" means "Clearly Seen:" It was a royal temple inside the palace during King Taksin period when the palace was expanded to the temple area. **Phra Prang Wat Arun** is the highest Prang Tower in Thailand and a symbol of Tourism Authority of Thailand. The Temple of Dawn joined the special event on St. Patrick's Day; The Global Greening Programme 2021, at 19.00 Pm., the Huge Phra Prang went green.

Not only the pagoda you meet but the main hall is enshrined with a very beautiful Buddha image. I would like you to get inside the hall before climbing the pagoda.

Admire the beautiful Rattanakosin art of Phra Phuttadhamma Mitsarath Lokathart Dilok; the principal Buddha image in the ordination hall of Wat Arun. The statue is made of bronze with gold gilded and lacquered. The ashes of King Rama II were enshrined at the base of the Buddha statue. It's said that the figure of the Buddha's face was made by King Rama II and the body of the statue sculpted by King Rama III. The temple and the stunning pagoda were renovated since King Rama I-IV period.

The beautiful pagoda or Phra Prang Wat Arun can be seen clearly from the boat ride. Phra Prang or the huge pagoda situated nearby the river-bank is surrounded by 4 Prangs. The original size of Phra Prang was only 16-meter-high built since Ayutthaya period. It was rebuilt in 1842 and renovated as it's seen nowadays in the reign of King Rama V period about in 1909.

The height of Phra Prang is 81.85 meters, made of brick covered with plaster and decorated with colorful porcelains from China made into Angels, Yak and Phaya Krut or Garuda (a mystical bird) images around the pagoda. You can climb to the top floor but be careful of the steep stairs. The wideview over the Chao Phraya River and Bangkok city can be seen beautifully from the top of Phra Prang.

The temples and city tours for one day trip are The Grand Palace and Wat Pho in the morning and have lunch at Tha Maharaj or Tha Phra Chan then continues with Wat Rakang, Wat Arun and Wat Kalayanamit by ferry boat, taxi boat or the routine express boat. Visit Tha Wang Lang and back to Wat Mahathat. Wow! you can visit many places in one day and it's worth it.

If you have time or your accommodation is at Khaosan road, you can ride the boat to **Tha Phra Artit** where it's full of café and restaurants. The areas are appreciated as the old-style city areas where it was the locations of many palaces since King Rama IV period. You will see a park called **Santichaiprakan Park;** a small urban park at the end of Phra Arthit Road, located at the east bank of Chao Phraya River. The park was built for celebration of King Bhumibol's 72nd Birthday Anniversary on December 5th, 1999, houses the Santichaiprakan Throne Hall and Phra Sumain Fort; built since King Rama I period, the last mangrove apples or called in Thai "Lumphu" (the name of Banglumphu Market came from this flower) is left within the park.

The scenery of Chao Phraya River is fascinating when you see from this park. It's the place for admiring The Royal Barge Procession during the most significant cultural and religious events. It's also a good atmosphere along the walkway by the Chao Phraya River, as for viewing the nice scenery of Rama 8th Bridge, quite a place where remind us of the old days here whenever we sit and relax awhile near the river. **I recommend Tha Phra Artit.**

WAT PRAYURAWONGSAWAT OR WAT PRAYUN

Wat Prayurawongsawat Worawihan is a one of the royal monasteries, located near the foot of the Phra Phuttha Yodfa Bridge on the Thon Buri side, on Prachathipok Road, Bangkok. The restoration of the temple resulted the temple being awarded the 1st prize (Award of Excellence) for the restoration project of Phra Borommathat Maha Chedi of Wat Prayurawongsawas. on cultural conservation in the Asia-Pacific region of the United Nations Educational, Scientific and Cultural Organization (UNESCO).

Phra Borommathat Chedi or the main pagoda is a large, round chedi, of the oval shape, height 60.525 meters, the lower base is around 162 meters, diameter 50 meters, there are 54 booths lined the ground floor of the chedi, and the upper floor next to the booth surrounded by the 18 smaller chedi. Somdej Chao Phraya Borommaha Prayoonwong; who donated the land to build this temple since the reign of King Rama III, was the one who started to build this big pagoda but he passed away before it's finished. The pagoda was complete in the reign of King Rama IV. The pagoda was ruined by lightning and was left damaged for 47 years. In 1918, the pagoda was repaired and had a celebration when it's enshrined by Buddha's Relic. The current abbot of the temple made the largest reconstruction of the Great Chedi in 2006. Many Buddha relics and old amulets were discovered on the main chedi on November 5 and 7, 2007. Her Royal Highness Princess Maha Chakri Sirindhorn Rajasuda was graciously presided over the ceremony to bring the relics to be enshrined on the Great Chedi on the occasion of the 180th Anniversary of Wat Prayurawongsawas Worawihan on December 11, 2008.

More places inside the Wat Prayun temple are such as the main ordination hall and the Principal Buddha image, the Viharn Hall (Pavilion of Buddha statue), Khao Mor; a small model mountain. Made of stone, located in the middle of the pond in front of the temple, there is a pavilion of 8 faces located beside the pond to enshrine a Buddha image and it is a place to relax There is a staircase leading up to the top of the mountain, the chedi of Khrua Khaew, and Buddha statues Museum.

RATCHA DAM NOEN AVENUE

Walk along **Ratcha-dam-noen Avenue**, the historic road in Bangkok, the main road is where some old buildings and temples are seen. You can ride taxi or Tuk Tuk for looking around after the Grand Palace tour. You will pass by this avenue before going to the Marble Temple which located near the Equestrian Statue of King Chularlongkorn the Great or King Rama V. But if you would like to explore places around the street areas, you can walk and ride taxi or tuk-tuk to see the monuments, Wat Saketh, Wat Ratchanadda and Wat Suthat with the Giant Swing.

The view of Wat Ratchanaddaram and Phu Khao Thong (Golden Mount) or Wat Saketh can be seen along the Ratcha Dam Noen Avenue as well as the Democracy Monument; a famous site for protestors of all ages.

The Democracy Monument was situated on Ratcha Dam Noen Avenue, which was commissioned in 1939 to commemorate of "Siamese Revolution of 1932". Most of the buildings located along the road are ministries and military company through the Equestrian Statue of King Rama V **and The Ananta Samakhom Throne Hall**; The Reception Hall for the king at The Dusit Palace, where you are still on Ratchadamnoen Avenue, at the end point of the road if you come from the Grand Palace. (By turning right, you will meet The Marble Temple and Jitlada Palace; the palace where King Bhumibol and Queen Sirikij and the royal family live.) The Equestrian Statue of King Chulalongkorn the Great or King Rama V is standing outdoor at the center of the Royal Plaza for honoring the king. The statue was cast in bronze and erected here on November 11, 1908 to commemorate his 40th anniversary of his accession to the throne which was the longest-reigning monarch at that time.

King Chulalongkorn the Great was the fifth king of Siam, belonged to Chakri Dynasty. He was born in 1853 and died in 1910. The king was characterized as modernization and reformation to Siam. His Majesty the king; King Chulalongkorn, from his important royal duties which changed Thai tradition and culture and best known such as; the abolition of slavery, prostration and commoners in Siam, defense of the colonialism of the French and British Empires and announced the independent to other religious people in the country like, those who were Christians and Islam. During reigning Siam; the other royal duties by King Chulalongkorn the Great, he established and developed modern systems for making people more comfortable living; by regarding of conveniences and benefits to the people in the country, he started such as; railway system; the first railway was opened in 1901 from Bangkok to Korat and the first power plant of Siam produced electricity and electric lights illuminated firstly along roadways, communication; post office and telegram, water supply to households, roads and canals dug for convenient transportation and traveling.

The king also developed education by establishing modern school and sent some of his people to study abroad and the administrative reformed by establishing ministers; like the defense ministry was established in 1887 and councils. All of his reforms were dedicated to ensuring Siam's independence from western powers at that time. **The Great King earned the epithet "Phra Piya Maharaj" which means "the Great Beloved King".** October 23rd was the day he died and announced by the government as the public holiday; the present king and queen and the royal family, people from different groups of professions and some from other provinces will put wreaths and beautiful flowers for remembering His Majesty's grace in front of the Equestrian Statue of King Chulalongkorn.

Photo of Anantasamakom Throne Hall

WAT SAKETH

Wat Sa Keth; or called as a **Golden Mount is a t**emple built since Ayutthaya period, it is where you can view a picturesque Bangkok of old areas from the top of the pagoda or at the temple's corner. The **golden** pagoda is seen outstanding on the high base of the temple by Ratchadamnoen Avenue. It's very beautiful sight if you pass by this area. The temple located near Mahanak Canal and recognized by the Thai for the temple's festival during the full-moon Buddhist Lent Day. Not only the festival is recocnized but also the famous legend about the **"Vulture of Wat Saketh"** has been talked all over the country.

The Pagoda on the hilltop; a model of a hill constructed in the temple with the pagoda similar to the pagoda at Wat Phu Khao Thong of Ayutthaya, was built from the wish of King Rama III at the beginning but finished in the reign of King Rama IV in 1865, contained Buddha's relic. The height is about 59 meters or equal to 19 storey-building. You can climb the staircases for 344 steps which built around from the bottom up to the top to view the Bangkok city. In fact, the most interesting area at Wat Sa Keth is on the top of the Golden Mount. When we reach here, we walk around the pagoda by right turn three times to pay respect and light the candle with incent sticks before chanting, afterwards; we usually sit still before viewing the landscape of Bangkok city where you can see the contrast of old buildings and houses and the new ones densely located around the temple.

The Buddha's Relic kept here was given by the government of India in 1899; which was excavated from the old pagoda near the hill at Kabinlapath City in India, the relics are put inside a casket with Brahmi characters inscribed that "This Relic belongs to Buddha (Samana Guatama). Sakaya Raj Family received this Buddha's Relic from the share at the time after The Buddha's Cremation. The Buddha's Relic is given to King Rama V." The king commanded to keep this Buddha's Relic inside the Golden Pagoda of Wat Sa Keth. The big and important event is held at Wat Saketh during Loy Krathong Festival every year is called "Phu Khao Thong Fair" for about 7-10 days where people come for paying respect to the Buddha's Relic.

"Reang of Wat Saket"; Reang means vulture. It is a famous legend of the vulture at Wat Saket, said that when cholera spread throughout Thailand during the reign of King Rama III in 1820 and about 30,000 people died in the capital. Wat Saket was the main place for receiving the body, with too many bodies here, the temple was unable to cremate all the bodies. Many of them were left at outdoor and let many vultures eat their bodies. It is a story that has been passed down from generation to generation when it comes to Wat Saket, and there is also a story about the fierce ghost at this temple as well. There is a sculptural stone of vultures and story along the way to the Golden Mount.

WAT RATCHANADDARAM

Wat Ratchanaddaram is the temple located opposite to Wat Sa Keth at the corner near Mahakan Fort; one of the 14 forts built in the reign of King Rama I, but it's one of the two forts left now in Bangkok. The temple was built in 1846 in the reign of King Rama III. This temple is one of the archaeological sites where **The Loha Prasat**; the first steel castle in Thailand and the only one Buddhist Steel Castle left in the world. King Rama III ordered to build this steel castle instead of pagoda. Loha Prasat are 3-storey building with 37 spire-roofs as Mondop, a beautiful Thai art of Rattanakosin era. The buildings were renovated in 2015 by cladding gold leaves on Mondops at the 2nd and 3rd floor. The courtyard is called the Maha Jetsadabordin which is an outdoor courtyard for the king to receive his guests during visiting Thailand. The courtyard was built in 1989 situated at the front of the temple where can be seen by the footpath along the road. The statue of King Rama III was built at the front monument before entering to the temple. The top floor is a beautiful spot for **viewing Loha Prasart**, Maha prakan Fort and the Golden Mount at Wat Sa Keth.

WAT BENJAMABORPIT OR THE MARBLE TEMPLE

The Marble Temple or Benchamabophit Temple was built in 1899 during the reign of King Rama V, near the Dusit Palace; his residence. Firstly; When entering the temple, there is a beautiful ordination hall in front of you, this is the main building of the temple. The courtyard and the statue of lions are made of Italian marble; the Carrara Marble. The front of the chapel is a beautiful photograph that has been selected for placing on a Five-Baht coin. You can get inside the hall for admiring the beautiful statue Buddha image and see the photo of King Chularlongkorn or King Rama V during his monkhood in front of the Buddha image.

The beautiful Sukhothai Art of Principal Buddha Image is called Phra Phuttha Chinnaraj; built in 1920, a copy of the original one in Phitsanulok Province. Within the base of the Buddha Statue are the ashes of King Rama V buried. The interior of the ordination hall; the main hall, decorated with lacquer and gold in paintings all the pictures of important pagodas of Thailand and some colorful stained glasses decorated above the windows are clearly seen when it's shone in the light. Along the cloister around the hall houses 52 images of Buddha in different attitudes. About the Buddha images that were built in various postures, they were all created from the history of the Lord Buddha, and the different beliefs about Buddha would be formed in different positions depending on the era of the kingdom and the beliefs of the people in that country.

The Buddha statues in many postures seen in Thailand were depended on the periods; such as Dhawaravadi, Sri Vichai, Lopburi, Chiang Saen, Sukhothai, Ayutthaya and Rattanakosin.

The postures are mostly seen in Thailand are: **Meditation Attitude** is the position of sitting cross-legged with both hands on his lap. **Mara Vijaya** Attitude or calling the earth to witness is the position of one hand on the lap but the other is towards the ground. **Leela** Attitude is the position of walking with stepping with one hand towards the front while the other swings. **Naga Prok** Attitude is the position of sitting position and sheltered by Naga; a mystical snake with 7 heads, after the Enlightenment. **Khor Phon** Attitude is the position of seated or standing position with one hand beckoning for rain falling. **Mor Ya** Attitude is the position of seated position with one hand holding the holy cauldron.

The First Sermon Attitude is the position of sitting cross-legged, with left hand supporting the right hand as the sign of wheel of dharma. **Um Bart** Attitude is the position of seated or standing images and holding the alms with both hands. **Pratan Pon** Attitude is the position of blessing by sitting or standing and or walking positions. **Siyat** or **Reclining** Attitude is the position of lying on the right side for sleeping and also might meant Nirvana posture or Buddha's last day. **Lei Laih** Attitude is the position of sitting on the stone, the feet placed on the lotus, the left hand is placed upside down on the knee and the right hand placed supine on the right knee included with images of crouching elephant using its trunk to hold a pail of water and a monkey holding a honeycomb. The Buddha's attitude which is the distinctive point of the Marble Temple is the position of Dhukkha; when the Lord Buddha abstained from food and drink during his intense meditation.

There are many more Buddha images built in different eras which are based on the history of the Lord Buddha. Some of them was an accompanying story from the Tripitaka which depended on the belief of the person who created the statue at that time. The group of **pavilions** near the canal is the residence when King Rama V was ordained. **Sala Si Somdet** is a stone-floored square pavilion, the roof is decorated with a bouquet of rooster leaves, built by King Rama V and his family, as a resting place for monks and novices, at present, Sala Si Somdej is used as a **drum tower**. The drum is for telling monks the time for meal and services of the temple, it's quite the same as striking the bell.

Early in the morning, people come to Wat Benjamaborpit or the Marble temple for offering to the monks' alms and meditate in the hall. The monk preaches in the hall during Buddha's Day and the hall may be crowded, but you are allowed to get inside here.

THE GOLDEN BUDDHA AT WAT TRIMITH

Travel to Wat Trimit can do by MRT: Hualumphong Statation; **THE HUA LUM PHONG RAILWAY STATION IS HERE, and walk to Trimit** Road for visiting Wat Trimit or The Golden Buddha Temple. When I was a tour guide, I started the temple tour from Wat Trimit because it's easy to continue the route to Wat Pho easily and the tourists could see the China Town areas when passing Yaowaraj. **Wat Trimith** is one of the oldest temples located nearby Yaowaraj Road or China Town Areas.The former name of Wat Trimit was Wat "Sam Chin" which means "three Chinese"; assumed that built by the three Chinese which were friends. In 1934, the temple was restored by the former abbot and after that the temple was named "Wat Trimith" in 1939. The areas of this temple consist of the religious rituals ground and schools; for monks and public school. People come here for the Golden Buddha.

Phra Sukhothai Trimit; the golden Buddha Statue is the biggest golden Buddha statue in the world, the height is 3.91 meters and the width is 3.01 meters, made of solid gold weigh 5.5 tons.

The Buddha was original covered with stucco and unknown about the origins; but from the art of sculpture, the sculpture would be the style of Sukhothai during 13th Century.

The statue was original covered with stucco and situated outdoor at Wat Phraya Krai near the Chao Phraya River before. It was assumed that the golden statue was covered to protect the gold and prevent from stealing; especially, preventing the enemies during the war.

The Buddha Statue was moved to Wat Trimit and situated outdoor nearby the road for 20 years because of the huge size. The plaster was clacked in 1955 during moving the statue for situating inside the new hall and the gold appeared. The abbot ordered for removing all the plasters from the statue. The plasters covering the statue are displayed to the public in the temple. King Rama 9th ordered to build a new Mondop Building; a square building with spire-roof, covering the Buddha Statue in 2007 for The King's 80th Birthday Celebration. Walk along the small alleys of the China Town from Wat Trimit. (Get some nice Thai-Chinese food at the opposite side of the temple such as noodles, rice with grilled pork seasoned with sweet sauce or "Khow Moo Dang" and Pad Thai by street, I recommend! **The China Town is started behind Wat Trimit. You can view the road on the top floor of the chapel.** Enjoy walking along **Yaowaraj Road** (about 1.5 kilometers) in the China Town area. If you ride the subway, MRT: Wat Mangkorn Station is the destination to explore China Town; the amazing markets which are full of everything you need, especially delicious food from many kinds of restaurants.

WAT MANGKORN OR WAT LENG NEI YI AT YAOWARAJ

Wat Mangkon Kamalawat or Leng Nei Yi Temple is a temple under the Chinese Sect of Thailand. This temple is sometimes called "Dragon Temple"; Mangkorn means Dragon and because the word "Leng" or "Leng" in Teochew means dragon ("Nei" means lotus and "Yi" means temple). Official name is "Wat Mangkon Kamalawat" bestowed by King Rama VI on February 16, 1911. This temple was established in 1871 and it took 8 years to complete the construction which was built in architectural style in the southern Chinese style of the Teochew artisan family. The plan was based on the royal temple style, which was the first viharn of Thao Chatulokban, in the middle was the location of the ordination hall or the Ubosot. The viharn of the gods was built behind the Ubosot.

The construction of Wat Mangkorn was made of wood and brick as important materials. The temple is located on **Charoen Krung Road** Between Soi Charoenkrung 19 and 21 in Pom Prap Sattru Phai, Bangkok, MRT: at Wat Mangkorn Station. It is familiar among Thai people of Chinese descent. and Chinese from abroad Pilgrims often come to pray for good fortune inside the ancient hall.

WAT LENG NEI YI 2 AT BANG BUA THONG

Wat Boromracha Kanchanaphisek Memorial the Creation Sect Chinese Sect or Leng Nei Yi Temple 2 is a Mahayana temple under the patronage of the Chinese Sect of Thailand. It is located at Bang Bua Thong District in Nonthaburi Province (**by taxi**), this large temple was built to honor His Majesty King Bhumibol Adulyadej the Great on the occasion of the 50th Anniversary Celebration of His Majesty's Accession to the Throne, June9, 1996.The temple has completed constructions for more than 12 years (1996-2008). The temple's area consists of various sanctuaries with architectural styles based on the philosophy and morals of the Mahayana Buddhist sect. The important buildings are such as Viharn of Guan Yin Bodhisattva, Viharn of Ten Thousand Buddhas, Viharn Burapha Chan Dharma practice room, monk's residence and Phrapariyattidhamma school.

Fun Kayaking along The Klong Ong Ang; it's a part of canals around Bangkok City but located at the center of Bangkok within the areas of The China Town and Indian Market. It's known as the important canal for journey since the past. The original canal was modeled from Rialto Canal in Italy and made in the reign of King Rama V, during that time it was very popular and unique spot for public uses but when the road was developed and constructed for giving people more convenient traveling then the area was covered with residents and commercial buildings, and then finally the canal become sewerage canal. Later in 2015, the government had demolished buildings along this canal and transformed the landscape into the walking street then the canal areas become a tourist attraction of Bangkok. It's where you can now see a Street of Art and can find some hostels in an old style of buildings nearby to enjoy and experience the living in other side of Bangkok instead of Khaosan Road and also you can taste variety of much Indian food. I like here.

THE GIANT SWING

The **Giant Swing is where you will see** the street of religious supplier shops near the Bangkok Metropolitan Administration. You are at Dinso Road; one of the old roads in Bangkok, built in the reign of King Rama V. "Dinso" means "Pencil", because it's the areas where people made a career by producing pencil and papers since Ayutthaya period (1350-1767) until Rattanakosin Period. When the road was expanded in 1898, the pencil-making career has already gone. The areas of **Dinso Road** and nearby roads like; **Thanow Road, Mahannop Road**, **Prangphuthon Road and Prangnara Road**, now are full of restaurants with delicious food and Thai desserts. There are some classic hostels and boutique hotels; adapted from old wooden houses, situated around the areas. The road started from the Giant Swing straight with the length of 850 meters, passing the Democracy monument and ending at Wanchart Bridge.

THE GIANT SWING; was built in 1784 and renovated many times, the swing is situated on the stone base with its height of 21.15 meters. The Swing Ceremony was a part of Hindu Rituals performed and celebrated here for until the reign of King Rama VII then it was cancelled because of accidents. Nowadays, the rituals are performed inside the shrine only. The Giant Swing or called as Sao Ching Cha was started since the reign of King Rama I, the first pair of swing pillars was erected in 1784, in front of the Brahmin Chapel. The pillar has a height of 21.15 meters with a round base made of white wash stone, built as the center of the city and to use the swing pillar as the main in the Tri Yampawai-Tripawai ceremony or swing which was a royal ceremony that brahmins have practiced since ancient times. Later in the reign of King Rama V, the swing was relocated, to be built a new one in front of Wat Suthat until nowadays. **The Fine Arts Department has announced to be registered as an important national monument on November 22, 1949. The swing has been renovated many times.**

WAT SUTHAT

The temple located close to the Giant Swing is called **Wat Suthat; a beautiful temple on Bumrungmuang Road,** built in 1807. The former name of this temple was given by King Rama I called as "Wat Sutthawath" but the temple was established completely in the reign of King Rama III in 1847 and the name was changed to "Wat Suthat Thep Wararam" was given. The King Rama 8th Monument is situated inside this temple and his ashes was placed at the base of The Principal Buddha Statue in the ordination hall. There are many beautiful architectures and sculptures inside **Wat Suthat** temple such as; the amazing ordination hall with its size; it is 72.25-meter-long and 22.60-meter-wide, the longest size in Thailand.

The Principal Buddha image in the ordination hall or **"Phra Sri Sakaya Munee" is** the biggest bronze-made Buddha Statue, built since Sukhothai Period (1249-1463). The other amazing size of the large **Phra Viharn** of the Buddha image is about 24-meter wide and 27-meter long with the Thai art style decorations and see the outstanding painting on the doors (front and back) that painted by King Rama II., and admire some Chinese dolls and animal sculptures put around the temple. I would like to talk about **Pret at Wat Suthat as it's a local legend of this area**. "Pret" is known as a kind of animal with abnormal tall with small mouth born in hell; according to the Buddhist's belief, told by the legend that if anyone who's greedy or steal or cheat others will be born to be Pret after death. It's assumed that Pret at Wat Suthat may have originated from a painting on the side pillar of Phra Sri Sakyamunee, the principal Buddha. **It is a painting** that was drawn during the reign of King Rama V, it's a figure of Pret lied on the ground and monks standing at the body. This picture was very famous in the past and become the rumors that if anyone has the opportunity to see Phra Sri Sakyamunee statue in the Grand hall then must see the painting of "Pret Wat Suthat" until it was said widely that see "The Vulture of Wat Saket, and the Pret at Wat Suthat"

In addition, there is also a story from mouth to mouth that there are frequent sightings of Pret at night near the temple. From this incident; it's assumed that it may be a misunderstanding of those who see the Giant swing pillar in front of the temple in the foggy morning, and from poor visibility, then mistakenly it is ghost or a Pret.

Be careful that "Pret" is a Thai slang bad word for calling someone who's really bad.

The areas outside the temple are many religious supplier-shops around the Giant Swing. The religious supplier-shops sell like, Buddha image statues, incent sticks and candles, god images, items for festival decorations, and tradition items used for religious rituals. Eating Thai food from a small restaurant and the night vendors here are cool. If you walk along Mahachai Road, you will come across Pad Thai (Thip Samai) and Jay Phai; the famous crab meat wrapped with eggs. The street vendors will come during sunset. I recommend here.

I think if you choose to visit within these areas, you need one day trip by starting Wat Saketh, Wat Ratchanadda, Wat Suthat, Wat Ratchabophit and together with the Giant Swing areas. It's nice to walk by the old shops, buildings, and old canals, and include Pahurat Market; the Indian market, if you have time. Many nice Indian restaurants wait for you to try. I always enjoy being here indeed.

WAT INTHARAVIHARN

From Khaosan Road, you can walk to Wat Intharaviharn; the famous temple where the huge standing Buddha situated. It's assumed that the temple was built before Rattanakosin Period, it was restored by Chao Int; the Laosian who lived by the temple that time, therefore; the temple was named from his name. The name was called "Wat Int" until it was changed to Wat Intharaviharn in the reign of King Rama VI because the name was the same name as "Wat Inthraram" at Bang Yee Rua. Luang Por Tho or the Standing Buddha was built in the attitude of holding the alm (the robe cover the alm) The statue is 32 meter high built in 1867 by Luang Por Tho (the former abbot of Wat Rakang) in the reign of King Rama IV but finished in the reign of King Rama VII, was named "Phra Puttasi Ariya Mettri" when the construction was finished in 1924. This head part of this sacred Buddha Statue was enshrined Buddha's Relic given from Sri Lanka in 1980. The statue was the highest statue in Bangkok before, until the Big Buddha Image at Wat Paknam Phasi Jaroen was finished in 2021 with the height of 69 meters and become the highest Buddha Statue now.

WAT YANNAWA

Wat Yannawa is a royal monastery, located on the Chao Phraya River Adjacent to Charoen Krung Road, Sathorn District in Bangkok, you can come here by Skytrain drop at Saphan Taksin Station; exit 3-4 and walk about 5 minutes to reach the temple. It is an ancient temple that has existed since the Ayutthaya period, formerly known as "Wat Khok Kwhy"; “Kwhy” means “buffalo”, due to the large number of Dawei people who settled there. and the Dawei people brought the buffaloes they raise to trade in the villages in that area which were later called "Ban Khok Kwhy".

During in the reign of King Rama III, the king was graciously pleased to restore and build a chedi or pagoda in the form of barge instead of the general stupa for future generations to see the style of junk boats that perhaps about to disappear from Thailand. Therefore; the name of the temple was changed to "Wat Yannawa". “Yannawa” means “Sampao” which is called as a kind of the boats in ancient time. There are also two large and small pagodas in the Sampao; in which the Bali room has a statue of Vessandhorn and Kanha in the Vessantara Jataka; it is one of the last Buddha’s past Lives, at the stern of a boat. The story of the statues is when Phra Vessandhorn persuaded his son; Kanha to devote himself together with the Father to create great merit like a large Sampao transporting humanity across the cyclicality of all life, matter, and existence to Nirvana. People come here to pay homage to the Buddha's relics enshrined inside the Sampao.

THE GIANT BUDDHA AT WAT PAKNAM PHASI JAROEN

When you are in Thonburi District, you have to visit the well-known temple with Big Buddha image located by Phasi Jaroen Canal. The boat trip along this canal is fascinating; full of beautiful temples and one of the popular and very famous temples is Wat Paknam Phasi Jaroen. **Wat Paknam** was established in about 1610 during Ayutthaya period. It locates near Phasi Jaroen Canal. You can go to this temple by MRT and get off at Bang Phai Station, but you have to walk along the narrow road of Phetkasem Soi 23 about 2 kilometers to reach the temple. I think you should get a taxi for about 40 Bahts here rather than walking.

The temple is well organized with many large buildings includes a huge Stupa and the large Buddha Statue. It was a royal temple during Ayutthaya Period according to evidences found in the temple area. The location of this temple is like a square island, surrounded by water. It was an important temple outside the capital city, in front of the maritime outpost. The temple was renovated by preserving the ancient arts from many kings. It was found dilapidated from its old ages and lacked of abbot, during the reign of King Rama VI, Luang Por Sod was sent from Wat Pho to be the abbot. He encouraged monks and novices to learn Dhamma (Buddha's Teaching) and practiced meditation strictly. The temple then became advanced school for teaching Pali and the center for learning meditation.

When you arrive at the temple, please go to the sacred stupa or called as Phra Maha Chedi by entering inside the huge tower-shape which is 80 meter high with five floors; the 2nd floor is a museum of Buddhist items includes the Buddha statues collected from old time, the 3rd floor has the Luang Por Sod statue; the former abbot and the 4th floor has a beautiful pagoda of Buddha's Relic decorated with naga around the base. You can admire the views and a large Buddha statue from the 3rd floor.Must see the Big Buddha; Phra Phuttha Dhammakai Thepmongkon; which is as tall as 20th floor building, with 69 meter high and 40 meter wide built in 2017 to honor Luang Por Sod and the Royal family. Luang Por Sod was the former abbot who has been widely known for starting "Dhammakai Meditation" method. You can see Luang Por Sod statue with beautiful devotional and people from different areas come to pay their respects with respect.

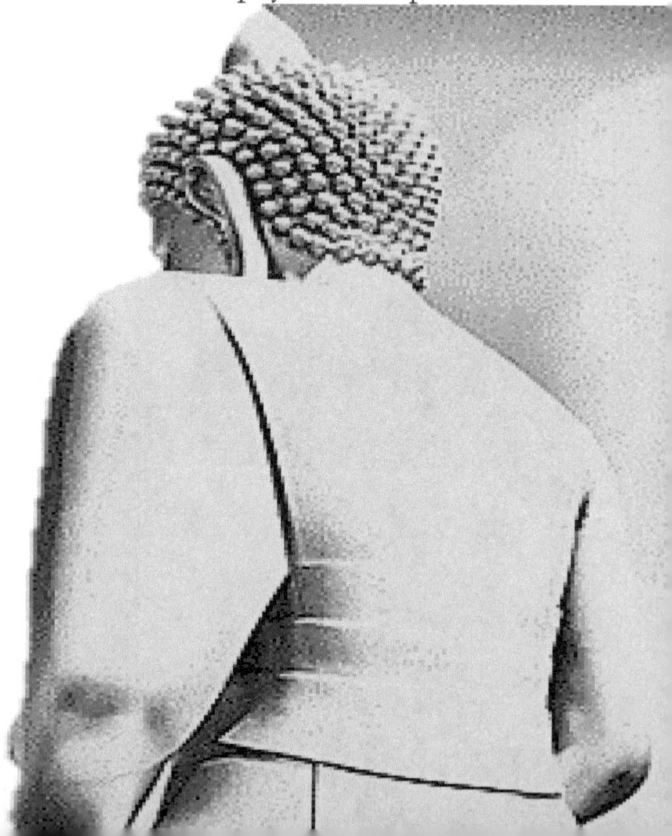

WAT DHAMMAMONGKOL, THE WILLPOWER INSTITUTE

Admire the **big green Jade Buddha** statue at **Wat Dhammamongkol** on Sukhumvit Road 101 alley. (BTS: at Pun-na-withi Station) When you get off the train here, get a taxi or local tuktuk to the temple.

Wat Dhammamongkol was built by Luang Por Viriyang Sirintharo; the forest monk who chose here as a pilgrimage accommodation during his journey to Bangkok. The owner of this land donated the land to him then the temple was built in 1963. There are many important architectures and sculptures to see such as; **Phra Viriyang Monkol Maha Chedi**; the pagoda where enshrined Buddha's Relic at the base; the huge pagoda is 94.78 meter high with 14 floors; composed of the exhibition room, museum, library, computer room and the ground hall is the school for Willpower Meditation, **Phra Yok** or the biggest green jade Buddha statue in the world which was named as "Phra Phuttha Mongkol Dhamma Sri Thai"; this jade was found under the Ice Lake in Canada. There is also a **cave** built for simulating the practice atmosphere in the forest-cave with screened door that can hold more than 200 people inside the cave.

The buildings inside Wat Dhammamongkol are dense because of the area is quite limited but convenient for people who wants to stay for practicing meditation at the institute of **Willpower** which found and initiated by Luang Por Viriyang. He had a reputation as a well-disciplined Buddhist monk and was highly respected among Thais and foreigners throughout approximately 80 years of his life in monkhood. Currently, it has spread throughout Thailand and some other countries. Luang Por Viriyang died when he was 100 years old. His previous position was not only the former abbot of Wat Dhammamongkol but also the Chairman of Dhammayuttika Nikaya monk in Canada.

MUSEUMS IN BANGKOK

BANGKOK NATIONAL MUSEUM

Open Wed-Sun and national holidays

8.30 am-16.00 pm.

This museum was the first museum in Thailand which was established in 1874 in the reign of King Rama V. The museum was originally located within the palace area for about 13 years until the Palace of Front or Wang Na position was cancelled and the palace become vacant so the museum was moved here till now since 1887. The entrance to the museum composed of Siwamok Phiman Hall and Phutthaisawan Hall.

There are ancient architectural halls (please see photo below) and sculptural items in addition to ancient art; like Ram Khamhaeng Inscription and Ratcharot Noi or the Royal Chariots; engraved with lacquer and gilded decorated with glass, made in the reign of King Rama I. The museum exhibits with all historical background of Thailand in each period. Bangkok National Museum still has a unique Thai architecture, one of the most prominent of the Rattanakosin.There are many throne halls exhibited Thai History, Archaeology, Arts, the architecture of the Palace of Front and etc. Please don't miss here.

THE ROYAL THAI AIRFORCE MUSEUM

Open Tue-Sun 9.00 am-15.30 pm (Closed on Monday and Public Holidays)

It is located near Don Muang Airport. You can come here by BTS Skytrain and stop at the Royal Thai Airforce Museum Station. (Phahonyothin Route) The museum was established in 1952 for collecting and restoring different airplanes and other aviation equipment used by the Royal Thai Air Force.

Some of the aircrafts displayed are rare like F11C and also includes one of 2 surviving Japanese Tachikawa Ki-36 trainers, the last surviving Vought O2U Corsair, one of 3 surviving Curtiss BF2C Goshawks, a spitfire and several Nieuports and Breguets. The museum provides also the details of Thailand's role during the World War II.

THE ROYAL BARGES NATIONAL MUSEUM

Open Mon-Sun 9.00 am-17.00 pm

It was originally a dock or barn for royal ceremonial boats, taken care and controlled by the Bureau of the Royal Household and the Navy. During World War II, some shipyards and ceremonial ships were blown up and damaged and disrepaired for many years.In 1947, the Bureau of the Royal Household and the Royal Navy commissioned the Fine Arts Department to renovate the royal barges and old boats used in royal ceremonies. All of them are of historical significance and artistic beauty. In 1974, the Fine Arts Department registered various royal barges as national heritages along with raising the status of the Royal Navy shipyard "National Museum ceremonial boat".

The tourists can admire **National Museum of The Royal Barges** of collection of 8 royal barges in Thonburi side by speed boat or by road. If you cross the river from Tha Chang or Tha Phra Chan to Tha Wang Lang; you have to walk along Siriraj Hospital to the main road (New Amarin Rd.) for ten minutes here. You can also come here by ferry boat from Bangkok Noi Train Station here.

The Royal Barges are still used during The Royal Barge Procession on the most significant cultural and religious events.

MUSEUM SIAM

Open Tue-Sun 10.00 am- 18.00 pm

It's near the MRT Snamchai Station. It's the museum of learning under the National Museum of Learning Institute which is the first learning museum focusing on creating a fresh experience in museum viewing. The Museum Siam was established as a model of a "New Concepts and Images" especially; for the Thai children and youth about creating a sense of self-knowledge, through modern technology and creative activities for learning history and stories for more fun. There are ancient objects displayed, knowledge center, souvenir shops, and restaurants in the museum areas.

BANGKOK ART AND CULTURE CENTER

Open Tue-Sun 10.00 am-21.00 pm

Bangkok Art and Culture Center is a contemporary art gallery; located at the northwest corner of Pathumwan Intersection. The location is opposite to the MBK Center and Siam Discovery in the Siam areas. There is a walkway connected directly to the National Stadium BTS Station as well as connecting to the surrounding shopping centers via Skywalk One Siam.

The building is 9 floors high designed to be cylindrical which can be connected between the buildings by a circular walkway inclined up so the people who come to see the work can view continuously on each floor. The exhibition room contains of many sections. The interior also includes a public library, art lab, a 300-seat multipurpose room, shops, and a 222 -seat cinema theater.

KING PRAJADHIPOK MUSEUM

Open Tue-Sun 9.00-16.00

You can visit **King Prajadhipok Museum** by Khlong Saen Saep Canal and drop off **Phan Fa Pier, it's close to Wat Saketh**. The museum was built in 1906, for the collection of King Rama VII and the Queen with royal displays; photo, documents, personal items and royal biography. The museum construction was designed in Neoclassic with the outstanding dome at the middle of the building. It was the location of John Sampson & Son Store; was settled as a branch store from London in 1898, which was persuaded by King Rama V for selling clothes, shoes and saddles.

King Rama V ordered to build the neoclassical building and opened for rent until the company went out of business. King Prajadhipik's Institute managed and renovated the museum to be opened in 2002 by King Bhumibol (King Rama IX). (see the photo below)

MOCA MUSEUM OF CONTEMPORARY THAI ART

Open Tue-Fri 10.00 am-17.00pm; Sat-Sun 11.00 am-18.00 pm

The museum of Contemporary Thai Art is a museum that keeps an interesting collection of Thai art history. The knowledge here is to honor the father of art Professor Silpa Bhirasri. The museum was founded by Mr. Boonchai Bencharongkul for exhibiting art works, visual art works from many generations of artists; which are the teacher's level including the gallery of Richard Green's works. It also shows the uniqueness of Thai art. It is a museum where you can indulge and enjoy the works of art.

RATTANAKOSIN EXHIBITION HALLS

Open Tue-Sun 10.00 am-19.00 pm

When you visit Wat Ratchanaddaram near Wat Saketh or the Golden Mount, you should visit the Rattanakosin Exhibition Hall; its location is at Wat Ratchanaddaram Temple. It is a 4-storey building holds the history of Rattanakosin as a learning center and a resource for information on historical knowledge, art and culture of Rattanakosin Era under the supervision of the Crown Property Bureau. The exhibition has presented various stories of the Rattanakosin Era through the exhibition rooms. There are also interesting points inside the 3 buildings and additional services such as Rattanakosin Exhibition Library; which is a specialized library book collection multimedia about Rattanakosin from the past till the present time, Multipurpose Activity Hall; the hall is for organizing exhibitions or rotating activities throughout the year, the viewpoint on the 4th Floor where you can see the scenery of Ratchadamnoen Avenue. The view of the top floor is the landscape of a beautiful architectural buildings of temples and surroundings in a wide perspective. The exhibition hall provides other services like food, drink, souvenir, and some local products.

QUEEN SIRIKIT MUSEUM OF TEXTILES

This museum (photo below) is located in the Grand Palace at Ratsadakorn Bhibhathana Building which was built since 1873. In 2003; the reign of King Bhumibhol or King Rama IX; Her Majesty Queen Sirikit requested for renovation of this building to be a museum of textiles; which was her efforts for promoting and supporting the production of Thai handicrafts in Thai silk and cotton to be known worldwide, she initiated the museum to preserve Thai textile for admiring the typical Thai Art; which is elegant and unique design, for the future generation. Please don't miss here when you visit the Grand Palace.

MADAME TUSSAUDS BANGKOK

The exhibition of Madame Tussauds Bangkok is located at Siam Discovery (at BTS Siam Station) where displays the life-size of wax statues of international famous people like leaders, scientists, artists, movie stars, sport legends, musicians, celebrities, and historic icons within the different themed rooms.

SUAN PAKKARD PALACE

Open daily 9.00 am-16.00 pm

You can ride BTS Skytrain to Phayathai Station and walk about 15 minutes here. This palace was originally a vegetable garden. It was the private residence of a prince who was a nephew of King Rama V and opened for the public to visit since 1952. When the prince died, his wife gave the palace to be under the care of Chumbot-Pantip Foundation and opened as a museum. There are many interesting artifacts on display in the museum include: Uma Devi sculptures in Lopburi Art, the lacquer-painting since the late Ayutthaya period Hall, and the antiques from Ban Chiang Archaeological Site in Udonthani Province. The Building and Houses in Suan Pakkard Palace are total 8 ancient teakwood architectural Thai Palaces which are the homes of many ancient objects such as paintings, ancient money, statues, and etc.

KUDICHIN MUSEUM

When you visit Wat Kalayanamit; the temple close to Wat Arun, then you should enter to this Kudichin Community for admiring the museum, Christian church, Muslim mosque and the old Chinese Shrine. The charm of Kudichin Community is the diverse cultures of the Thai and Chinese merchants who lived near Wat Kalayanamit during Thonburi period. It's been more than 200 years since the Thai of Portuguese descent have settled along the Chao Phraya riverbank. The long history of the Kudichin Community passed through many generations; from the way of living among Buddhists, Christians, and Muslims, as well as the diverse cultures of the Thai and Chinese in the same neighborhood. **Ban Kudi Chin Museum** is open to visitors for free of charge. The ground floor opens as a small café, the upper section displays and tells the origins of the Catholics with Portuguese, Vietnamese, and Chinese descents together with the foreigners who came into Siam in the reign of King Rama III, especially; the famous historical figures such as Doctor Bradley; an American who lived within this community. It shows the cultural diversity through real items that existed in that era very well. You can go up to the mezzanine level of the museum to enjoy the atmosphere of the Chao Phraya River and the local livings. Don't forget to taste an old-fashioned cake of Kudichin Community.

SUAN MOKE BANGKOK

Open Mon-Sun 9.00 am – 18.00 pm

Phuttha Thart Intapanyo Archives; or called as the Moke Gardens of Bangkok, was situated at Suan Rodfai Park near Jatujak Park. The place is to be a source of collection, conservation, and dissemination of the Dharma (Buddha's Teaching) inherited from Phuttha Thart Bhikkhu given to the future generation. It's a Sacred place designed from the image of the original Suan Moke in Suratthani Province. The original Suan Mok was the famous temple where Phuttha Thart Bhikkhu lived during monkhood. The place is as a modern spiritual learning activity center for creating a calm environment conducive to the practice of meditation, such as using natural light as a backlight to promote the holiness of the sacred objects and the humble architectural design for letting the nature manifest its power and be a spiritual teacher to man; as said by Phuttha Thart Bhikkhu, "Dharma is nature".

Phra Dhammakosajarn (27 May 1906 – 8 July 1993) has been a person registered as an important person in the world by UNESCO. He was known as Phuttha Thart Bhikkhu which means "Buddha's Slave"; was a native of Chaiya District in Surat Thani Province. He was born in 1906, began to study at the age of 20 at the hometown temple then he came to study the monk-school in Bangkok and received the 3rd class of Dharma. **Phuttha Thart Bhikkhu** found that the Buddhist society at that time was very corrupted and distorted and could not reach the heart of Buddhism at all, so he decided to go back to practice Dharma at Chaiya District on his own. He called himself a Buddha's slave because he wanted to devote and dedicate himself to serve Buddhism until the end of his life. The outstanding works of Phuttha Thart Bhikkhu are books such as the Buddha Dharma book, Following in the Footsteps of the Arahants, and Human Manual. He was the first Thai monk who pioneered the use of modern audiovisuals for spreading the Dharma to public. You can arrive at Ha Yak Lad Prow BTS Station and walk here. On the way back, you can have a look at the food court at Central Ladprow. Awesome food.

JIM THOMSON HOUSE

Jim Thomson House is a museum with a collection of Southeast Asian art especially; the art of various Buddha sculptures kept inside the building built in a typical Thai style house; awarded the Architectural Conservation Award in 1996. Jim Thomson was an American businessman, the owner of Jim Thomson's house who was one of the famous Thai silk traders in Thailand for a long time. He mysteriously disappeared at the age of 61 in 1967. I recommend this place. (photo below)

OLD MARKETS IN BANGKOK

At Krungkasem Road near Mahanak Canal is an old market which is called Bobae Market; since 1927 before World War II, it's the big wholesale and retail shopping areas of mainly cheap clothes and some other goods. The market is opened day and night; 9.00-15.00 and 23.00-05.00. Most of retail sales merchants come here from not only from Thailand but also the neighbor countries like Laos, Cambodia, Vietnam, Singapore and Malaysia.

The biggest markets for exporting clothes from Bobae are Arab countries. MRT: at Hua Lumphong Station and connect the local bus no. 53. **Bo Bae Market is** the large and old wholesale clothes market located near Klong Mahanak. It was established since 1927 before World War II until the war happened, the all consumer goods were lacked like clothes. People brought clothes from the dead and the second hand clothes by cleaning all of them and sold. The merchants were increased and the market was expanded rapidly then the commercial buildings were constructed and the clothes selling here came from the manufacturers and clothes factory direct to the customers who want to buy bunch of clothes for selling. "Bo Bae" was assumed come from "Bonk Benk" which means "Noisy". The market opens early in the morning and closes about 4 pm. **Pahurat Market** or Indian Market was named from the road built in the reign of King Rama V. The market is started from Ban Mo Square to the east. It's not so far from Yaowaraj and it's where you can find fabric shops, delicious Indian food and cheap accessories. Ride BTS to Samyod Station or Wat Mangkorn Station and continue by walking. You can also see a plaza mall; called **The Old Siam**" with many types of goods and much delicious Thai food inside the building. Talking about walking in Pahurat market; you have to walk and dodge with the motorcycles, vendors with tricycles, and it's crowded with people around. I can't imagine where to escape if something happens here, but I did enjoy everytime I was there. **Ban Mo** is the road located in between Jaroenkrung Road and Maharaj Road. It's built in 1863 in the reign of King Rama IV.

Ban Mo was the area where Vietnamese refugees; since the fall of Ayutthaya, settled homes and communities. "Mo" means "Pottery"; the primary trade for these areas during that time. At present, Ban Mor is famous for jewelry making such as diamond and gold jewelry. **Sampeng or Chinese Bazaar is like a trading town** area located at Yaowaraj Road and the most popular market among shoppers. The market is opened 8.00-17.00 and night time from 23.00-dawn. If you look for things for gift shop, accessories for clothes and hair, fashion clothes, hats, watches, dolls, toys and also material for cooking, please don't miss Sampeng. **Pratunam Intersection is one of popular markets of all time.** You can find the market easily by riding sky train from the airport to Ratchaprarop station. It's a shopping district full of shopping centers, mall, open-air markets, hotels and restaurants. "Pratu" means "Gate" and "Nam" means "Water"; it was the former water gate built in the reign of King Rama V in 1905 to drain water from San Saep Canal to distribute to people for agriculture and leveling the water for boats and raft transports. Pratunam is a heavy traffic area and a center where people get transport; either by road or canal. Visit **Pak Klong Talat or the Flower** Market by River boat. The name of the pier here is called Pak Klong Talat; where you can cross the river to Wat Kalayanamit. This flower market is one of the old markets in Bangkok, selling flowers, vegetables and fruits. You can also come here by MRT stop at Sanamchai exit 4. Many Café are located at the flower market. Enjoy Yodpiman River Walk and local market where you can see the shrine of King Rama I where people come for paying homage to the statue here.

LARGE SHOPPING MALLS IN BANGKOK

Ride a river boat to **ICON SIAM**; one of the largest shopping malls in Asia. It's a fantastic mall with variety of things. I like this mall because it's large and nice to walk inside the mall, especially Suk Siam at the ground floor; a small local market full of delicious food by modeling floating market in air-con room. There are 5-star hotels located nearby this mall. The sky train to Icon Siam Station is available and when you reach here, it's very convenient to visit other parts of Bangkok by river boats from Icon Siam Pier. I love the riverside view at the pier and hope you don't miss here! There are shuttle boats to go to the **Asiatique the River Front**, a large open-air mall in Bangkok. **The Asiatique the River Front** is a place full of shops and restaurants.The free shuttle boats are from Sathorn Pier near Taksin Bridge. BTS: Saphan Taksin Station. You can enjoy The Calypso Cabaret Show with dinner and Jo Luise Puppet Theater here. Calypso Show is for those who like to enjoy the show from her male. The location of Asiatique is he former docks of the **East Asiatic Company**. (photo of river view from Icon Siam)

There is a hospital called Taksin Hospital located near Icon Siam. It's one of the old hospitals in Thailand, established in 1904. "Taksin" came from the name of the king of Thonburi Capital. The location of the hospital is not so far from the King Taksin the Great Memorial at Wong Wien Yai Circle. On December 28th every year is recognized as King Taksin's Day. The present king with the royal family will come to lay the wreaths at the monument. People also come to this memorial for laying flowers for expressing their gratitude to King Taksin the Great for his brave fighting with Burmese Army and brought freedom back to Siam and established Thonburi to be the capital. If you have a boat trip along Chao Phraya River, you will see a beautiful old building located on the eastern bank of the river, opposite to The Mandarin Oriental Hotel which is **East Asiatic Company;** the old company which was a unique significance to the relationship between Thailand and Denmark. The company was found in 1897 by Mr. Hans Niels Andersen; a Danish ship captain who arrived Bangkok since 1873, and was a captain for the royal barge of King Rama V. The company building; built in Renaissance Revival architecture about in 1900, has been well –conserved as it's registered as a historical site by Fine Arts Department and also it was received the Architectural Conservation Award in 1984. The building commemorates as one of the most important historical time in terms of international business for Thai-Danish trade. It's closed for public now but open for rented in filming location.

Other large malls; Samyan Midtown by MRT: Samyan exit 2, **Siam Paragon** and all Siam Malls nearby at BTS Siam Staion, **Central Ladprow** at BTS Ha-Yak Ladprow Station,

Central RamaIX MRT Station, **Central Festival Eastville** at express way of Ramindra (near the Suwannaphum Airport), **Central Chidlom** at BTS Chidlom Station, **Fashion Island** (near the Suwannaphum Airport), Central World near Siam Station areas, Emquartier at BTS Prompong Station, Terminal 21 at BTS Asoke Station, **Platinum Fashion Mall** at Pratunam, **MaboonKlong** (MBK)near Siam Square, Big C Ratchadamri Road opposite to Central World, **The Mall Nonthaburi, Mega Bangna** (near the Suwannaphum Airport), River City near the Royal Orchid Sheraton, at Si Phraya, Intra Square, King Power Outlet is at Rangnam, Kehson Plaza is at Ratchaprasong Intersection, Fortune Town, the IT mall at Ratchada, Gateway at the Ekamai BTS station, Central Chaengwattana (near Pakkret Pier), Central Rama II, Central Pinklao (Thonburi side; not so far from the Thawanglang Pier), Silom Center, Robinson Samutprakan, The Crystal near Ramindra Express way, and etc.

LOCATION IN BANGKOK

Inner Bangkok with premium quality;

Silom, Sathon, Ploenchit and Sukhumvit Roads are dense with high-class hotels, luxurious condominiums, high-end malls, superstores, convenient stores, and restaurants. Many of luxurious hotels are located on the riverbank of the Chao Phraya River and boats are available for avoiding traffic in the city. BTS and MRT Lines are available for inner Bangkok.

Phahonyothin Road, Mo Chid, Bang Sue and Ha Yak Ladprow

There are 7 lines of Sky trains in total. Bang Sue - Bang Yai is the extension of the Blue Line Project, Bang Sue - Tha Phra is the red line project, Bang Sue - Rangsit and Bang Sue - Taling Chan and the green line Mo Chit - Saphan Mai make the largest access point in the urban area. Although it's outer Bangkok, it's easy to go in the city and nice to stay in the hotels or condominiums around here in lower prices than the inner Bangkok, if you don't mind traveling for longer time to reach the main attractions at the center of Bangkok.

Ratchadapisek Road

It is the new Complex for the New business center like the stock exchange building, the Super Tower 125 which is the highest building in ASEAN included with the Makkasan Complex Project of the Railway, Chaloem Ratchamongkhon Skytrain, Airport Link and Orange Line Sky trains for Cultural Center - Ramkhamhaeng – Minburi, MRT Yellow Line Ladprao - Bang Kapi - Phatthanakan make Ratchadapisek Road become the good areas to stay and convenient for going around. The areas are full of entertainments, commercial buildings and some luxury hotels.

Ladprow along the Express Way

The yellow line train Ladprao-Bangkapi, the gray line train Watcharaphon-Thonglor, MRT Pink Line on Ramintra Road and Eastern Zone of Retail District as the Central Department Stores, etc. are under construction. The areas are mainly the residential areas which are not so far from the airports, full of homes, condos, apartments, automobile business, plaza, amusement parks, and department stores. There are not many hotels located at the present but maybe more in the future when the Sky trains are ready.

Jaransanitwong, Bang Wha and Petchakasem Road

The MRT blue line, the Bang Sue - Tha Phra Hua Lamphong - Bang Khae and BTS Bang Wa make the areas booming and although it's on the Thonburi side; the west riverbank of the Chao Phraya River where there are old buildings and wooden houses, there are interesting areas like the floating markets and old temples located within the areas make the land prices increased and interesting.

Bangyai-Bang Bua Thong

The areas will be soon the new city and the sub-center in the future. Bang Yai and Bang Bua Thong in the past were the location in the perimeter that have been popular in buying homes as the top priority. Always (alternating with the Rangsit area), but after the construction of the MRT Purple Line, Bang Yai, Bang Bua Thong, including Nonthaburi province have been continued to be popular in number one for residences until today. In the future, this area will be upgraded to be a regional center with the motorway project which is the Bang Yai – Kanchanaburi; the Gateway to the West of Thailand and to Myanmar's Dawei in the future. The two giants of the Retail Companies developed shopping centers and convention centers namely; Mega Bang Yai and Central Westgate with hotels within a combined area of nearly a million square meters.

It's quite close to the west border of Bangkok where you can go to **Nakonpathom, Ratchaburi** (for the Damnoensaduak Foating Market), **Kanchanaburi** (the Bridge over the River Kwai), **Samutsongkram** (Train Market at Mae Klong and Amphawa) and to the beaches at **Cha-Am and Hua Hin** easily.

Chaeng Watthana-Pakkret

The Pink Line Chaeng Watthana Government Center Muang Thong Thani is under the constructions and will be expanding. At the present, this area is considered one of the important residential areas of Nonthaburi Province which is a part of Bangkok Metropolitan Region. It is an area that has continuously expanded from Bangkok since almost 20 years ago. There were only a few housing estate projects before but later on, there was an expansion of more housing; due to the presence of an expressway system, the emergence of the Muang Thong Thani project, which includes both large residential projects, the Exhibition center with trade shows at Muang Thong Impact, and the hotels.

Regarding to the relocation of the Chaeng Watthana Government Center, the construction of a bridge over the river, and the emergence of the MRT Pink Line project; Khae Rai-Suwinthawong that runs through Chaeng Watthana Road now causing this area to grow rapidly and has developed various housing projects occurred massively in the present, make the commercial projects to occur to support dense living, such as Superstores like Big C, Makro Lotus, Central Department Stores and the Major Cinema Complex included with there are some hotels located at the Impact Muang Thong Center such as; Ibis Bangkok Impact and Novotel Hotel and within the surrounding areas like Don Muang Airport area are mostly condo with rooms for rent cause the areas become traffic jammed and crowded. You can reach the Pakkret Pier which is where you can explore Koh Kret and the Mon community within this location.

Saphan Mai, Khu Khot and Lam Luk Ka

The MRT Green Line Extension with the New Cut Road; Saphan Mai-Watcharaphon-Nimitmai included with the Green Line Metro Project Mo Chit - Saphan Mai - Khu Khot section will soon make the area become the potential area for business. The route for Sky train is from Lat Phrao, Ratchayothin, Bang Khen, Saphan Mai to Khu Khot and Lam Luk Ka Road around Khlong Song with a distance of 19 kilometers and the 16 elevated stations. The areas are at the eastern side of Bangkok which is near to Ayutthaya, Khao Yai, and the northeastern region.

The hotels are still only small hotels around for the Thai tourists from other provinces because it's the suburban area of Bangkok but anyway, the area is not so far from the airports; Don Muang and Suwannaphum Airports. Fahion Island Malls seems to be the attraction for the Thai tourists during weekend, it's the large mall complex of the variety of goods and delicious food, it's crowded with people from other nearby provinces on Fri-Sun. Most of the people come from Cha Choeng Sao, Ayutthaya, Saraburi and Nakonnayok.

Minburi, Sukhapiban 3 and Ramindra Road (the late No. to Minburi)

Minburi in the past may not be flashy but the future may be changed due to the arrival of the two Sky train lines. Minburi is quite a less prominent location, because it is located in the outer area of the city especially, near the Floodway line where the overall city plan defines it as a green striped area (Rural preservation and for agriculture areas) which is very limited in development. Some are affected by the sound of planes because it's close to the two airports, therefore; the population is not very dense. The current land used in this area is a combination of residential and agricultural or green spaces in the east side of the Minburi market along the Nimitmai Road and Suwinthawong Road which head to Cha Choeng Sao Province. But in the near future, the location in this area may become more active; due to the coming of the 2 train lines, namely the Pink Line (Khae Rai - Min Buri) and the Orange Line (Cultural Center - Bang Kapi - Min Buri).

The location here is nearby the Suwannaphum Airport, Cha Choeng Sao, Chonburi and Pattaya City, and the east shorelines, and having the express way to reach the North and the Northeastern regions conveniently.

Rangsit-Klong Luang

The red line Skytrain is along the location of **Rangsit** and Klong Luang in Pathumthani. The area along the Rangsit-Nakhon Nayok Road makes the development deep into the area along the canals, various sub-lanes, starting from Khlong Song (2), Khlong Sam (3), Khlong Si (4), onwards, which have roads along the canals. Both the northern side of Rangsit-NakhonNayok Road connects to Bang Khan Road and the southern side that connects to Lam Luk Ka Road. Most of the developments in the present era are housing projects located along various canals, especially Khlong Song, Khlong Sam, Khlong Si, which has a particularly dense project. If driving along these canals nowadays, you can see that there are dense with residential areas like home projects and condominiums.

But it's a location that was mostly flooded in 2011. The areas are in Pathumthani Province (part of Bangkok Metropolitan Region) at the eastern side of Bangkok which connect to Nakonnayok Province (a Waterfall and forest land); the nearest place where people in Bangkok choose to go for drinking oxygen and enjoy the nature atmosphere.

On-Nuj, Bangna, Bearing and Samutprakan

These locations have an important sub-commercial center started at the On Nuj Market, Udom Suk Market, Bang Na Road with a large shopping center and Malls included with **BITEC Bangna Center**; the exhibition center for trade fairs all year round and **Samutprakan province;** the location of the Suwannaphum Airport. The Green Line Extension Skytrain On-Nuj-Kheha in Samutprakan makes people enjoy all tourist attractions in Samutprakan. (see Samutprakan details)

I recommend you to stay at the inner Bangkok areas because you can roam around other areas by Sky trains and Subways. But if you accidentally get the hotel from online booking, you can see what you can do or explore.

Kha Jao

FLOATING MARKET IN BANGKOK

KLONG LAT MAYOM FLOATING MARKET

Sat-Sun 8.00-17.00

Khlong Lat Mayom Floating Market is a mixed floating market with a land market. There are shops selling products on board and inside the multipurpose building. The area is spacious, divided into 4 zones, with more than 600 shops. Most of the products are local savory and sweet desserts, such as grilled fish, seafood, pork satay, boat noodles, rice topped with curry, khanom jeen (steam noodle eat with curry), pad Thai, fried clams, Hormok (steam/grilled curry inside the banana leaf basket), grilled pork, Kanom Bueng Yuan, Luk Chup, and many cups of desserts, banana snacks, ice cream, and more, and organic agricultural products from villagers in the community and nearby areas.

There are also recreational and learning facilities in the surrounding area, such as the Jeamton Park near Zone 2 and Zone 3. There is a self-sufficient farming lifestyle and a boat museum.

Travel to the market by car; from Kanchanaphisek Road, enter Bang Ramat Road for about 1 kilometer to reach Khlong Lat Mayom Floating Market. Take another route from Phutthamonthon Sai 1 Road into Bang Ramat Road and go straight for about 1.5 kilometers. But if you can join the tour, I think it is more convenient.

TALING CHAN FLOATING MARKET AND SONG KLONG WAT TALING CHAN MARKET

Sat-Sun: 8.00-17.00

Taling Chan Floating Market is a floating market along the canal Chak Phra. or the Bang Khun Si River at Khlong Chak Phra Subdistrict, in Taling Chan District. It's the Bangkok Floating markets near the center of Bangkok; there are two floating markets, which are Song Khlong Wat Taling Chan Floating Market and Taling Chan Floating Market located at the Taling Chan District Office. Both of them are popular with many items for sale but very crowded near to the Taling Chan Office which seems to be more popular for visitors. The entrance to Taling Chan Floating Market is full of small plants, cacti, flowers and flowers. The food continues at the middle of the pathway until reaching the raft tied by the canal. There are tables and chairs for relaxing and you can enjoy the music from typical Thai instruments during eating.

There is also a boat tour to take you around; a one-hour tour around the market-island. Take a boat to see the atmosphere through Taling Chan Floating Market, Khlong Chak Phra, Khlong Mon Intersection to Bang Chueang Nang Canal, stop by to feed the fish in front of Wat Paknam on the south bank. When you enter Bangkok Noi Canal, you can visit Thai houses and temples in the Ayutthaya period and pay homage to the Buddha image at **Wat Koh**. There are several rounds, starting from 12.00 - 15.00, the price is 60 baht/seat and takes about 1-hour tour.

How to go; take a boat to **Wang Lang Pier** (opposite pier to Tha Phra Chan Pier near the Grand Palace area) and walk along the pathway to the direction of the Siriraj Hospital for riding Songthaew-pickup near Thonburi Railway Station. Get off in front of the Taling Chan District Office.

KWAN-RIAM FLOATING MARKET

Sat-Sun and public holidays from 7:00 to 18:00

Kwan-Riam Floating Market is a floating market in Khlong Saen Saep which located between 2 temples, Bamphen Nuea Temple and Bang Peng Tai Temple where there are two bridges connecting the two temples, the bridge is a boat-shaped bridge. The original bridge was called Somboon Uthit Bridge built in 1887 between Wat Bamphen Nuea and Wat Bang Peng Tai which was narrow and dilapidated. The new bridge was built about 100 meters away, down to the west of the Saen Saep Canal making the walkway easily for walking around.

The idea for the design of the ship-shaped bridge came from the design of the bridge where Mr. Chaovalit; the owner of the project, saw in Spain but adjusted to be a boat shape in accordance with the Thai style. There will be a novice rowing a boat to receive alms from people in the areas every morning. A 2-storey building was constructed parallel to the canal at Wat Bamphen Nuea. The ground floor sells food like street food. The upper floor is a way to connect to the other side of the canal. It is a shop selling things such as clothes, glasses, bags, and etc. Along the canal, there are many items for sale, including food, and some souvenirs. In the Saen Saep canal, there are boats of various sizes that stop selling food such as coffee and drinks for you to sit and drink in the boat or raft. On the side of Wat Bang Peng Tai, it is an old market like a hundred-year-old market; **hundred-year-old market is called for an old market** which found every province with commercial wooden buildings or houses with thatched roof with homemade food by using charcoal stove. There is a coffee shop and an antique photo shop. The thatched roof areas sell food and some products that looks like a flea market.

Kwan and Riam are the names of the characters from a famous love-story novel called "Plae Kao" which means "the past sad memory". It is the first written work of Mai Muang Derm (the author's name), first published in 1936. It was made into a movie for the first time in 1940 and the second time in 1946. Later, Cherd Songsri; one of the famous movie producers, brought it back to make the movie touching the audiences than the past.

The film again in 1977 was the highest grossing record when it was first released, which deleted the record for every movie that was released at that time for both Thai and other countries. It also won the first prize at the 1981 Film Competition in Nantes, France and being the most famous at that time. The story has been made into TV series and movies many times and the last time (as of now) was a movie in 2014.

At the floating market there is also a statue of Kwan-Riam riding a buffalo, located next to the Banyan Tree Shrine. On the side of Wat Bang Peng Tai along the Saen Saeb canal in front of the court facing the canal side, there is also a pet show such as dwarf horses and rabbits.

You can travel to the Kwan-Riam floating market via the MRT Orange Line, Min Phatthana Station. which has a way up - down near the entrance of Soi Ramkhamhaeng 187, the entrance to Wat Bang Peng Tai where you can go to the market.

KLONG BANG LUANG FOATING MARKET

It is a daytime market open from 9 am to 6 pm.

Klong Bang Luang Floating Market is a local floating market along the Bangkok Yai Canal which is an old community since Ayutthaya Located in Phasi Charoen District in Bangkok. The floating market consists of communities with two-storey buildings made of old wood line along the banks of Bang Luang Canal.

There are souvenir shops, restaurants, barber shops, and community exhibitions which collects various kinds of antiques. In addition, around the floating market, there are also Wat Kamphaeng (Bang Chak) which was an old temple built within the community for a long time. Inside the floating market, there are also interesting things, including the Artist House which is the former home of "The Rak Samroud Family", an old family of goldsmiths which has been renovated to be a place for an art exhibition and become the gathering place of a group of artists who love art. Currently, Klong Bang Luang Floating Market is classified as one of the attractions along the canal in Phasi Charoen District as well as Wat Nimmanoradee Floating Market. This floating market has received interest from both Thai and foreigners who would like to get the old atmosphere of this ancient community. It’s the route of the long-tail boat and a cycling route tour. You can go to the floating market by riding the MRT to Bang Phai Station and keep on walking for about 400 meters along Phetchakasem Soi 28. You can admire the Big Buddha at Wat Paknam as well.

BOAT TRIP IN KLONG SAEN SAEP

Klong Saen Saep is one of main waterways in Bangkok for avoiding the road-traffic. It's a canal nearby Jim Thomson House. It is the important canal for public transports like express boat-service within the center of Bangkok. The length of the canal is 72 kms passing 21 districts and joined with sub-canals for more than 100 canals. Khlong Saen Saep was dug in the reign of King Rama III for not only for connecting Chao Phraya River to Bang Pakong River, but also, it's for facilitate the travel and transportation of food and weapons during the conflict between Siam and Annam (Vietnam); situated at the north of Cambodia, for about 14 years. The method of digging the canal that period of time was by using buffaloes trampling into the sludge dug. You can ride a boat to see the local living life style by canals; like a canal tour and drop by the places you like. Rush hour time is in between 7-9 am and 4-6 pm. The Center pier of Khlong Saen Saep is at **Pratunam Market**; getting in the boat on the **right-hand** side, it will pass Phan Fah Lilat (near Wat Saketh), Bo Bae Market, Chidlom, Nana, Asoke, Soi Thong Lo.

For the left-hand side will pass Hua Chang Bridge (for going to Siam), Witthayu or Wireless Road (for going to Ploenchit, Silom, USA Embassy), Ramkhamhaeng University. Those piers I mention here are the diversity of attractions you may like to visit but there are more piers for drop off too.

THE CHAO PHRAYA RIVER TOUR

I hope you have a chance for enjoying a **Dinner Cruise especially; if you are** during Loy Krathong Day Festival (in November), you will enjoy the beautiful Fireworks and the lighted candles are glittery on all decorated banana-leaf baskets floating on the river. It's a Full Moon Day after Buddhist Lent Day. I think it's quite a fantastic night as I experienced before, some cruises have classical dances show during dinner (buffet). **Cruise to Ayutthaya** for one day trip at the River City or join the package tour. **The Chao Phraya Express Boat** at **Sathon Pier**; Blue Flag 6.00-18.00 for one day trip, pay one time for hop on-off. **The Chao Phraya Express Boat to Koh Kret** in Nonthaburi. (see details of Koh Kret)

TALAT NOI

You should experience a traditional Chinese quarter at **Talat Noi;** a cultural attraction with several historic buildings from 300 years ago. (By the River Boat with orange flag, stop at **Ta-Krom-Chao-ta** or say "Talat Noi"). There are many things to do here such as:

- ❑ Hire a bicycle for roaming around Talat Noi areas.
- ❑ Admire the Kalawa Church near Talat Noi.
- ❑ Admire the old aged Chinese Temples/ God's Shrine in Talat Noi.

- ❑ Taste a popular stir-fried noodle dish and famous curry puffs at Talat Noi.
- ❑ Admire the streets of art and try the local coffee and charcoal grilled breads at Talat Noi.
- ❑ The old Chinese Mansion **"Lhong 1919"** and the old styles of the Chinese resident areas, located opposite to Talat Noi Pier are now closed since Dec1, 2021. (Because of Covid-19 situation)

JATUJAK MARKET

Jatujak Market is the world's largest weekend market with many thoudsands of shops of all things you need. It always crowded every weekend. Jatujak Market's quote for Thai is "We can find from toothpicks to battleships in Jatujak Market." If you get lost here, try to stand at the clock tower and you will notice that it's a popular meeting point here.

Jatujak Market is located near the Jatujak Park and **Or Tor Kor Market; the high-quality market for cooking ingredients and materials, the wonderful** Food Court, and some of them are local handicrafts, located opposite to the Jatujak Park. You can ride the BTS sky train to Morchid Station or the MRT to the Kham Phaeng Peth Station to Jatujak Market. The market is opened about **6 am-6 pm during weekend**. You have to check the schedule for available time you have if you wish to come here during in transit of Thailand, otherwise; you may miss your flight. I heard many tourists missed their flights because they thought that the time arrived in town was the same as the returning back by taxi. Well! As I always remind you in many chapters that the traffic in Bangkok is unpredictable except; you ride a sky train; but not during the rush hour. There are more than eight thousand shops with 27 sections and about 8 kinds of goods included with street vendors around here. **The Jatujak Market** was established in 1978 for vendors moved from Sanam Luang; which was a flea market during weekend at that time, the government had the policy to make Sanam Luang to be the place for organizing the big event of 200th Anniversary of Rattanakosin Celebration so the flea market here moved to Jatujak. In fact, the Park Complex at Jatutak district is a public park for relaxations which are composed of Jatujak Park, Wachirabenchathat Park and Queen Sirikij Park; where Children's Discovery Museum 1 is situated. Right now, the MRT train station which is laid under the park is **Chatuchak Park Station.**

Bang Sue Grand Railway Station is located near Jatujak Park, it's the largest railway station in Southeast Asia with 26 platforms and the size is about 600 meters long. You can experience riding the trains for some sight-seeing.
Bang Sue Grand Railway Station was constructed since 2013 and opened in 2021 as Thailand's new railway hub for replacing Hua Lum Phong Railway Station; it is divided as two parts; Bangsue I and II which are close to each other. The first one is for the north and northeast lines and the other is going to the south region. You can go anywhere you want except; to the east line, you have to go to Hua Lumphong Station for the east line. Please check the website of Bangsue railway schedule for the place you want to go. If you come by BTS, stop at Mochid and connect MRT to the Klang Bang Sue Station.

PHAHONYOTHIN ROAD AREAS

The Phahonyothin areas in the past was like a suburban area of Bangkok though it's in the city areas. It's because there were few old shops and small hotels with residential areas along the sub-lanes. Nowadays, the area is dense with many tall office-buildings, superstores, and condominiums then you won't feel lonely at the Phahonyothin Road areas anymore. The popular places you have to go are **Soi Aree; a place of** street food and the community mall. (BTS: at Aree Station) Soi Aree is now popular for its location which is suitable to travel anywhere conveniently. It's an alleyway with many sub-alleys for the locations of apartment, condominiums, houses, shops and restaurants. You are still at the center of Bangkok when you stay at Soi Aree.

Along the BTS to Phahonyothin route; you can drop at the Central Plaza Ladprow; the plaza that has been a legend of meeting point for enjoying shopping and restaurants since 1983; it's an old and famous Department Stores and the hotel was constructed later; which is very convenient for tourists. The mall is very popular among Thai and foreigners for decades. I have still chosen this store for walking around even for window-shopping since it's firstly opened. Right now, it's full of variety of shops and business center like, banks and Store Company and it's where you can enjoy the Thai and international restaurants. It's a modern plaza with many product-brands where I never get tired of walking. Don't miss here! You can ride the **BTS Sky train to Ha Yak Lad-prow Station or the MRT to the Pha-hol-yo-thin Station.**

If you ride a Sky train along Phaholyothin route a little bit further from the department store, you will see the **Ratchayothin Station** for visiting the busy corner of **the Major Cineplex; the grand theater for watching movies** and enjoy eating the varieties of food from many international restaurants around the area. It is where there is a flea market at night in Bangkok.

VICTORY MONUMENT

The **Victory Monument is** the gate to downtown in Bangkok. If you come by Airport Link, the last station is at **Phayathai Station** at the Victory Monument; from here, you can choose where to go easily; connect BTS for Sukhumvit Route: to **Siam Station; the main station to go other places; and** at Siam Station you will find Siam Paragon Shopping Mall and others, or go direct to Samut Prakan Province for The Erawan Museum, etc. You can also catch a train to Suburban Route along Phaholyothin Road to the northeast of Bangkok areas.

The Victory Monument was established to honor heroes; soldiers, policemen and civilians who died in Franco-Thai War (Oct 1940-Jan 1941) in the dispute of border improvement between Thailand and French Indochina; the 59 people lost their lives.

The shape of the monument was meant the bayonet; a military weapon, its height was 50 meters made of concrete and decorated with marble, built above the large hall; the Great Hall, which stored artillery shells containing the ashes of the dead people in the war, the bayonet was surrounded with 5 warrior-statues; Army, Navy, Air Force, Police and Civilians. Outside the walls of the Great Hall was a copper plaque engraved with the names of the deceased. The total names right now are 801 names who sacrificed their lives from different wars from 1940-1954. There are important places located around the Victory Monument such as; Rajchavithi Hospital, Queen Sirikij National Institute of Child Health, Phra Monkut Hospital, Century the Movie Plaza, Center One the Shopping Plaza and Sri Rath Express Toll Way. The monument has been the center for transportations to other provinces by private vans and the center of public transports.

If I don't mention about noodles at the Victory Monument, I must miss a legend of delicious noodle from a small boat in the canal of the monument which was black color. It's at the corner near the exit route to Phaholyothin Road and close to the toll for express way. When I was teenager, me and my friends rode a public bus to Siam during weekend for fun time, all buses stopped at the ended route at the victory monument for connecting the other bus to Siam and we always loved to eat noodle here every time we passed or dropped by the monument. It cost only 1.50 Bahts per bowl; I could eat about 8-10 bowls while my friends could do to 16 bowls. Each bowl contained a little noodle, bean sprouts, a little meat and meat ball, seasoning with spicy taste for eating about 3-4 spoons or chopsticks; it's so much-fun and delicious in eating these tasty noodles. The merchants sold noodles from their sampan boats that lined the dirty canals at that time. There are seats like long wooden seats along the canal for all customers on the canal bank. Some people talked about the taste of the noodles here which seemed coming from marijuana as a part of ingredients to make delicious noodles; well! either good or bad that time, but we loved to eat anyway. The noodle merchant we usually stopped for was a nice lady with a kind smile and kept on making noodle bowl after bowl for her clients. I have never forgotten the moments **of joy here!**

SIAM BTS STATION

If you stop by BTS: Siam Station, I bet you have fun walking, eating and shopping around inside **Siam Paragon Mall, Siam Center, Siam Discovery and Siam Square** at the opposite side. I remember me and my friends worried about the clothes that we should wear to be the most fashionable; by following the upcoming fashion trends and show them off when we visited Siam Square, which was the Fashion center for teenagers that time. The area still has been popular till now. By Siam Square you can take a walk to the **Maboonklong Shopping Mall** or **MBK** Center (big mobile market), you have to be careful of your bags during walking in this area when it's crowded. MBK locates near The National Stadium. It contains thousands of shops and restaurant included with activities center for concerts, movie-houses, hotel, club, game center, studios and exhibition hall for special events and performances. Its concept is "One Stop Shopping".

You can come here by air-con flying bridge from Siam Square, BTS National Stadium Station joining pathway to second and third floor or from Chulalongkorn University to the third floor of MBK. you can visit the **Bangkok Art and Culture Center;** a very interesting contemporary arts center of art education with book shop, library and commercial art galleries. It also aims for cultural exchange at the **BTS the National Stadium Station.**

The national stadium is called **Suphachalasi Stadium**; the sport complex in Bangkok. It was established in 1937 and expanded for multiple stadia and sport facilities in 1941. The stadium was served for Asian Games in 1966, 1970 and 1978 and right now it's used mostly for football matches. The new stadium with sport complex is at Rajamangala National Stadium; located at Hua Mak which was opened in 1998. I had a good memory at the Suphachalasai National Stadium once, when I came to this stadium for watching Michael Jackson Concert in 1993 during his "Dangerous World Tour" where crowded with about 150,000 attendances, the performance was great in the open-air football field of Suphachalasi National Stadium at that time. I felt joyful and excited in watching my favorite singer during this concert with my friends and other people. He was a great music artist. RIP Michael Jackson.

Walk along the sky Bridge **from Siam to the World Trade Center; a large mall, to** see Ratchaprasong Intersection. When you reach the world trade center mall, you can go to Pratunam Market easily by TukTuk or just by walking. (see the detail of this market in "Old Markets in Bangkok")

Ratchaprasong Intersection has been recognized as one of the important areas of Bangkok where it was the place gathering people during political crisis many times in the past. It was told that the land around the intersection was a mysterious land; this property belonged to the king where a palace was settled during the reign of King Rama IV. There were many incidents occurred here after the land was rented for business buildings, hotels, and department stores. It was believed that the land was cursed and evil spirits covered all over the land, many of business like; department stores and hotels that time were shut down sooner or later. Some of business men tried every way including arranging auspicious ceremonies for worshipping the sacred spirits from their beliefs for enhancing their business to grow and part of their beliefs was making God Shrines. This intersection was called as the God Intersection from Thai. There are many God shrines; mostly from Hindu beliefs, situated around the intersections as the guardians for protecting the evil spirits which was the advice from the experienced Bhramis that time. This God Intersection (Ratchaprasong) has now: Phra Tri Murati Shrine is situated in front of Central World Mall, Phra Pickaneth Shrine is situated in front of Iseton Mall, Phra Mae Luxamee Shrine is situated on the fourth floor at Kesorn Plaza, Phra Mae Umathevi is situated in front of Big C Superstore at Ratchadamri Road, and the Four face God Shrine is situated in front of The Grand Hyatt Erawan Hotel. The well-known God Shrines among Thai and Chinese tourists is Four-Face God Shrine or Brahma God or God of Creation from Hinduism which was built and put at the corner of the intersection since 1956, right now is in front of The Hyatt Erawan Hotel.

FOUR- FACE GOD SHRINE OR ERAWAN SHRINE

If you pass by the **Erawan Shrine; which is called as Four–face God Shrine from tourists**, you will see lots of people with incent sticks with their smoke all over the area, and see features performances by Thai Dance troupes hired by the worshippers who succeeded in what they wished. The statue was renovated and repaired and has been respected by many Thai and Chinese worshippers every day. Many Chinese tourists come to Thailand for making wishes from this shrine and return back here again when they succeed.

THE PARKS IN BANGKOK

The MRT at Silom Station is where you will see a popular park called **Lumpini Park**; where you can relax and exercise in a giant garden at the center of Bangkok which is called as the Bangkok's Lung. It's near Chulalongkorn Hospital; a state hospital and very well organized for medical service. If your accommodation is close to Silom Rd., Sathon Rd., Ploenchit Rd. and nearby Hua Lumphong railway station, you can come to the park easily by sky train BTS at the Saladaeng Station for refreshing yourself. There are almost 40 parks in Bangkok but the main parks which are popular with large sizes are mentioned here for your information, please check if you are close to one of them.

LUMPINI PARK

Lumphini Park is the Bangkok's first public park and the land was given by His Majesty King Mongkut (King Rama VI) in 1925, when he reigned for 15 years. It's also because of the economic downturn after World War I, he therefore, had an idea to organize a museum exhibition and natural resources like the Western countries had already done that time. It was scheduled to be held in the late winter of 1925 called the Siam Rath Museum and had the idea that when the event finished, this place should be made into an arboretum for people to study and relax. His Highness chose the area of Thung Sala Daeng (the park), the rest of his land to be the place where the event was held and His Royal Highness donated his own money as the initial capital for expenses in construction. At that time a large pond was dug, a floating island was built in the middle of the water, the roads were constructed and permanent objects such as a clock tower and a Greek-style building were built. King Rama VI gave the name Lumbini Park, which meant the birthplace of Lord Buddha; at Lumbini Wan Sub-district in Nepal. King Rama VI (photo below) passed away before the day of the Grand Opening of the Lumpini Park.

The statue of King Rama VI was situated in front of the park built in 1942 to commemorate the royal benevolence of the one who gave birth to this Lumpini Park. It is the lung and a nice park of Bangkok people. I love here in the morning time but afternoon time is also good for walking too. There's an aerobics dance for a fun exercise here. You will have a good time here! MRT: at Silom Station or BTS: Saladaeng Station and walk back to the direction of Silom intersection for 10 minutes.

SUAN LUANG RAMA IX PARK

BTS: at Udomsuk Station and walk through Sukhumvit Soi 103 then catch the red bus to Prawet route; where it's passing the park. It is the largest urban park and botanical garden in Bangkok, with an area of approximately 500 Rai located at Prawet District, east of Bangkok. The park was built in the occasion of His Majesty King Bhumibol (King Rama IX) the Great for his 60th birthday in December 5, 1987. You can admire and see the Chaloem Phrakiat area or the areas for the collects the story of His Majesty King Bhumibol; consisting of the **Ratchamongkhon Hall** and **Maharaj Park.** Inside the Ratchamongkhon Hall, it exhibits stories about the royal duties and his personal equipment. The Botanical garden is an important objective in constructing this Royal King Rama IX Park with a total area of 150 rai. It is a collection of various Thai plants, including rare plants, and herbs as well as international gardens such as Spain, France, Italy, Japan and England. The park is open to visitors from **Monday to Saturday**.

This park area has the following buildings: **The Botanical Hall** houses a collection of plant specimens and plant documents.

Takon Phrakiat Building is as a meeting academic seminar and organize various activities throughout the year. The **Desert plant (Giodesic Dome)** and the exterior of the building is a collection of desert plants. and various succulents both in the country and abroad. **Indoor plant Building** is planted with various types of indoor plants. There are also ferns and orchids. **The water storage tank dug here is** with an area of 40 rai, serves as a water storage facility to solve the problem of flooding in the inner city and for water sports as well as to conserve aquatic animals. There is a rowboat service and water bikes. The **Rommanee Park is** an area of 50 rai, which is a landscaping to imitate local nature, with waterfalls, streams, and decorative materials with ornamental flower species and local symbols. This area also has a Chinese garden and the Cliff Garden which were built by the Chinese Embassy in Thailand offering to pay homage to His Majesty King Bhumibol Adulyadej the Great. **The Water Park of** an area of 40 rai is a collection of various beautiful aquatic plants planted in the stream and on both sides of the water bank. The **Rat Stadium and Multipurpose Ground is t**he area of about 70 rai, consisting of a wide field area with outdoor stage for being a venue for cultural performances, Traditions and Agricultural Produce contest. The **Desert plant** is a collection of desert plants and both Thai succulents and from abroad. There will be an event called "Arham Suan Luang Rama IX Plant Fair"; "Arham" means "Brilliant", organized by Suan Luang Rama IX Foundation in cooperation with Bangkok Metropolitan Administration.

CHATUCHAK PARKS; WACHIRABENCHATHAT PARK, QUEEN SIRIKIT PARK AND CHATUCHAK PARK

BTS: Mo Chid Station

MRT: Suan Jatujak Station or Kam Phaeng Phet Station

Chatuchak Park is a part of the Group of Chatuchak Parks within the areas of 726 rai; consisting of 3 public parks with consecutive areas: Chatuchak Park, an area of 155 rai, Wachirabenchathat Park; an area of 375 rai, and Queen Sirikit Park; an area of 196 rai. The State Railway of Thailand offered 100 rai of land to build a public park in 1975 according to the wishes of His Majesty King Bhumibol Adulyade, the Great and for on the occasion of his 4th cycle or 48th birthday on December 5, 1975.

His Majesty King Bhumibol graciously gave the garden's name "Chatuchak Park" on January 8, 1976. The name means "four rounds". The Chatuchak Park opened for business (market) and to be the park for the public on December 4, 1980. The memorial which has been a witness from when it was first built as a symbol of the park are the clock tower, flower clock, sculptures from 6 ASEAN countries. In the summer (Mar-May) of each year; on the side of Phaholyothin Road; the road pass by the park including Wachirabenjathat Park or nearby the Train park, it is the period when the pink flowers of the Rosy Trumpet Trees are in full bloom and they fall to the ground in a pink contrast with the green grass causing an extremely beautiful image. You can admire the time you visit Chatuchak Market or JJ Mall.

BENJAKITTI PARK

Benchakitti Park is the first Forest Park in Bangkok and considered as a neighborhood-level park. It was built in 1992 to honor Her Majesty Queen Sirikit; The Queen Mother of King Vachiralongkorn, the present king, on the occasion of the 60th of her Birthday Anniversary. It is located in the area of the former tobacco factory next to the Queen Sirikit National Convention Center on Ratchadaphisek Road; between Rama IV Road and Sukhumvit Road belongs to Khlong Toei District, Bangkok. This park project is part of the Tobacco Factory Substitution Area Development Project Phase 1, by following the Cabinet of the government resolution, to move the tobacco factory outside Bangkok. The name Benjakitti Park was given by Her Majesty Queen Sirikit.

Her Majesty the Queen came to perform the Opening Ceremony of the Benjakitti Park on December 9, 2004.

In 2014, Benjakitti Park was used as a venue for stage plays and music with spectacular techniques in honor of His Majesty King Bhumibol Adulyadej the Great, titled "Phra Mahachanok The Phenomenal Live Show", with a stage in the middle of a lake over 100 meters long. Subsequently, the Tobacco Factory gave an additional area of 61 rai to make the park as the "Benjakitti Forest Plantation" for the use as a large perennial plantation area such as Canada, Sela and Kradon in the form of a shady forest garden with the light shines through the Benjakitti Park which is the first **forest park in Bangkok**.

MAHANAKORN SKYWALK

BTS: at Chongnonsee Station

You have to experience walking on a 314-meter-high glass floored sky where it's at the highest peak outdoor of the building in Thailand, at 78th floor of King Power **Mahanakorn Skywalk. I**t is the largest Glass Tray Observation deck for 360 degrees panoramic view with the fastest elevator in Southeast Asia, the best rooftop in Bangkok which is perfect for thrill seekers. It's located on Silom Road which is not so far from Lumpini Park.

SUKHUMVIT, NANA, ASOKE, SOI COWBOY, THONG LO

Sukhumvit is the main road in Bangkok going to the east region and homes of numerous hotels, malls and entertainments. The Skytrain from Siam Station is the route on Sukhumvit Line till Samutprakan Province; at Keha BTS Station where there are many attractions. If you come by **Sukhumvit Road you are on the way to Nana, Soi Cowboy and Thong Lo** areas where they are the popular places the most tourists love to spend nightlife because they are the zones of bars and pubs. Nana or Soi Nana is an intersection at Sukhumvit Road Soi 3, it's after Ploen Chit BTS station. Nana is home to a large number of shopping centers, Arabic restaurants, International restaurants, pubs, night clubs, bars and condominium where mostly popular among Arabic tourists since long time ago. When you stop at BTS: **Asoke Station** or MRT: Sukhumvit Station, you will hear about **Soi Cowboy**; its location is between Sukhumvit Soi 21-23 near The Grand Millennium Hotel.

Soi Cowboy was named after the retired American Air Force T.G. Edwards whose nickname was "Cowboy"; he's very fond of wearing cowboy hat and opened a bar called "Cowboy" on the alley in 1977. Some of popular culture which made Soi Cowboy well known were songs released called "Soi Cowboy" by Norwegian group and American rock band and some movies shot from here.

BTS: **Thong Lo Station** is at Sukhumvit Soi 55 where there are many shopping malls, international restaurants and superstores, apartments and condominiums where mostly Japanese stay. Soi Thong Lo in the past was the place where Japanese troops settled during World War II and it's the private land before. There is a bridge across San Saep Canal within this alley. One of the popular malls is **The Commons Community** Mall; a contemporary shopping complex with outdoor spaces full of arts and a market.

TRAIN MARKET IN BANGKOK

Ratchada Local Night Market or **Train Market** or "Talat Rodfai". (MRT: at Rat-chada Station) was like a flea market for selling many things; sold from vendors who brought their own products and food. It's a popular place for people after work. Actually, the Night markets are popular anywhere in Bangkok because the weather is not so hot.

The Train Market at Ratchada was temporarily closed since July 2021, but I heard that it might be close permanently very soon because of the Covid-19 pandemic situation. The market looked like a little town which was sparkling with neon lights when you watch from the top floors of the parking building nearby, but afterwards the lights were shut one by one from little shops gathered in this huge area. It's a tragedy for traders and tour business around Thailand from the Covid-19 situation. I hope it will come again when everything is OK.

SILOM ROAD AND PAT PONG

Experience nightlife of **Soi Pat Pong areas**; one of the Red-light districts in Bangkok. (BTS: at Saladaeng Station) When you enter **Silom** Road, you will see many tall buildings with heavy traffic most of the time, because Silom Road is the business center areas and like a "walking street" in Bangkok where many shops and restaurants situated through the street; its length is about 3 kilometers. The famous temple which is located on Silom Road is **Wat Khaek** or **Sri Maha Mariamman Temple**; the Hindu temple in Bangkok which was built in 1879 by Vaithi Padayatchi, a Tamil Hindu immigrant. It is one of the oldest and most important temples in Thailand where a large number of Thai Buddhists and Chinese come for worshiping the Hindu God here.

The famous venue is full of go-go bars, pubs and nightclubs, as well as a "special night show" and a fake Rolex watch found in a small alley known as "Pat Pong", which is a "risk zone" for tourists or commuters who did not come here for any of the above locations. In the past, I have received "wake up calls" from tourist customers, this often happened after midnight at the go-go bars many times, most of the cases such as; expensive drinking and unfair extra charges, lost camera, money, and etc. Watch out!

Sincerely, I never hesitated to help all my clients, although I felt that I might not solve the problems awaited, but at least I could stand by my tourist-client who's become like a good friend during the tours. I drove from home suddenly, always came with some policemen so everything was all set every time. That's the talk of Pat Pong from my experience; it's the red-light district area, but it calls all tourists to see what it's like till now. **Pat Pong** has been widely known for variety of night entertainments as one of the famous red-light districts when you are on Silom Road, it's also one of the entertainment areas which is famous among foreign tourists. The land at Patpong alleys are the private land; original gave for rent as shops and business buildings, but later on the nightclubs and bars were settled in Patpong for the American soldiers as the entertainment's venues during Vietnam War (1972-1992). Patpong is also an area where night-time stalls sell products such as; CDs, DVDs and imitations brand names of watches, bags etc. Please use discretion in negotiation with vendors and bar criers during walking around in these areas.

The Red-light districts like, Patpong or Soi Cowboy are places of beer bars, go-go bars, pubs, nightclubs and inter-restaurants, but there are some street vendors for goods and food all over the places. You may only walk through with friends or your companions for having a look. I don't recommend the ladies walk alone. Anyway, Patpong alley connects Suriwong Road and Silom Road where you can enjoy walking at night time for some delicious street food.

Thaniya Alley near Patpong is recognized as the areas of Japanese tourists because it's full of special nightclubs for Japanese; with Japanese alphabets of each place. There are many Japanese restaurants and Thaniya Plaza; which is famous for golf equipment center where you can find the most golf equipment in Bangkok.

KHAOSAN ROAD

Roaming around the streets **at Khaosan** Road and find a nice guest house for settling yourself to feel the atmosphere of this popular place for backpackers. It's an area of some old temples located, old style of Thai restaurants, the Banglumphu Market, and a popular nightlife spot in Bangkok you should take a look if you don't stay around here. **Khaosan Road** is the road started from Chakrapong Road in front of **Wat Chanasongkram** to the southeast until Tanao Road near Khok Wua Intersection (keep walking till you meet Ratchadamnoen avenue from here). The name of "Khaosan", which means "Rice"; came from the history told that it was the old alley built since 1892 in the reign of King Rama V and it was famous for a big center for selling rice in Bangkok. The rice here was transported from mills on the barges along the Chao Phraya River to Banglumphu Pier and brought to vendors at Khaosan Alley for selling to the people in these areas and nearby areas.

Khaosan Alley was developed and expanded to be wider lanes, with many buildings and houses built along the road, and changed from the alley to be the road afterwards. It was popular among foreign tourists in 1982; during the 200th Anniversary Celebration of Bangkok, but the guesthouse business boomed when the Hollywood Movie Making needed Khaosan Road to be the movie location; there were no hotels in this area that time so they had to rent the houses from people who lived here, finally; the guest houses and small homestays include some hotels were established and made the Khaosan Road has been very popular among backpackers and become one of a nightlife spot in Bangkok for many tourists. You can ride a public bus from Suwannaphum Airport directly to Khaosan, it's on the first floor exit 10. **From Wat Chanasongkram, you can cross** the street to **Banglumphu Market** and admire **Wat Bowonniweth Ratchavoraviharn. T**he two temples here are one of the important temples in Bangkok where you should not miss if you stay close to Khaosan.

WAT CHANASONGKRAM NEAR KHAOSAN

Wat Chanasongkram was built since Ayutthaya period but unknown when. It was called Wat Klangna and the name was changed to Wat Thong Pu when it's restored by King Rama I and made the temple as the Mon Temple like Wat Thong Pu in Ayutthaya which was ruined because the three battles supported by the Mon people were victorious army during the wars against Burmese Army in 1785-1788. The army was led by Phra BowornrajchaoMaha Sura Singhanat or Prince of the Palace of Front; who was King Rama I's brother.

Wat Chanasongkram has always been restored. But in the reign of King Rama VI, the main construction was started for the aim of keeping the ashes of the high royal family at the back veranda of the ordination hall and the ashes of the Prince of Front Palace was enshrined here in 1927. The beautiful Principal Buddha Image at Wat Chanasongkram was named Phra Phuttha Norasi Tri Lokacheth or called by local "Luang Por Phu". The statue is 2.5-meter-wide and 3.5-meter-long made of stucco with tin lining situated with 25 Buddha Statues enshrined around the base. The statue of the principal Buddha contained the clothes with talisman belonged to the Prince and his soldiers which were used during the war many times.

The temple was renamed to Wat Chanasongkram which means "Victory of war" and it's one of the royal temples.

WAT BOWONNIWETH NEAR BANGLUMPOO

Wat Bowonniweth Ratchavoraviharn is the temple where the former abbots stayed and the first Monk's College called Mahamakut Buddhist University located. The temple was original called Wat Mai built in the reign of King Rama III. It's where the 4 former Thai Supreme Patriarchs resided. The architectures of the temple are mixed between Thai and the Chinese. You should get inside the ordination hall of this temple for admiring **the two Principal Buddha Statues**; the base of one of the Buddha statues enshrined the ashes of King Rama VI and King Rama IX; both of the kings ordained here. The areas close to the temple is called **Banglumpoo** Market; an old market for clothes and food.

At the present, the market is full of many bars, shops, and restaurants surrounded. In the olden days, Banglumpoo was a famous market for buying clothes but it's changed to be the tourists' intersection for pubs, bars, Thai massage by the street, vendors and tour agency when Khaosan has been crowded with foreign tourists. The old restaurants selling noodles here are recommended.

AIRPLANE GRAVEYARD

This abandoned place used to be a beer garden called "Runway" or "Runway Beer Festival" with the idea of being a permanent beer garden and expected to be the popular hangout place on Ramkhamhaeng Road. It was the huge areas for carparks which seemed to be very necessary for customers in Bangkok and quite suitable for people from the nearby areas. The decommissioned plane wreck was only bought to match the atmosphere and its concept. It was opened for the first time in 2012 with the attraction of the large jumbo jet decorated with twinkling lights. The area in the back was used to be a gathering place for vendors which looked like a flea market sold to hip-teens such as clothing, hats, bags, and all handmade items. Many visitors here like some couples came here for posing themselves for pictures with planes. Previously, a foreign media office has been ranked as the 2nd most amazing place in Bangkok with some of the written reviews of this cemetery travel route. In fact, the abandoned of these 747 planes and two smaller MD-82 planes lying in pieces becoming homes of the families who collect garbage. When a tourist or a photographer asked them to take a picture with their home, 100 baht per time would be charged.

You can discover this **Airplane Graveyard** on Ramkamhaeng* Road 103 alley, by Airport Link to Ramkamhaeng Station and ride a taxi there. There's not much to see at the abandoned plane-graveyard; but tourists who visit here love to experience this amazing spot and get some shots of the plane wreckage parked around.

***Ramkamhaeng areas** are the rural side of Bangkok at Bangkapi District which is quite far from downtown of Bangkok. It's like an empty land in the past until **Ramkhamhaeng University was settled**; it is a government university conducting teaching and learning called as "The Market of Subjects" which accepts all people to study without qualifying examinations and accepted unlimited numbers students. The university has made the areas crowded with busy road. Many of entertainment places was built and has been one of the business trade areas.

ENTERTAINMENTS IN BANGKOK DAY AND NIGHT

The popular places for your entertainments I would like to recommend: The Siam Niramit Bangkok was the large theater which has been recorded by Guinness Book of World Records that the stage is the tallest and the largest in the world. The show performed with amazing special effects by using high technology to introduce Thailand's history and culture, performed by about 100 performers with colorful costumes. This theater's capacity was 2000 seats and 25 wheelchair spaces. The duration of showtime was about1.5 hours. The attractions inside The Siam Niramit Theater also included Traditional Village of 4 Regions in Thailand, outdoor entertainment with Thai music and dance, Thai Massage, and restaurants. It was opened in October 27, 2005 and closed in September 2021, but The Siam Niramit Phuket has been closed temporarily. I hope it will be open again when the pandemic situation is better. The place can be reached by MRT at Thailand Cultural Center Station Exit 1.

Dinner with Classical Thai Dance is almost everywhere even on the cruises. If you join dinner tour, Khon dance is always be a part of the show. "**KHON**" is a Thai traditional dance, performed on stage with masks; most of the expressing characteristics of Dancers in the drama based on the ancient epic; Ramayana. The Thai traditional shows at the dinner tour mostly included with the Khon Dancing which is more interesting than the normal classical dances.

- ❑ Enjoy **the Safari World; the open zoo of Safari Park and Marine Park** with some special shows. It's one of the fourite tourist attractions in Bangkok. (it's not so far from the airport) When you get inside here, the park-bus will take you to see the wild animals along the way around the park. The Marine Park comes with shows; where you can see water-ski show and elephant show, while the Jungle Walk is newly opened for feeding Giraffe, the Birds Shows, and etc.
- ❑ Enjoy **the Wonder World Fun Park** opposite to the **Fashion Island** shopping malls which is close to the Suwannaphum Airport.
- ❑ **The Siam Amazing Park still** remains as the **oldest amusement** and water park complex in Southeast Asia. This park has been a fun place for decades for family entertainment. (the location is quite near Suwannaphum Airport) It composes of Bangkok World and amazing adventure; water world, extreme world, family world, adventure and small world; for a little child. The park's areas are also included restaurants, shops, facilities in water world, locker service and so on. Siam Park has been popular for the "Bangkok Sea"; the imitated sea with waves for the Bangkok people who don't want to travel far.

- **The Dream World;** is a **large outdoor amusement** park in Thailand. It is located at Km 7 of Highway No. 305 (Rangsit-Nakhon Nayok) at Thanyaburi District, Pathum Thani Province (one of Bangkok Metropolitan Region). This amusement park covers an area of more than 160 rai. Dream World theme park opened for the first time on November 12, 1993. **Dream World theme park has 4 areas:** "Dream World Plaza" a quaint village, "Dream Garden", a land of gardens and a large lake, "Fantasy Land", the land of the world. Fairy tales and "Adventureland", the land of adventure. You can come to Dream World by Skytrain BTS: at Victory Monument Station and catch the van no.84 or the public bus no.538 for Dream World at **Phayathai side**. The van return trip to the Victory Monument is about until 17.00 Pm. Otherwise; you need to come back by taximeter or a public bus for Victory Monument. Dream World is not so far from both airports. **Open Mon-Fri: 10.00-17.00, Sat-Sun 10.00-18.00.**

The indoor amusement land in Bangkok is available like the **Harbour Land or Harborland which** is the largest famous indoor playground in Asia, the excursions for children with world-class standards designed by SPI Global Play, Sweden. It's a leading player manufacturer. As for an amusement park for children that is assured of quality and the safety of the toddlers. There are different zones for each branch for enhancing the imagination of kids to learn along with having fun as well. The indoor amusement parks can be found within the large malls such as;

- ❑ **Fashion Island**, 3rd floor, open from 10:00 a.m. - 8:00 p.m.
- ❑ **Gateway Bangsue**, 6th floor, open from 10:00 a.m. - 8:00 p.m.
- ❑ **Mega Bangna** 1st floor is temporarily closed.
- ❑ **Gateway Ekamai**, 5th floor, open from 10.00-20.00
- ❑ **Sindhorn Midtown Hotel** opens from 8:30 a.m. to 7:30 p.m.
- ❑ **Central Westgate**, 4th floor, open from 10:00 a.m. - 8:00 p.m.
- ❑ **Seacon Bangkae**, 4th floor, open from 10:30 AM to 8:00 PM. Weekends and holidays 10:00 AM to 8:00 PM.

- ❑ **The Mall Lifestore Ngamwongwan**, 6th floor, open 11.00-20.00 hrs., Saturday-Sunday holiday 10.00-20.00 hrs.
- ❑ **ICONSIAM**, 6th floor, open from 10.00-20.00

ROOFTOP BARS

Take a moment to see the beauty of Bangkok. in the sunset with the one you love and soak up the atmosphere in the wide angle of the city. You might even stay up late to enjoy a wonderful party with friends or someone in the midst of a night where millions of lights shone below. The famous rooftop bar is located on the high rise building and on the top floor of the hotel. The place is where you can eat or drink cocktails, listen to a lovely music with someone. The best and most popular rooftops such as Banyan Tree, Lebua, Sofitel, Sathorn, Millennium, Hilton, Centara, Grand at Central World, Cielo Skybar and Restaurant, Indigo Hotel, Ban Wang Lang Hotel, Avani. Bangkok Hotel and more. Enjoy the view of Bangkok on the rooftop bar with your special someone!

WATERPARKS IN BANGKOK

Suan Siam; The Sea of Bangkok is a water park in Bangkok surrounded by trees which is suitable for bringing the family to relax and unwind. You can play all day in the artificial sea with giant slide large winding gutter and relax with a wellness spa, or to lie in the wind on the canvas bed. It's close to the two airports in Bangkok.

Pororo Aquapark; it's the world's first floating water park at the Central Plaza Bangna 6th Floor in Bangkok. There are many play zones with 9 pools and 4 highlight slides for people of all genders and ages. A water park themed with cute little penguins. Kids will be amazed by the colorful rides. There is a wide variety to choose from many play zones an amazing slide. There is a special zone for children. Best for the whole family who wants to have fun in Bangkok.

Saimai Waterpark; is a water park in Bangkok that has been called the first and largest inflatable water park. Have fun in the water park with many players to beat the heat. There is no need to wear a bathing suit or rent it. This is close to Don Muang Airport.

- ❑ You can also go to **Jungle Water Park in Nonthaburi and Fantasia Lagoon at The Mall Shopping Mall; Gnam wongwan in Nonthaburi.** Hang out and enjoy at the **Chocolate Ville** International restaurants for varieties of food (Kaset–Nawamin Road) it's not so far from Suwannaphum Airport and a good place for family.

SEAFOOD RESTAURANTS AT THE BANGKOK SEA

If you stay by Silom Rd. and nearby, you can enjoy a nice seafood and sea view of Bangkok at "Talay Krungthep"; "Talay" means "Sea", located at Bangkhuntien district on Rama 2 Road which is near the Gulf of Thailand and Samutsakon province. The famous seafood restaurants in downtown of Bangkok are all around within each district that you can try one of them (50 districts). The top and famous fish markets in Bangkok are on Charoen Krung Road, Talad* Thai; the most comprehensive wholesale market in Thailand, Talad Or Tor Kor, Talad Bangbon, Talad Wong wien Yai at Thonburi side, Talad Paknam in Samutprakan, and etc. They are the source of fresh sea creatures delivered directly to merchants every day for wholesale, to famous restaurants or retail for all customers to come and buy. All the sea creatures transport trucks will arrive at the fish market for delivery of crabs, scallops, shrimps, squids, as well as freshwater animals. Most restaurants sell seafood by weighing each type of seafood. It depends on the size and the rare marine animals of each season. * Talad means Market.

THAI MASSAGE

The historical evidence that records stories about the oldest Thai massage came from a stone inscription of the Sukhothai period which was dug within a mango forest which corresponded to the era of King Ramkhamhaeng. It has inscribed the image of healing the by massage. Later, in the Ayutthaya period, there is clear evidence of Thai massage in 1455 during the reign of King Borom Trai Lokanat with a royal decree dividing the duties of doctors according to their specific expertise. Later in the reign of King Naresuan the Great; this was the era when Thai massage was very popular. It appears in the archives of the French ambassador named La Lou Bear in 1687 that if someone was sick in Siam, first aid was by stretching the body-lines from having the specialist stood up on the patient's body then use the foot pedal for massaging. It was said that some pregnant women often used their children to step on them to make childbirth easier and less painful in the ancient time. In the reign of King Rama III, he chose Wat Pho to become a university for Herbal Medicine; by making Herbal medicine texts around the monastery and the king ordered to make sculpture of Hermits in 80 postures; the statues were cast in zinc and tin, along with writing poems describing those postures for curing the diseases, and inscriptions of Thai massage techniques on marble plates are now 60 images; for showing the massage points in detail decorated on the wall and a pillar of Sala Rai near the entrance to The Reclining Buddha Hall at Wat Pho.

Wat Pho is now considered as a systematic collection of knowledge in Thai massage. Later, in the reign of King Chulalongkorn (King Rama V), in 1906; the textbook of Thai massage or called as "The Royal Thai Massage Textbook" was applied in studying among the Royal Physicians or a doctor in the royal court. The famous for massage at that time was Doctor Inthevada who was a royal court chiropractor, he transferred all massage subjects to his son, Dr. Chit Dechphan, who later passed on his knowledge to his students. The knowledge of traditional massage became widespread and opened to the general public. It's also one of the subjects of the Thai Medicine. UNESCO has announced the registration of Thai massage under the English name **"Nuad Thai" or means the traditional Thai massage. "Nuad" means "Massage", as** it is an intangible cultural heritage in the category "List of representative cultural heritage of humanity". **I recommend** a **traditional Thai Massage at a clean and registered place in a wide space room (not so crowded)**. There are many types for you to try like foot massage, full massage for the whole body and massage some points like; neck and shoulder, and oil massage. The massage parlors are seen everywhere or even by street. You should not trust them to massage as they want but you want instead; say to them for **"Relax"** only otherwise; you may get hurt after massages; some can't walk awhile and you really won't enjoy your day. Be careful and let your body be relaxed during massages! If you feel hurt; just warn him/her to be slow down. Foot massage is a good start for trying at open air area during in the pandemic situation.

BOXING STADIUMS IN BANGKOK

Muay Thai or Thai Boxing was very popular in the early Rattanakosin period. The era that was considered the most flourishing was the reign of King Rama V who studied and trained in Thai boxing and favored to organize boxing competitions in front of the throne. The competitions were done by selecting skilled boxers from various regions come to compete and be bestowed and titled. The king also pleased the Department of Education for including teaching Muay Thai as a compulsory subject; in the physical education teacher training school.

There was regular boxing in front of the throne until the reign of King Rama VI; the fighting tournament were between the boxers and the Thai boxing teachers and fighting between boxers with foreign boxing teachers such as the boxing match between Muay Lie Pha (Kung Fu) Overseas Chinese Names of Mr. Jee Chang and Mr. Young Harntalay, major students of Krom Luang Chumphon Khet Udomsak; the prince, which showed a boxing pose in the style of Korat boxing; emphasized on stretching body to stand and got ready to attack and defend with an emphasis on the use of feet and swinging punches.

Later; the pose became a model for practicing Muay Thai in most physical education institutes. In the reign of King Rama VII; during that time, Muay Thai fighters were wrapped around the hands with ropes for boxing, until Mr. Phae Raising Prasert; the Boxer from Tha Sao in Uttaradit Province punched Mr. Jeer, a Khmer Boxer with a "buffalo throwing punch" to death. Therefore; Muay Thai was changed to wearing gloves instead of wrapping hands. The rules for the fight began to be established at standard arenas namely; Lumpini Boxing Stadium and Rajadamnern Stadium, hosting Thai boxing competitions until the present. You can experience a **Thai Boxing or "Muay Thai" competition,** the exciting and popular sport, at the Lumpini Stadium on Raminthra Road (30 Kms. from Suwannaphum Airport) or Ratchadamnoen Stadium on Ratchadamnoen Road. You should get the matches information from websites before going to a stadium.

When I was a tourist guide, I remembered one of my clients who loved Thai boxing asked for a school for learning Thai Boxing and I found one camp for him to practice for about 2 weeks. He was selected to be amateur boxer in competition. He's brave and really did a good job. Right now, the Thai boxing camps can be found easily in Bangkok. Thai Boxing is an art of fighting by using the body to be the weapon in fighting and the mind to focus where to knock down your opponent. It's also a part of exercises nowadays.

MORE ATTRACTIONS IN THE FUTURE

There will be some new places coming in the future; The huge People's Park built by the present king (King Rama X), which is honored King Bhumibol; King Rama IX, located in front of Jitlada Palace and The Marble Temple, it's built for being a people's park for exercises and relaxation and will be finished by 2026. The land of this park was the horse racing tracks before. The other one will be the new Zoo at Pathumthani Province and finished by 2027.

There are more attractions in Bangkok for visiting. But if you go on a trip as I stated in this book, you can experience Bangkok like a local, I mostly mentioned the highlights that you shouldn't miss when you are in Bangkok. If you stay anywhere please try walking around the area where you stayed and look for a train or subway station to begin your own journey. The temple's buildings are easily distinguishable with their spires and Buddha images. You may be able to walk in and see inside the hall.

Some temples may have nothing interesting because they may be small, insignificant temples or newly built.

I recommend you to eat at the food court inside the mall or department store where you can see what the food looks like before trying the street food. Another thing is that I recommend wearing modest clothing and wearing a mask at all times. Although the epidemic was reduced, but it makes you safer to travel by wearing a mask or keeping your social distance when you're in a community or inside every building in Bangkok.

I don't recommend that you take a taxi or tuk-tuk often because you may waste time with traffic and you may find that the service is not good for you. If you join the tour or choosing the professional local tourist guide you can trust (see the registered ID) at the beginning, you can do your own later on easily. But in case; your time is limited, it's much better for you to go with a local tourist guide for the tours you want. I believe my **guidebook** for Bangkok be one of your best friends when you are in Thailand more or less. It can save you a lot of time searching on the website and also help you identify easily for more details on the topic you might need. The spelling of Thai words in English may not seem the same but as long as the pronunciation is very similar, you will find a list of your locations. I guarantee you will enjoy the places in Bangkok by following this guide book.

TOUR KOH KRET IN NONTHABURI

Nonthaburi is a province of Bangkok Metropolitan region which is at the northwest border of Bangkok, established since 1561. It is the most densely populated province after Bangkok. I lived here many years and still love it.

Nonthaburi is really a part of Bangkok if you don't notice the sign shown direction to Nonthaburi. When I was young, I went to high school in Bangkok but I lived in Nonthaburi. I rode the public bus and it took about 45 minutes to reach school. Many people lived in Nonthaburi at that time earned their living by growing fruits; durian was the top fruit within Nonthaburi land and because the cost of living was cheaper than in Bangkok; therefore, people chose to live in this town with nature surroundings rather than Bangkok. I remembered that it's commonly seen old teakwood houses by canals with Durian gardens and some rice fields around this old town. Nowadays there are few left to see the rice field and garden of fruits because the land is priced higher and higher, and the owners of these land sold the land to the property companies for building the residential projects and department stores.

You can ride the Express Boat from Sathorn Pier; the major pier on the Chao Phraya River, to **Nonthaburi Pier** where the largest market of this province located, **or** to get off at the **Pakkret Pier** for exploring **Koh Kret**. The boat trips are the most easy and fascinating trip. You can go to the piers at BTS Saphantaksin Station for Sathon Pier or MRT: at Yaek Tiwanon Station and get a taxi to the Nonthaburi Pier if you stop at the MRT Ministry of Public Health Station then get a taximeter for about 15 mins to Nonthaburi Pier. **Nonthaburi Pier** is a main spot for visiting many attractions such as **the Former Nonthaburi Provincial Hall**, established in 1936, which is now the Nonthaburi Museum, Wat Chaloem Phra Kiat, Wat Pleang, local market, and eat at a restaurant or street food by the riverbank.

WAT CHALOEM PHRA KIAT IN NONTHABURI

You can stop at **Wat Chaloem Phra Kiat** Pier for exploring this beautiful temple if you ride an express boat or get a boat ride across the river from Nonthaburi Pier here. The temple was built in 1849 in the reign of King Rama III to honor his mother. It was built at the former residence of his grandfather and grandmother. The monument of King Rama III or Somdej Phra Nang Klaoa Chao Yu Hua is seen at the riverbank. The ordination hall is surrounded by unique walls which are fortified like The Grand Palace which is the only one seen like this in Thailand, as it was the old fort here before. The ordination hall is the art combined Thai-Chinese styles with a very beautiful principal Buddha image inside; named as "Phra Phuttha Maha Loka Phinantha Patima" sculpted from copper. Many buildings within the temple are around the areas and besides; there's a wonderful park; **Chaloem Kanchana Phisek Park located** near the temple.

WAT PHLENG IN NONTHABURI

Wat Plaeng was abandoned for more than 200 years since Ayutthaya Period but it was restored and registered as a temple in 1987. The highlight of Wat Phleng is the pink ordination hall which was painted with faith in His Majesty King Chulalongkorn (King Rama V); because the pink color was his favorite color. In addition, the temple area also has a statue of King Rama V and enshrined also with Luang Pho Tho Buddha statue; the statue is very tall Buddha image in the subduing Mara posture made of red sandstone cladding with lacquer and gold lacquer, the lap width is 3 in 4 of the width of the ordination hall. From the characteristics of the Buddha's such as the face, the mouth, and the hair were assumed as the Buddha images built in the art of U-Thong period. This temple is located in Nonthaburi downtown. The highlight tour for Nonthaburi is the exploration of the **Koh Kret;** the small island in the Chao Phraya River where is promoted as a cultural tourism destination of Nonthaburi. Here, you can ride bicycle around this island and learn about **the traditional earthenware making** which is the main career of people here. After visiting Nonthaburi Pier then ride a river boat to Koh Kret, but it should be during Sat-Sun and public holidays 9.00-17.30. The Ferry routes can be done from many piers like Pakkret Pier or Wat Sanam Nua Pier.

Koh Kret is a subdistrict belong to Nonthaburi; it is the land where **Mon people** live. The Mon people; according to the history, were the first people settled in Burma for centuries. It's assumed that they had migrated from Central Asia to establish their kingdom in the South of Salawin and Satong rivers of Burma and the land was mentioned in Chinese and Indian documents as the "Suwannaphum Land". The archaeological evidences in Thailand said about the Mon people was since the 11th-13rd Century from the 19 mm diameter of silver coins found in **Nakonpathom** and Uthong, with inscription of "Si Tharavadisuan" and a figure of cauldron on the other side of the coin, made them to believe that the ancient Mon established the Dharavadi Empire in the central region of Suwannaphum Land where Nokonpathom was the city center. The Mon people was invaded and be in the war many times with Burma and lived very badly until they did not have their own territory. They evacuated to Thailand since Ayutthaya period (1351-1767). Although there was no community of Mon descendants within Ayutthaya, but there were Mon people scattered their communities along the banks of the Chao Phraya River from **Ayutthaya** down **to** Bangkok; His Majesty the king bestowed arable land for Mon immigrants in all regions in Thailand, and one of them was Koh Kret. (The photo of Pakkret Pier and can see Koh Kret the other side of the riverbank. Many local restaurants and a big market located here. I always enjoy coming here for a bowl of noodle and set free some fish to the river. **Koh Kret's area** is about 4.2 square kilometers composed of 7 main villages; with population about six-thousands of Thai-Mon living within the island.

In fact, the island was originally a meander located on the Chao Phraya river which delayed maritime to Ayutthaya. King Taisa of Ayutthaya planned a canal dug here for reducing shipping time in 1722 and the canal was called by locals "Klong Lat Kret"; "Lat" means "Shortcut". The canal was become wider when the time passed; due to erosion made canal became a part of the river, then causing an island which is Koh Kret nowadays. You will see the Leaning Pagoda or "**Phra Chedi Mutao**"; a white tilted pagoda built by Mon people inside **Wat Paramaiyikawat** on Koh Kret from the boat ride. The temple was built in the late period of Ayutthaya and was left empty during the fall of Ayutthaya. When the Mon migrated in Koh Kret in 1774 during King Taksin period, the king ordered to restore the temple. The Buddha's Relic was enshrined inside the pagoda since 1884 by the King Rama V. The age of this Mutao Pagoda is about 300 years old, made of brick and mortar on octagonal base recess, it has five-tiered on the top which is the Mon style art. The pagoda was announced as an ancient monument in 1935.

From the first-time construction of this pagoda, it was built upright but the water eroded the bank made the pagoda collapsed and tilted approximately in 1895. Later in 1992, a wooden and a cement dams were built for preventing the erosion but it could not solve this problem. The Department of Religious Affairs and many people repaired by making the concrete dam for the pagoda base to be firmly fixed but The Fine Arts Department allowed the conservation of the pagoda to be restored in a tilted state. Mutao is now the symbol of Nonthaburi province as "the tilted Pagoda" known all among tourists all over the world.

WAT CHEDI HOI IN PATHUMTHANI

Pathumthani is another part of Bangkok Metropolitan Region. The Province is an old city which located at the north of Bangkok. This province has been established since the Ayutthaya Period in the reign of King Narai the Great (1656-1688). The former name was "Sam Khok" where the **Mon people** evacuated during the war. Many parts of this province are hard to notice for being in Bangkok or Pathumthani province.

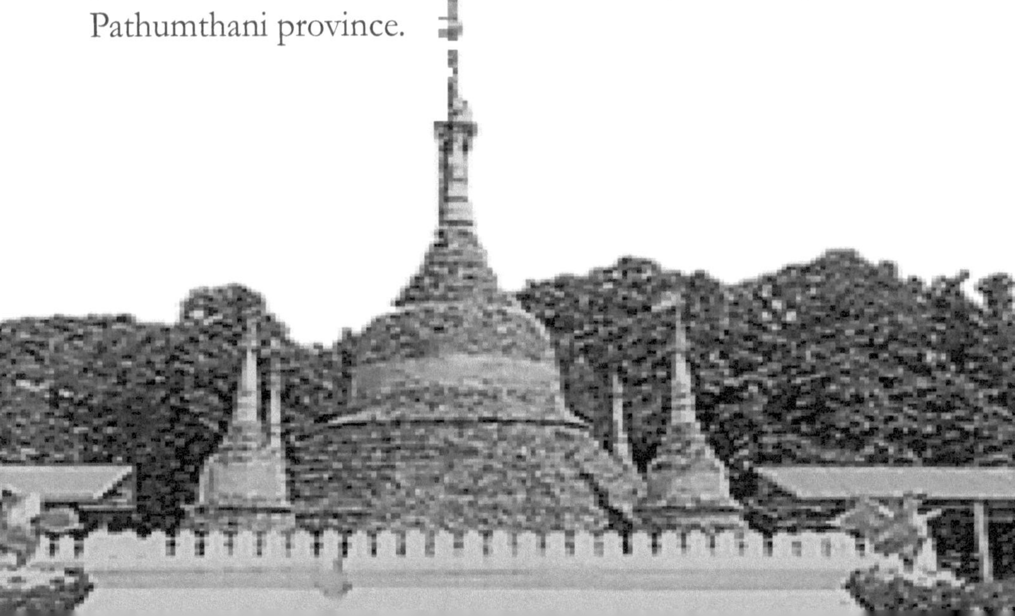

Even the Thai usually call Rangsit instead of Pathumthani (Rangsit is a subdistrict belong to Thanyaburi district in Pathumthani) and some still think that is a part of Bangkok, anyway; it's nice to look around this small **town.** The lines of the MRT Green Line Extension to reach Pathumthani are **Mo Chit - Saphan Mai - Khu Khot.** It's the red line suburban trains between Bang Sue to Rangsit. **T**he best way for us to notice Pathumthani is when you ride a car passing many Klongs or Canals on the roadsides which are numbered at Rangsit town; there are 55 natural canals with the length of 180 Kms, the other 29 canals are irrigation canals. You can ride a taxi and ask him to go to Rangsit to admire the atmosphere of Bangkok's suburb which is in Pathumthani province areas. It's the direction where you can go to Nakonnayok province easily from Rangsit by passing along these canals. The location of Dream World; the amusement park, is not so far from here. **Wat Chedi Hoi** is the first attraction where most people look for in Pathumthani. It's located in Lat Lhum Kaew District. The temple was registered as a temple in 1988. Many of ancient oysters' shell from million years ago were found here and the abbot built the huge pagoda from them in 1995. If you have time, see a nice temple called **Wat Sing;** the first Mon style temple, located on the west bank of the Chao Phraya River, has been one of the oldest temples with old pagodas, where the ordination hall here are for the Thai history research, then visit **Wat Phuet Udom at Klong 13 or Canal No.13;** known for the imaginative arts of Heaven and Hell from the Buddhist's belief about doing good will go to heaven but doing bad to hell.

Admire the mural paintings depicting the story of The Ten Lives of Buddha which is called the "Tosssachart Chadok" at **Wat Chinwararam,** located on the west bank of The Chao Phraya River. (Travelling by Boat or car to reach here.)

- ❑ Visit **the National Science Museum of Thailand**, the great place for enjoying and knowledge (the children love here), located at Klong 5 or Canal No.5 in Pathumthani Province. (The place is close to the Suwannaphum Airport)
- ❑ Admire **the Mon Golden Pagoda and the white jade Buddha** Statue at **Wat Chedi Thong**, on the west side of The Chao Phraya River in Pathumthani Province.
- ❑ Pathumthani is famous for **noodle on the boat** or we call "Kua Tiew Rue Rangsit", you will see a big boat on each canal as a noodle restaurant on each canal and very popular among the locals and tourists. The boat is the same size as the rice barge; having seats for customers and sometimes the merchant cooks on the boat. I never miss those whenever I pass by these canal-road in Rangsit. Please try.

THREE-HEADED ELEPHANT IN SAMUTPRAKAN

When you arrive Thailand, you are entering Samut Prakan Province; or called by Thai as **"Pak-nam"; means "the mouth of river" which** located at about only 30 kilometers from Bangkok. It's the place where the Chao Phraya River flows into the Gulf of Thailand. Samut Prakan was an old town since Ayutthaya Period. The motto for this attractive town is "Naval Fortress, Chedi Klang Nam (Pagoda in the middle of river), big Crocodile Farm, beautiful Ancient City, Happy Phra Pradang Songkran Festival, delicious dried salty river fish (Salid Fish), "Rab Bua Tradition" (throwing lotus for worshipping Buddha) and the main location for all industries". From the province's motto, you should explore here and of course, there are more attractions than that. It's the province where you can get closer to the sea. Most of tourists think they are in Bangkok. This little town can make you find something to do while you have a short time for transit in Thailand by Sky trains from Suwannaphum Airport.

I knew this town when I visited Wat Asokaram since 1986 and found that not only the temple was a nice place to visit but also the Ancient City was very interesting place included with the Crocodile Farm that made my clients excited and enjoyed. Many tourists I guided here loved the local canals scenery and the wooden houses with along the road, some of the houses remained but many of them become condominiums and department stores. Although it's quite modern, different from the old days, but Paknam has its own charm and it's hard to be forgotten. If you ride Sky train (Sukhumvit route), you can stop at BTS Chang Erawan Station for admiring **The Giant Statue of Three-Headed Elephant Art** and see antiquities or priceless collections of Buddhist objects contained inside the statue as it's called The Erawan Museum which is regarded as the Copper Elephant Floating Sculpture by using hand-forged technique, depicting a three headed elephant which is called in Thai Erawan Elephant from the literature that actually has 33 heads, due to convenient construction, then the architect reduced to only 3 heads with the height of 43.6 meters (approximately the height of 14-17 floor-building). The Three-Headed Elephant Sculptor was built from the idea of Mr. Lek Viriyaphant, a businessman who owns Viriyah Insurance Company, one of the leading insurance companies in Thailand, for preserving ancient collectibles with sacred idols as a heritage of Thailand. The construction was started in 1994. The building has three floors; designed from the imagination of Trailokya (three worlds) in Buddhist's belief; Badan World (Water World), Human World and Heaven World; with the collections of old Buddha statues kept inside.

A chance for discovering the Temple of **Phra Samut Chedi; located** on the island of the mouth of the Chao Phraya River, is not so often for the people who's not the local here. If you have time, you should do once in Samut Prakan Province. (BTS: at Paknam Station exit 6 and connect the Ferry Boat at the Viboonsri Pier)

Phra Samut Chedi is the name of district which derived from the Phra Samut Chedi; the large pagoda situated at the middle of the river, built in 1827 in the reign of King Rama II who established Samutprakan province with 6 forts for preventing the enemy to invade the capital (Bangkok) and also ordered to build this pagoda at the same time. The constructions of the forts and the pagoda were finished in the reign of King Rama III period together with 3 more forts. **Phra Samut Chedi Pagoda** was restored in 1859, in the reign of King Rama V with one of the forts was added that time; the fort is called **"Pom Phra Chulachomkrao";** ("Pom" means "Fort") located by the shore. At the present, there are only the two forts left in Samutprakan; Pom Phra Chulachomkrao and Pom Phi Sue Samut.

Come and enjoy **the Crocodile Farm**; the biggest crocodile farm in Thailand and recognized as the biggest farm in the world. It's where you can enjoy the exciting shows in this zoo. If you ride BTS Sky train, please stop at **Keha Station** and get a taxi for 10 minutes to reach here. This crocodile farm was opened since 1950 with 40,000 crocodiles and contained some other animals and dinosaur museum. Right now, the Crocodile Farm in Samutprakan is announced "permanently closed" because of the Covid-19, in my view; it will open again. The lovely days during weekend for tourists is feeding the flock of seagulls at **Bangpoo Seaside**; the nearest seaside to Bangkok, located in Samut Prakan Town. If you would like to relax and have a nice seafood dishes, you should try a restaurant in Samutprakan areas which is not so far from Suwannaphum Airport. The Seafood restaurants are crowed with mostly Thai during weekend here. **Bang Poo** is also well known among Thai tourists for having a Balloon Dancing at Bang Poo Seaside during weekend and have a nice seafood here. Ride along the road to Bang Poo, you will see the big sign of **The Ancient City or** the Ancient Siam which is like the museum park, dubbed as the world's largest outdoor museum located on the opposite side to Bang Poo.

The Ancient City is recommended because it's where you can admire the replicas of the remarkable places in Thailand that were built within this huge land. It's really worth coming here when you have a short visit to see the remarkable places in Thailand to be gathered in one area.
The famous temple in Samut Prakan is called **Wat Asokaram which is t**he center of the locals joins together for religious rituals on the Buddha's Days. The place has been well known for practicing meditation and observing precepts. Here; you can see the stunning of the pagoda grouped total of 13 Pagodas which is called Phra Thu Thangkha Chedi situated opposite to the large Viharn or the multi-purpose building for religious rituals; these pagodas represent Thudong Khawat 13 or the 13 disciplines strictly for the Forest Monk to practice which are: **1.**wearing Bangsukoon Robe; the used clothes, **2.**wearing 3 pieces of monk clothes as usual, **3.** going for alms, **4.** going for alms by walking in line, **5.** eat one time a day, **6.** eat in a monk bowl only, **7.** do not get any more offerings during sitting in a place and ready for eating, **8.** stay in a forest, **9.** stay under the tree, **10.** stay outdoor, **11.** stay by the cemetery, **12.** no attaching to any residence where offered by other, and **13.**no lying on the floor; sleeping in sitting position. The group of pagodas was initiated for construction by the first abbot named as Luang Por Lee. He has been respected among Buddhists for both Thai and foreigners from his well-disciplined during his monkhood and intense practicing for mindfulness by way of Buddha's Path. The temple seems to be well known for those who want to observe precepts and are Dharma practitioners.

I experienced staying at the temple many times and realized that the rules at the temple should have made the practitioners feel the difference from staying home such as chanting, calm, and listen to the preaching from a monk daily. You can admire the chedi and Phra Viharn Hall where enshrined a beautiful Buddha image and Luang Por Lee's coffin; of his body. There is a small pier by the shore at the temple. Besides; the temple is famous for a well-preserved mangrove forests where you can trail nearby the shore. It's also fantastic for this nature trail because you will see many lizards and many foot-fish on the mud, some of the lizards here is huge and walk inside the temple. The picturesque of the 13-pagoda group should be shot from the top floor of the Viharn Hall during sunrise or sunset.
One of nice places in Samutprakan is at **Sri Nakhon Khuean Khan Park and Botanical Garden**, it's the best Urban Oasis of Asia, for viewing birds and walking paths along the mangrove forest. The park is located at Saladeang* District in Samutprakarn Province.
***Saladeang District** is very famous in nationwide for Songkran Festival, it is where the locals play Songkran for a long period of time, about 10 days.

THE FIRST HOLY STUPA IN NAKONPATHOM

Nakonpathom is a small province at the northwest of Bangkok which is very near; about 56 kilometers. This province has been known as the ancient city since Dvaravadi Period (around 11th -16th century) from the archaeological evidences such as; a polished stone ax, bronze vessels like bowls, human bones, stone beads and etc. If you join "One day trip for Damnoensaduak Floating Market" in Ratchaburi Province or a Tour to Kanchanaburi for the Bridge over the River Kwai, you may add **Nakorn Pathom** on the way back to Bangkok for seeing the landmark of this old province which is one of the largest pagodas in Thailand; located at the center of town.

But if you drive to Nakonpathom, you can go by Phra Borom Chonnee Sky Bridge from Bangkok, straightforward directly to Nakonpathom town easily. This is not just the passer-by province for traveling to the western provinces of the country like Kanchanaburi, but Nakonpathom has more attractions and delicious food than you expect, besides; you will love a picturesque of the rice fields and scenery when you ride a train to come to Nakonpathom.

PHRA PATHOM CHEDI or the first pagoda of Siam is the symbol of Nakornpathom Province and one of the tallest and largest pagodas in Thailand, the name given by King Rama IV which means "the first holy Stupa", situated inside the area of Wat Phra Pathom Chedi Racha Worawihan. You can reach the pagoda by riding a train at Hualumphong Railway Station, or Bang Sue Grand Railway Station, or buses at the Southern Bus Terminal, or get a public bus no. 84 at Punnavithi BTS Station or Thonburi BTS Station for **Sampran District** and connect the local bus to the huge pagoda in Nakonpathom. **Phra Pathom Chedi** is an important sanctuary of Thailand; has a long history inside Wat Phra Pathom Chedi Ratchaworawiharn. It is believed that the Buddha's relics are enshrined inside this pagoda. Phra Pathom Chedi is a large chedi in the shape of an inverted bell with a gigantic mouth, a log structure. fastened with a huge chain of bricks, holding mortar, decorated with tiles over it, consisting of a viharn in 4 directions and a 2-tiered glass wall, the kind of the pagoda is considered the largest chedi in Thailand as well. It is worshiped by Buddhists all over the world.

The temple stipulates that there is a festival to worship Phra Pathom Chedi on the 12th day of the 12th lunar month to the 5th day of the waning moon of the 12th month, a total of 9 days and 9 nights annually. In 1908; when His Majesty King Mongkut was appointed as the Crown Prince, he visited the northern city and had seen many ancient Buddha images, he saw one Buddha image at Si Satchanalai (Sukhothai Province) consisted of a beautiful character to his heart but the statue was greatly damaged, leaving only the Buddha's head, hands, and feet therefore, the Buddha image was graciously to be summoned to Bangkok and let the potter built up his fullness and graciously organized the ceremony of pouring gold-liquid for the statue on December 30, 1913 at Wat Pho and named **Phra Ruangrojanarit; the standing Buddha next to the pagoda wall.**

The height of **Phra Ruangrojanarit**; the Buddha statue is about 7.42 meters, the Buddha image built in the posture of prohibiting relatives in Sukhothai art stamped standing on a brass pedestal with a lotus-backed lotus pattern, wrapped in a thin robe covering the body facing to the north, and made of heavy brass metal. You can visit **Sanam Chandra Palace;** a unique style palace located nearby the pagoda, **which was** the former palace built by the King Rama VI. The palace is composed of a group of the building complex and a shrine. Well! if you would like to have a lunch here, you should walk to a market areas, crossing the road (at the Standing Buddha's side) and enjoy a local restaurant for a dish of rice topped with grill pork and sweet sauce or called as **"Khao Moo Dang";** the signature of the town, I think it costs you 40-50 Bahts a dish, reasonable and good taste for you. It's superb! Or let's eat **Khao Rham,** baked sticky rice with coconut milk and nuts mixed with sugar and put inside a bamboo flask, for your snack. It helps stave off hunger quite well like eating a meal and a dessert at the same time. I love it with a cup of coffee. Khao Rham is the signature souvenir from Nokonpathom Province, please don't miss to try it! On the way back to Bangkok, you can stop by **The Don Whai Market; one of the top attractions in Nakhonpathom. It's located by the river like a floating market but most of the vendors sell the products on land; you can pick some of** variety of local goods and food plus enjoying the scenic view of Tha Chin River; the main river of this town. The boats are for hired here. You will discover the old-style houses built since King Rama VI period still remained of beautiful architecture at The Don Whai Market.

The food vendors at Don Whai Market travel by boat along **Tha Chin River to sell their products** here. This market is located at Phutthamonthon Sai 5 Lane which can be reached from Bangkok conveniently. You will notice that the sub-roads here are called Phutthamonthon Road and lied with its numbers. The name of the road come from the place called **The Phuttha-Monthon which** is one of the important religious sites with 1000 acres built for the celebration of 2500th year of Buddhism. It is where the huge Buddha image built in walking attitude (photo below) situated and being seen from the Phuttha Monthon Sai 4 Road; as the symbol of this road area; if you don't know where you are, when you see the Buddha image, you will know that you are at Phuttha Monthon Sai 4 Lane. The site is as interesting as a collection of many gardens and decorated with buildings. Sculptures created by private communities and business corporations created for charity by planting flowers and planting forests to make this park beautiful with a good atmosphere for exercise and it is a public park for recreation of the general public. The big event of Buddhist Day is usually performed here.

Samphran Elephant and Cultural Show at the Rose Garden has been very famous for its cultural show and elephant show since I was a tour guide in the past. It's a place for many activities right now such as; cultural show, Thai dance, and the hotel which is a place organized for some wedding party. The garden area is by the Tha Chin River. The popular activity here is for biking around **Sampran Riverside** and participate in workshop for Thai handmade products and get your handicraft back home. Visit the **Thai Human Imagery Museum on the way;** it is a museum of the wax/fiberglass sculptures of vivid details created by the group of Thai artists, located next to the Phuttha Monthon Park. The **Woodland Museum is the new attraction along the way from Nakonpathom to Bangkok which is an interesting gallery. The place is a large gallery of** thousand pieces of wood carvings and wooden artwork Collections. This place is along the way to Phuttha Monthon. Well! The places I mentioned in Nakhon Pathom here are all easily accessible for a day trip to enjoy the suburbs of Bangkok. I recommend if you have time.

SALT FARM IN SAMUTSAKON

Samutsakon; is a province on the southwest of Bangkok which borders Samut Songkram, Ratchaburi, Nakhon Pathom and Bangkok. **It** was the trading port where Chinese junks arrived since 1548 A.D. The familiar name for Thai calls this province is **"Mahachai".** Sometimes it's not noticeable that you are in Samutsakon or Bangkok until you see the exit sign showing the direction to Samutsakon downtown. Riding along the highway to the south, you will notice many salt fields both sides of the road.

Samutsakon is located at the mouth of Tha Chin River; distributed from The Chao Phraya River, flow into the sea at the Gulf of Thailand. People usually visit Samutsakon for enjoying the seafood at variety of restaurants in both downtown and by the sea. One of the famous restaurants is called **Krua chai Talay located** near the Gulf of Thailand at Phanthai Norasing Subdistrict. You can get a **free boat** to see the scenery and viewing some teal birds and small freshwater duck when you come to the restaurant and discover the shrine in the middle of the sea or called **as "Phra Klang Nam",** the **unseen of Samutsakorn Province** by getting a boat from this restaurant.

Tha Chalom Samutsakhon

Don't forget to take a boat for **watching the dolphins** and swarm of fish during in **May-October** where they appear near the Gulf of Thailand. The **Red Boardwalk Bridge** along the seashore surrounded by the mangrove forest during sunset is known as **"Dolphin Viewpoint". Enjoy the picturesque view with a** cool breeze in between November-January. Admire **the Wooden Ordination Hall at Wat Leam Suwannaram**; the oldest temple located on The Tha Chin River bank in Samutsakon Province.

This beautiful city gave me good memories of my time working as a salesman in a car showroom long time ago. I found the people here to be friendly and kind. Many of my customers for cars were fishermen and merchants in urban markets. When they pass the the car showroom where I worked, they would always stop by and had some fish or shrimp for me and my colleagues as souvenirs. I love this place and will stop by on my way every time I travel to Hua Hin Beach.

TRAIN MARKET IN SAMUTSONGKRAM

Samutsongkram; or called as "Mae Klong" by locals, is the smallest province of Thailand with the least population. It's located next to Samutsakorn Province where is recognized by tourists for Amphawa Floating Market and Talad Rom Houb. **The popular transport is the train to Maeklong Station** but if you join a tour for Damnoen Saduak Floating Market, please request for adding The Train Market or **Talad Rom Houb** in your program. The trip to Mae Klong is great for one day trip in the suburb which is not so far from Bangkok to experience many local places and delicious fresh seafood.

The main destination for tourists is for seeing the "Talad Rom Houb"; or The Train Market on the Mae Klong Railway Track, "Rom Houb" means "Closing Umbrella"; because the vendors here have their goods under the tall umbrellas; it's for preventing the sunshine and the heat. Those umbrellas will be suddenly pulled down and removed with all the goods from the tracks when the train approaches the market. All the goods will be replaced again and the umbrellas will be opened when the train has already passed the areas. It's an amazing market you should not miss! (the schedules are **8 times a day; in Maeklong Station at 8.30, 11.00, 14.30, 17.40/ out of station at 6.20, 9.00, 11.30, 15.30)**

The Thai Buddhists who come to Samutsongkram never miss going to **Wat Petchsamut Voraviharn or "Luang Por Ban Leam Temple**"; an old sacred Buddha for the Thai Buddhists nationwide. The statue is a standing Buddha image in the posture of holding an alm bowl, with the height of about 2.8 meters, cast in brass and gilded with gold. It is enshrined in the Ubosot or the ordination hall of Wat Phet Samut Worawihan or it's known as Wat Ban Laem.

The Thai people come to pay respect for wishing a good health and luck. This Buddha statue is one of the centers of faith among Thai people. When you arrive at the temple area here, you will notice the local way of life in a small province which is quite similar to each other in Thailand; a market, roads, people, etc.

The Amphawa Floating Market is a famous tourist attraction for eating the local food especially grilled seafood with hot sauce. It's nice to ride a speed boat to enjoy a scenic view of the Mae Klong River to the market indeed but don't forget to visit the **Tha Kha Floating Market;** a nice old market selling the food and souvenirs from the vendors in Sampan Boats as well. The area of this market is surrounded by coconut trees and gardens. Admire **Wat Chulamanee; a beautiful** ancient temple on the bank of Amphawa Canal will make your trip quite complete. The buildings and some old items inside the halls are the uniqueness of the art since Ayutthaya period.

The amazing ordination hall covered with the Huge Banyan Tree and the ancient Buddha Statue inside the hall at **Wat Bang Koong** is one of the top attractions for tourists who visit Samutsongkram province. I recommend here. But don't miss the old aged Mural Paintings; which is rarely found other places, left faded color but showing the techniques of monochromatic painting on the four walls of the old Viharn or a ceremonial hall which depict the Buddha's Life at **Wat Bang Kapom** which is about 3 kilometers from downtown of Samut Songkram.

Actually; there are many resorts and hotels nearby the Amphawa Floating market. If you enjoy here and would like to drink the local atmosphere at night by riding a boat to see thousands of beautiful fireflies of countryside (May-Oct), please stay by the canals, you will get something different from Bangkok. The big sign on the main road within Samutsongkram area is "Don Hoi Lort", it's where anyone who visit or pass by Samutsongkram will drop by a restaurant for Stir fried spicy **"Hoi Lort";** it's a kind of mollusks found in Samutsongkram at Don Hoi Lort which is a shoal located at the mouth of the Mae Klong River. The area is about 3 km wide and 5 km long at Bang Cha Kreng Subdistrict, Laem Yai Subdistrict, and Bang Kaew Subdistrict. The land was caused by sedimentation of sandy soil where the villagers called "Duck Sand", the land of plenty Hoi Lort. It's much fun when you go to **Klong Khon** for wading in the muddy land; you can hire a speedboat to admire a beautiful nature surroundings and drop by **Bang Khontee Floating Market** along the way. Don't miss **The Rama II Park too; it's the park** for admiring the wooden houses built in a typical Thai style which made for being the museum in the park. Whenever we dropped by Samutsongkram, we continued to travel to Petchaburi province and Hua Hin Town-Resort before heading to the south of Thailand. The road to the southern region is called Petchakasem Road; the main road to the south of Thailand started in Bangkok for the length of 1,277 kilometers till Songkha province. If you ride the bus from the Southern Bus Terminal along the road, you will see the signs of each province when you enter its area.

AYUTTHAYA

The official name for Ayutthaya is now called **"Phra Nakorn Si Ayutthaya", which** is a province away from Bangkok to the north about 75 kilometers. The trip for Ayutthaya; can do for one day tour by road and by river cruise or the express boat from Bangkok. Throughout Phra Nakhon Si Ayutthaya, there are still many old ruined temples, the Royal palaces and shrines with many sacred Buddha statues. The Prime Minister of Burma visited Thailand and gave 200,000 Bahts to help restoring the temple and Phra Mongkhon Bophit Hall and it was the beginning of serious restoration of the ancient sites in Ayutthaya. Finally, the Fine Arts Department was an important unit in the operation until there was a resolution from the United Nations Educational, Scientific and Cultural Organization or UNESCO to register the historical city of Ayutthaya as a "Cultural World Heritage Site" on December 13, 1991, with an area covered in the ancient city of Ayutthaya located in the heart of the city, which is called **"The Ayutthaya Historical Park".** Ayutthaya is a province in the central region with a long history and also an important industrial economic zone.

Ayutthaya was famous as an important rice planting area of the country. Phra Nakhon Si Ayutthaya Province is the only province in Thailand that does not have a Muang District; Muang means "in the city", that usually the name of the main district in all provinces which is the most prosperous area. Muang District seems to be the center of administration and business for the province. Phra Nakhon Si Ayutthaya District is like the Muang District where it is the center of management in various fields. King Naresuan the Great was the beloved king of Ayutthaya period who restored the independence to Siam from Burma in 1584. Ayutthaya was attacked and was lost to the Burmese army on the second time in 1767. King Taksin the Great was able to recapture the city from the Burmese Army the same year and changed the capital to Thonburi later. Ayutthaya was the former capital city of Siam for 417 years (1350-1767) and had 33 monarchs who ruled the kingdom successively. There were 5 dynasties taking turns occupying the kingdom which were U-Thong dynasty, Suphannaphum Dynasty, Sukhothai Dynasty, Prasat Thong Dynasty, and Ban Phlu Luang Dynasty. Although King Taksin established the new capital in Thonburi, Ayutthaya was not an abandoned city because there were still people who loved the former homeland. The villagers who had fled to the forests were united and returned to live around the city until the official raised it to be a quarter called "Old City" or **"Krung Kow";** "Krung" means "City", "Kow" means "Old". From the history; Phra Nakhon Si Ayutthaya Province was the former royal capital of Thailand, a city in the Chao Phraya River Basin since about the 16th - 18th Buddhist century.

The location of the city, ancient sites, antiques and stories of events in nature chronicle legend included with the stone inscription was considered the contemporary evidences to the past events. From the history; it's said that the city was called "Ayothaya" or "Ayothaya Sri Ramthep Nakhon" was located on the eastern side of Ayutthaya Island. It was a land that had a prosperous culture with powerful politics and administration. Ayutthaya had a history of ruling, salvage independence, Heroism, and many traditions and has been recognized from generation after generation. Many of film makers have produced the movies and series movie about Ayutthaya and could hit the audiences in nationwide. It was a city that was fertile with cereal crops, as the local usually says as a motto that "In the water there are fish, in the fields there are rice." If you would like to relax and see more details than the package tour arranged, you may have to stay in Ayutthaya Town and explore by yourself. There are TukTuk taxi for taking you anywhere you want. It's an amazing city and attracts anyone who enters the town to see the ruined, old style houses, river view, food and all the temples around this old capital of Siam. I usually choose to go to Ayutthaya during weekend if I have a chance for traveling and I have a one-day trip to guide you for an example; in case you don't have much time.

TRANSPORT TO AYUTTHAYA:

RAIL: Trains for Ayutthaya Railway Station is in town, Ban Phachi Junction and Bang Pa-In Railway Station which is close to Bang Pa-In Palace. **ROAD:** Buses at the Northern Terminal.**BOAT:** The Express boats at Sathon Pier or other piers you are close to. Join a cruise tour for Ayutthaya.

ONE DAY TRIP IN AYUTTHAYA

The one-day trip in Ayutthaya should be started early in the morning to avoid the traffic; if you leave Bangkok about 7 am, you should arrive by 9 am. But it depends on the location of your hotel. Riding to Ayutthaya is heading to the northern region of Thailand along the Phayonyothin Road about 75 km then you will see the sign to the downtown. The first impression; as I feel every time I come to Ayutthaya, is when you meet an old pagoda situated at the middle of the intersection which is called the **Chedi Wat Sam Pluem**; This pagoda was assumed to be built before the Fall of Ayutthaya. In 1937; this Chedi was supposed to be demolished because the government that time decided to cut off the road connecting from Phahon Yothin to Phra Nakhon Si Ayutthaya Province and re- planned the city. The Fine Arts Department suddenly announced in the Government Gazette in March 1941 that the Chedi Wat Sam Pluem was a historic site therefore; the government could not dismantle the pagoda and then needed to build a road around the Chedi as the circle.

The government of Field Marshal Por Phibun Songkhram had a policy to restore ancient sites in Ayutthaya Province, including Chedi Wat Sam Pluem in 1956 – 1957 and designated the Chedi Wat Sam Pluem to be a landmark of Phra Nakhon Si Ayutthaya Province as well. When you turn left at the Chedi, you will see an old temple called **Wat Yai Chaimongkol.** The temple is considered an important historical temple for many periods and a very popular temple among both Thai and international tourists. There are many outstanding architectures like the tallest chedi in Ayutthaya, the ordination hall, the reclining Buddha outdoor, the shrine of King Naresuan the Great, and the surrounding area has a beautiful garden to relax as well. This beautiful temple is the first temple you visit when you enter Ayutthaya Town. **It** was an old temple built since the beginning of Ayutthaya Period. The highlight of the temple is a **large pagoda; which found the incantation kept inside,** that is believed to be restored in the reign of King Naresuan the Great and a monument of the great victory that King Naresuan the Great won the war.

The war at that time was when the Burmese had brought troops into the border of Siam, King Naresuan and Somdej Phra Akha Thotsarot, who was his younger brother, led the army to fight and drove the elephant into the encirclement of the enemy waiting to fire their guns at him and his brother, it was the bad time because the king and his brother were without the soldiers running after him in time. Suddenly King Naresuan proclaimed in a loud voice to the Burmese Crown Prince or called as Maha Uparacha who was the leader of the Burmese troops; **"Shall we get out from the shade of the tree and come out for doing Yutthahatthi to honor this land, because in the future; there will be no kings who will be able to do Yutthahatthi* Fight anymore." the viceroy; The Crown Prince of Burma immediately drove his elephant out to King Naresuan to accept the challenge.** When the elephants were close enough, King Naresuan used Phra Saengphon or the long-handle sword to beat Maha Uparacha torn apart and fell on his elephant's back.

Yutthahatthi or Elephant duel was an ancient custom of warfare on the elephant's back by the kings of the Southeast region. It was an honorable war because elephants are considered large animals and it's a face-to-face clash, the loser can be fatal.

From the history record; The Chaimongkol incantations discovered inside the large pagoda of Wat Yai Chaimongkol was the Chanting that King Naresuan usually prayed with faith. This incantation depicts about how Buddha overcame the Mara or obstacles during Enlightenment. The sacred incantation has been prayed by many Buddhists for receiving luck and success nowadays.

You are allowed to climb up the top of the historic huge Pagoda here, it's the tallest pagoda in Ayutthaya and be as the memorial for the Victory of King Naresuan the Great. Walk around the pagoda and enjoy the scenery of the Historical Park from the highest viewpoint on the top of the pagoda.

You should get inside the **Ubosot or the main hall** of the temple. It is enshrined Phra Phutthachai Mongkol, the principal Buddha image which is the sacred Buddha of the temple where the Thai Buddhists visit the temple for paying respect to. In addition, inside the temple is also **the shrine of King Naresuan** the Great. The construction was completed in the year 2001.

There's an old **Reclining Buddha outdoor** at the entrance with the building left ruined; only the brick walls and some columns remain for the shape of the hall. I usually stayed awhile inside the temple for feeding the fish in the pond and sometimes I guided the tourists for having a lunch snack at the famous noodle located in front of the temple before proceeding to other places. Have a nice grilled pork Sa-te with peanut sauce too!

After Wat Yai Chaimongkol, I turned to the left-hand side along the road for about 10 minutes to **admire Luang Por Tho at Wat Phanan Choeng;** the statue is the biggest Buddha Statue in Ayutthaya, with the width of 14.20 meters and the height is 19.20 meters, made of stucco cladded with gold sheets. This sitting position Buddha image is in the attitude of calling the earth to witness or Maravijaya attitude. **Wat Phanan Choeng** is one of the oldest temples in Ayutthaya, the historical background has been unknown, but assumed that it's the temple before Ayutthaya was the capital. The temple is located on the east bank of The Chao Phraya River. The famous Buddha statue here is called "Luang Por Sum Por Khong" as the Chinese Name or "Luang Por Tho" by the locals, "Tho" means "Big" because the statue is the biggest Buddha image in Ayutthaya. If you will notice among the Buddha statues put in the hall, there is a Golden Buddha statue in front of Luang Por Tho which is made of pure gold with 1.5 meters wide and 2 meters high.

There is an interesting spot in the temple which is The **Chao Mae Soi Dok Mak Goddess Shrine; it is located nearby the main hall; it's** a memorial of love story between a Thai king of Ayutthaya and the Chinese Princess. The beautiful shrine was built in the mixed art of Thai and Chinese style.

The legend of the goddess was said before Ayutthaya was the capital. It's a slightly sad love story; the story of Phra Nang Soi Dok Mak who was the daughter of the ruler of China which was bestowed upon the King Sai Nam Phueng of Ayodhaya. When both of them traveled back to Ayutthaya, King Sai Nam Phueng told the queen to wait on the royal barge because he wanted to arrange a procession to welcome her with honor. The procession came to pick up her without the king; so, she preferred to wait for him on the boat instead. The Little Queen was waiting at the boat, refused to go up if the king did not appear for picking her up. King Sai Nam Phueng was amazed and joked to her that "When you've already arrived and don't get out of the boat, then stay there." The king said like that twice until the Queen became discouraged and grieved and finally died on the boat. King Sai Nam Phueng was very saddened, so he ordered a shrine to be built to commemorate the late queen. However; the importance of this shrine is a confirmation of the close relationship between Thailand and China for a long time since before the Ayutthaya period. This neighborhood has a densely settled Chinese community until the present.

THE AYUTTHAYA HISTORIC PARK

Phra Nakhon Si Ayutthaya Historical Park has the area boundaries as announced by the Fine Arts Department regarding the boundaries of ancient sites are total area of approximately 3,000 rai. It was announced as the national archaeological Site in 1976 and was renovated the ruins and specified areas within the park until the sites were **declared a UNESCO Cultural World Heritage Site in 1991, which has been the evidences of a culture or civilization that is still appeared or has been lost.** The lists of important historical places within the archaeological land are **The Royal Palace, Wat Mahathart, Wat Phra Si Sanphet, Wat Ratchaburana, Wat Phra Ram, and The Viharn of Wat Monkon Borpit Hall.** But later in 1997; the 22 places were added in the lists of the park site. It's not enough for one day to see all of those but you can start the UNESCO world heritage right after touring Wat Phanan Choeng. Some of the tourists come to the historical park before heading to Wat Phananchoeng and Wat Yai Chai Mongkol and maybe have a nice dinner in a restaurant and chill nearby the river before leaving for Bangkok.

When you arrive the park, I think you should take a walk inside Wat Phra Sri Sanpetch and the grand palace area for the first step. Wat Phra Si Sanphet has an important interesting point which are the Lanka-style pagoda, there are three figures of the pagodas lined up along the east and west; the first one on the east side was built in 1492 by King Ramathibodi II for containing the ashes of Somdej Phra Borom Trai Lokanat (his father), later in 1499, he ordered to build the center one for King Borom Rachathirat III (the half-brother of King Ramathibodi2) and the third chedi was built on the west side in the reign of King Boromrachathirat IV for the ashes of King Ramathibodi II; who was his uncle. **Wat Phra Sri Sanpetch** was originally the residence of King Ramathibodi I. In the reign of King Borommatrailokkanat; he built a new palace in the north then raised it to be the royal temple for performing various important ceremonies of the country. It was a temple in the palace area where there were no monks like Wat Phra Kaew inside the Grand Palace in Bangkok and both of the temples were established as a tradition for having a temple built as a royal temple in the palace area. **Wat Phra Sri Sanpetch** was established in 1448, the ruined was left located at the north of Wihan Phra Mongkhon Bophit Hall. Imagine the plan of the three pagodas here are the same model as in Wat Phra Keaw in Bangkok.

The Old Palace or the ruined Grand Palace

The royal palace that appears in Phra Nakhon Si Ayutthaya today, only the base of the building remains. It is assumed that King U-Thong built the palace since when he was in Wiang Lek; small palace in 1890 and when the construction of the city was completed in 1893, he moved to stay at the new palace near the lake called Nong Son, the first throne halls were built of wood in the area which is now Wat Phra Si Sanphet, later in 1991 when Somdet Phra Borommatrailokanat raised the land at the palace grounds for buiding a temple in the palace area, which was called **"Wat Phra Si Sanphet"** and then built the new royal palace at the north of the temple which was close to the Lopburi River consisted of various royal residences known today as the ancient palace; the residence of all Ayutthaya monarchs, located along the walls to the north of Ayutthaya City. From here; there is a road around the city that passes from The Chankasem Palace about 2 kilometers. According to the historical evidences; the area of the Grand Palace consists of 8 forts around the palace, 2 Water Gates or called as Pratunam in Thai, 20 Gates on the land or called as Pratubok. The ground of the Royal Palace, assumed having about 7 important throne halls and the outstanding throne hall that is still in perfect condition is called as **Trimuk Throne Hall. The Trimuk Throne Hall** was made as a wooden pavilion with clay tiled roof located next to the Sanpeth Prasat Throne Hall; a place where the King welcomed the guests of the city with a white elephant shed on both sides, the year the Trimuk Throne Hall built was not appeared.

Wat Mahathat

Wat Mahathat is one of the royal temples located near Wat Ratchaburana in the area of Ayutthaya Historical Park, built in the reign of King Boromrachathirat I or Khun Luang Phangua in 1374, but it was completed in the reign of King Ramesuan who graciously built the main pagoda and brought the Buddha's relics to be contained under the base in 1384, this evidence appeared in the royal chronicles of the royal letter. The main constructions of the temple are:

❖**The large prang** (dome shape pagoda) which is now completely destroyed.

❖**The octagonal pagoda** which built in a four-tiered, octagonal chedi, the top floor enshrined with a small prang; a strange pagoda found only one in Ayutthaya.

❖**The Viharn hall at the Chukachi base** of the principal Buddha statue in the temple where The Fine Arts Department found that some smugglers had dug down to a depth of 2 meters, so they continued digging for another 2 meters and found 5 small pottery containers containing light gold leaf in various shapes.

The famous photo of **“The Face of Buddha Image”** inserted in the hollow at the base of a large tree is here; it’s t**he small temple** with roots spreading all over the wall Part of the tree roots surround the Buddha's head. The Buddha’s head is made of sand stone and assumed that the Buddha’s head was broken during renovating and fell to the ground of Bho Tree about 50 years ago, afterwards; the tree’s roots cover the head and become the famous unseen Thailand to the world. The photo was one of the selected photos by UNESCO from all the world heritages.

❖ **The Medium-sized Prang**; found Ruen Kaew Painting depicts a part of the Buddha History inside the prang.

❖ **The Patriarch's Palace; t**he vacant area on the west side was the location of the Patriarch's pavilion. It was told that a pavilion carved in gilded patterns, with gold embroidered curtains, carpeted floors, and rows of embroidered flowers in a row on the ceiling, hanging lamps. There were two thrones here.

Wat Ratchaburana was established in 1424, one of the oldest and largest monasteries during Ayutthaya Period which has been appreciated as "The Treasure Trove of Ayutthaya"; found at the temple's crypt at the main shrine or "Phra Prang" inside the temple. **The Prang of Wat Ratchaburana** has a large and deep dungeon. The Fine Arts Department completed the excavation in 1957 and is now open to visit the dungeon. The prang of Wat Ratchaburana has a total of 3 large rooms arranged vertically downwards. The lowest floor is in the ground level as follows:

The 1st floor dungeon is the top floor. Originally, there was a wall covering all the pictures (of Chinese people, gods and angels, etc.) behind the wall made a small hole filled with prints and Buddha images. The villains found 3-4 gold Buddha images inside.

The 2nd floor dungeon is in the middle layer, there are 3 gold trays full of gold artifacts. The Fine Arts Department has demolished the floor, therefore; the 2nd and 3rd rooms are connected together, there are paintings depicting the past life of the Buddha drawn in squares and small bronze tables are around. The thief testified that the gold jewelry and gold cloth found here turned into powder when it's only touched.

The 3rd floor dungeon is the room in the end which is the most important room containing relics; which is well preserved in the golden pagoda with various Buddha images around.

The discovery of the dungeon in 1956 made headlines across the country.

There was a large group of thieves smuggling to dig the dungeons of Wat Ratchaburana in the following year. Lots of gold and gems were found at the dungeons. But with the heavy rain and rushing, the thieves couldn't carry all their belongings. The police took about a few days to seize the gang of thieves and seize some of the belongings. After that, the Fine Arts Department started to dig and found more than 2,000 items like over a hundred thousand of Buddha Amulets and more than 100 kilograms of gold which are currently kept at the **Chao Sam Phraya National Museum in Ayutthaya**.

Wat Phra Ram is a temple located outside the palace area on the east side, opposite to the Vihara Phra Mongkhon Bophit Hall. The temple was estimated to be built in 1369 during the reign of King Ramesuan. This was the area where King Ramathibodi I (King U Thong); his father was cremated. The area in front of the temple is Bueng Phra Ram; Bueng means Lake. At present, only ruins within the temple remain like the Pillars in the Ubosot, 7 viharas, and one wall. Phra Prang; which was built in a large ancient Khmer prang Style contains murals on both sides. It is a picture of the Buddha sitting in the attitude of subduing Mara on the throne where the colors used are red, indigo, yellow and black in the art of an early Ayutthaya period painting. Now a lot of color from the painting has faded.

Wat Monkolborpit

The hall of Phra Mongkhon Bophit is located at Pratuchai Subdistrict of Phra Nakhon Si Ayutthaya District at the South of Wat Phra Sri Sanphet. It is an old temple in the city wall that has been restored well. There is Phra Mongkhon Bophit; the large main Buddha image that was damaged since the second time of the loss of Ayutthaya but has been completely restored with the current gold-clad bronze. **Wat Mongkolborpit was** assumed to be built in 1448-1488 in the reign of Phra Borom Matrai Lokkanat, the eighth kings of Ayutthaya Kingdom. The temple was renovated many times. In 1956, the building and the Buddha image were renovated as seen nowadays.

❖ **Phra Monkon Borpit;** the huge Buddha Statue in the hall was made of bronze and lacquer gilded, has been assumed that the statue was built at the beginning of Ayutthaya Period with the size of 9.55 meters wide and 12.45 meters high. The statue was put outdoor before and restored many times.

*For one day trip of Ayutthaya town were mainly mentioned from the beginning till here in town but some of the trip may include the **Bang Pa-In Palace for the optional tour of Ayutthaya** as well.

BANGPA IN

Bang Pa-In Palace was an old palace built in 1630-1656 during the reign of King Phra Chao Prasat Thong; the 24th king of Ayutthaya Kingdom.

The palace was a temporary overnight stay for the kings during travelling in these areas. Bang Pa-In Palace was abandoned for a while after the loss of Ayutthaya to Burma in 1767. The palace came back to be recognized again by Soonthornphu; who was the famous poet of Ratthanakosin Era, who followed His Majesty King Phra Phuttha Yodfa Chulalok the Great or King Rama I to worship the Phra Phutthabat; the sacred Buddha's Footprint found in Saraburi. He expressed his poem about the Bang Pa-In Palace in the "Nirat Palace"; Nirat is a kind of the long lyrical Thai poetry with eight or nine syllables per line.

It was until during the reign of King Mongkut (King Rama IV), the palace was restored again and later on, King Chulalongkorn (King Rama V) ordered to start major renovations by building many royal residences and a royal guest house with banquets on various occasions

Currently, Bang Pa-In Palace is under the supervision of the Bureau of the Royal Household. It is also used as a place for a royal residence of His Majesty the King and the royal family including performing the royal ceremony for some occasions. It is open to the public and tourists to visit as well. Please kindly dress modestly.

The palace is about 18 kilometers from Ayutthaya downtown. Ride a train from Bangkok to Ayutthaya and enjoy the scenic rice-fields along the way to get off at Bang Pa-In Station for reaching the palace.

Bang Pa-In is also the name of a district in 16 districts of Phra Nakhon Si Ayutthaya Province, formerly known as Phra Ratcha Wang District (Ratcha Wang means Palace), it was renamed to Bang Pa-In district in 1917 and it is the second most populous district of Phra Nakhon Si Ayutthaya Province. The area of Bang Pa-In Palace is divided into 2 parts; The outer and the inner court areas.

The Outer Court Areas was the area where His Majesty the King used for the ceremonies of the Great Society or various royal ceremonies, the areas consisted of four halls, a medium-sized Gazebo-style tent built during the reign of King Rama VI, and the royal houseboat for King Rama V was built in Thai style; from golden teakwood with a thatched roof, divided into sections.

The Inner Court Areas are connected to the outer court with a special bridge which having a screen separating at the middle along the bridge to divide the walkway of the front courtiers and the inner courtiers, the person who walked at the inner courtiers was not seen by the other side during passing along the bridge. This bridge connects to the Warophat Phiman Throne Hall, the outer court area and the Devarajakhanlai Gate was the entrance to the inner palace which was the residence of the King and the royal family. The buildings of the inner Court Areas consisted of a hall for a royal guest house, a resting place in the royal park. Hor Withun Thatsana was built in the reign of King Rama V to be as the place for observing the herd of wild elephants. The Queen Sunandha Kumariratana Monument and the Rajanusorn Monument were situated in the palace.

The Aisawan Thipphaya-art Throne Hall (photo page 301) is at the middle of a large pond in the palace areas. It was the throne of King Prasat Thong. His Majesty the king graciously built to celebrate the birth of his son; the Crown Prince, by giving the royal name "Aisawan Thiphaya-art Throne Hall" which means the place where his child was born here and became the King of the Siam Kingdom. This throne was the residence of the kings of the Ayutthaya period until the loss of the city to Burma in 1767 then the throne hall was ruined and abandoned.

His Majesty King Mongkut traveled to Ayutthaya one day and passed by the Bang Pa-In Palace. His Majesty the king graciously ordered for restoration of the throne by using wood to build a new throne at the original location and still called "Aisawan Thiphaya-art Throne Hall".

In the reign of King Chulalongkorn (King Rama V), he expanded the pool to be more spacious and built a new throne which was a replica of the royal throne from the Abhon Phimok Throne Hall in the Grand Palace in Bangkok. The throne was made of wood in the middle of the pond and still remained the royal name as original called as "Aisawan Thiphaya-art Throne Hall". Later, His Majesty King Rama VI gave the royal throne to be restored again by changing the floor and pillars which formerly made of wood to be concrete and built a bronze statue of King Chulalongkorn; the real size of the King, in his uniform full of Army Field Marshal* ranks, to be enshrined at the Aisawan Thiphaya-art Throne Hall until now. * King Rama V or King Chulalongkorn gave birth to the Cadet School in 1887 and later this institute was named by King Bhumibol-

(King Rama IX) as "Phra Chulachomklao Royal Military Academy" in honor of His Majesty King Chulalongkorn. When you visit Bang Pa-In Palace, you will discover **Wat Niwate Thammaprawat located o**pposite to The Bang Pa-In Palace. It's an amazing temple built the same as Christian Church. The main hall was an architectural style of Gothic Revival but become as a Buddhist Temple. Wat Niwet Thammaprawat Ratchaworawihan is a royal monastery built by His Majesty King Chulalongkorn and used as a private place for the royal merit making like praying and meditation during staying at Bang Pa-In Palace. The beautiful hall was decorated with stained glass windows and a Gothic altar for Buddha image that built in 1878. The temple received the ASA Architectural Conservation Award in 1989.**Ayutthaya** has been a city full of charms and memories of the past. It never lacks people to come here. I always dropped by to admire this old mysterious town whenever I drove from the north, and I always choose Ayutthaya as my weekend trip if I have a chance to do.

The Department of Fine Art in Thailand declared more places to be national archaeological sites within Ayutthaya areas after Ayutthaya was praised as a cultural world heritage by UNESCO, by renovating and developing in order to preserve the old capital city to be more interesting. If you stay few days in Ayutthaya, you can roam around the city for more places, but I recommend you to ride taxi or Tuk-Tuk to visit all the places instead of biking because it's quite dangerous to bike in this town except; riding within some areas where there are lanes for bicycles or you have a local guide with you. **Please check carefully before crossing the road or cycling and make sure everything is neat and tidy. I don't blame you, if you want to have fun, but you have to stay away from the dangers of unfamiliar roads especially; you only come here for tourism only.** I would like to give the lists for you to explore more if you have more days in Ayutthaya as follow (Most of the temples and places are not so far from each other, please look around when you stop at any place):

- ❑ Chantara Kasem Palace
- ❑ Wat Suwandararam Ratworaviharn
- ❑ Wat Lokhaya Sutharam
- ❑ Wat Thamikarat
- ❑ Wat Senasnaram Ratworaviharn
- ❑ Wat Suan Luang Sop Sawan
- ❑ City walls and Fortifications
- ❑ Wat Chaiwattanaram
- ❑ Wat Putthaisawan
- ❑ Wat Na Phramain
- ❑ Wat Kasatti Ratworaviharn

- ❑ Wat Kudi dao
- ❑ Wat Dusitaram
- ❑ Wat Phu Khao Thong
- ❑ Wat Phraya Man
- ❑ Portugal Village
- ❑ Holland Village
- ❑ Japanese Village
- ❑ Paniet Klonk Chang
- ❑ The Cathedral of Saint Joseph ETC.

Wat Chaiwatthanaram: the beauty of this monastery can be seen at the west bank of The Chao Phraya River outside the city. It's built in Khmer or Cambodian architecture like, "Angkor Wat" style. **Wat Kudi Dao is a temple from** the late Ayutthaya architecture, has been the legend for Thai talk of "The Hidden Treasure" possessed by the spirits of the owners from Ayutthaya Period. **Phra Chedi Suriyothai is** the memorial of The Brave Queen Suriyothai who joined the war with the Burmese Army by riding on the elephant to fight and sacrificed her life in the battle. **Wat Phu Khao Thong is a** huge pagoda, built in mixed Thai and Burmese architecture with 90 meters high, located about 2 kilometers away from town. **The Elephant Kraal Pavilion or Paniet Klonk Chang is** the place where the elephants were round up in front of the royal family. Must visit **Japanese Village and** the **Sam Phraya Museum** for admiring many ancient items and some treasures found from the ruined monasteries.

THE BRIDE OVER THE RIVER KWAI IN KANCHANABURI

Kanchanaburi was one of the important outposts in the war between Thai and Burmese Armies during the Ayutthaya Period until the Thonburi and Rattanakosin periods. The former town was located at Tambon Lat Ya. (The area of Khao Chonkai at present) until 1831; in the reign of King Rama III, the city was moved to the southeast about 16 kilometers to set up at the confluence of the Kwai Yai River and the Kwai Noi River which is the location of the present province nowadays. Kanchanaburi is well known to the world for The **Bridge over The River Kwai;** a part of "The Death Railway" built in 1940-1944 during The World War II.

The railway route is 415 kilometers between Ban Pong in Ratchaburi Province to Than ba yu zayat in Burma.

This Death Railway was in Thai Zone around 304 Kilometers and crossed The Three Pagodas Pass and The River Kwai in Kanchanaburi. The estimated 100,000 allied POWs and Asian laborers were forced labor to construct the railway to supply troops and weapons in the Burma Campaign of The World War II, caused almost all of the forced prisoners died from these horrific working conditions. The pictures and stories of the atrocities during World War II appear in many museums in Kanchanaburi.

Kanchanaburi is a province located in the western part of Thailand with the total area of about 19,473 square kms It is the third largest area in the country after Nakhon Ratchasima and Chiang Mai and has the largest area in the west, the distance is about 129 kilometers from Bangkok or 2 hours ride. It borders with Burma at a distance of about 370 kilometers and borders on neighboring provinces such as Tak and Uthai Thani at the north, Ratchaburi at the south, Suphan Buri at the east, and Nakhon Pathom and Myanmar at the west. Most of the Kanchanaburi areas are forested and mountainous. Although Kanchanaburi has an area adjacent to Tak Province in the north but there are no roads connected, because it's the seam of the wildlife sanctuary in **Thung Yai Naresuan;** a world heritage site by UNESCO and has fertile forests interspersed with intricate mountains of the two provinces. If you want to travel in a row, you must detour to Suphan Buri Province and passing Chainat Province, Nakhon Sawan Province, and Kamphaeng Phet Province to enter Tak Province which is a total distance of more than 490 kilometers. It's also weird for; if you want to travel to Umphang District; the location of a well-known Thi Lor Su Waterfall in Tak Province, which borders Kanchanaburi Province, you must travel back to the south of the province for a total distance of more than 700 kilometers. The average low temperature here is about 22.7 degrees Celsius, an average high of 36.0 degrees Celsius; some of the areas may be as the lowest temperature like 3.7 degrees Celsius (on January 17, 1974), but in the hot season in April; the highest could be 44.2 degrees Celsius. There is a lot of heavy rain, with an average rainfall of 1496.2 mm per year.

TRANSPORTS:

RAIL: Must try traveling by train from Bangkok to Kanchanaburi. You can check the rail routes from the website so you can get the train from the nearest station you are convenient. You can travel from Bangsue Railway station or some other stations you are close to. Kindly check at the station. The schedule of the usual train along "the death railway" is **Thonburi Station-Namtok Station every day**, but **the special route scheduled from Bangkok to Nam Tok Station is during Sat-Sun and Public Holidays.**

By Bus from the Southern Bus Terminal, **Booking a tour or a package tour** for one night in Kanchanaburi and add Damnoensaduak Floating Market, Nakhonpathom into your lists, and **by Car or Taxi; p**lease check and agree the price before leaving from the lists you want to visit; if for one day, you can only have the Bridge over the River Kwai and the death railway, Museum, and the cemetery then see the downtown.

TOP ATTRACTIONS IN KANCHANABURI

The Bridge over The River Kwai is one a very important historical sites of Thailand. It is the most important bridge of the Death Railway and the landmark of Kanchanaburi Province. The Bridge over the River Kwai and the Death Railway is a cultural heritage of the world that has sentimental value to many people who visited the place. It was like a symbol of the Great Eastern War that took place in Thailand.

The bridge was built by the lives of more than a hundred thousand forced-labor people from 14 nations which seemed to be the only railway in the world that was built by the most people. One of the POW wrote in a book that; "A train that runs on this steel track is like running on the bodies of human lives that have been lost". You should walk along this historic bridge; it's for about 300 meters for crossing the river which is as one of a highlight parts of the trip. **Have you tried walking on the railroad tracks once?** Perhaps you could feel the tragedy of the past at this deadly railway like I did. **The Bridge over the River Kwai** was originally built by the labor of Allied prisoners of war (POW) under the control of the Japanese Army and the construction took only a year to be complete before being bombed by Allied airborne troops until the middle bridge collapsed. After the end of the World War II, the Thai government bought this railway from England for 50 million baht and renovated it in 1946. The repair at that time was by collapsing the central pier (the 5-6th) and built the 2-span steel bridge instead of the original one, replaced a steel bridge for the wooden bridge of the ends. The total length of the bridge is approximately 322.90 meters.The current bridge over the River Kwai has become an important symbol of Kanchanaburi; regarded as "A symbol of peace". The story about this bridge was made into a Hollywood movie called; The Bridge on the River Kwai in 1957, based on the novel of the same name. The other movie "The Railway Man" was a movie in 2013; which was based on the biography of a prisoner of war.

Kanchanaburi organizes an annual River Kwai Bridge for featuring light and sound performances every year to reminiscing about the past World War and the bridge.

You will discover **"The Death railway"** route by riding the train from Kanchanaburi Station to Nam Tok Station for about 77 Kilometers. The schedule of this train is **Thonburi Station-Namtok Station every day**, but **the special route scheduled from Bangkok to Nam Tok Station is during Sat-Sun and Public Holidays.** Please check from the website or train station at Hua Lum Phong or Bang Sue Railway Station.

The reason why this railway line is called The Death Railway was because the Japanese Army recruited approximately 61,700 Allied prisoners of war during World War II; from the information recorded by the Australian authorities states that, Japanese army used workers in both projects (building rails from Thailand to Myanmar and the other from Burma to Thailand) about 180,000; 61,700 were the westerner-prisoners of war and died 12,621; they were 6,904 British soldiers, 2,802 Australians, 2,782 Dutch (Dutch) and 133 Americans, and thousands more died in Burma's construction sites.

The workers were included with many nationalities such as Chinese, Vietnamese, Javanese, Malay, Burmese, Indian laborers to construct this strategic railway as a route through Burma to transport weapons including personnel to continue attacking Burma and India which at that time was a British colony. The route had to cross the Kwai Yai River; so, a bridge must be built. The construction of this bridge and railway line was full of difficulties, the brutality of war, and diseases as well as food shortages caused many thousands of prisoners of war to death. This railway was completed on 25 October 1943 and opened for service in December. The railway line becomes a monument to the world that inscribes the atrocities of World War II and also commemorates those who died in the war.

Start riding the train in Bangkok will make you move into a different atmosphere; by seeing the tall buildings become the rice fields and forests until you reach the bridge over the River Kwai which is approximately 48 kilometers, the place where you will arrive at another highlight point with millions of views that pay for the train ticket only in hundreds and that is **'Tham Krasae'** or Krasae Cave in Sai Yok District; the most exciting of this route During World War II, this cave was used as a shelter for prisoners of war when building the Death Railway from Thailand to Myanmar, the hardest point for building this railway because of the curvy path along the hill. On the way before reaching Krasae Cave is filled with forests, the train will gradually slow down, traversing along the foothills along the Khwae Noi River, a 400-meter long route, giving you a scenic view.

The cave and the railroad are right next to each other. If you view from the train into the cave, it's clearly seen inside; there is a sacred Buddha image enshrined and on the other side, when looking back, there is a view of the curve of the train moving along the hill with the Kwai Noi River as a backdrop. At present, this railway ends at Ban Tha Sao or Nam Tok Station. The distance from Kanchanaburi Station to Nam Tok Station is a nice route approximately 77 kilometers. Must try the train trip. You can discover the beautiful viewpoint of The River Kwai from **The Krasae Cave** by walking from Wang Pho Railway Station about 100 meters along The Death Railway track.

- **The Thai government and the Allies agreed on August 24, 1954 to build these two war cemeteries; at Don Ruk Cemetery and Chong Kai Cemetery. Don Ruk Allied War Cemetery** or "United Nations Military Cemetery" or what people in Kanchanaburi generally call "English Cemetery" is a large cemetery on an area of 17 hectares, it was the main prisoner of World War II cemetery, containing the bodies of 6,982 prisoners of war who died during the construction of the Death Railway. The 300 prisoners of war died of cholera and were buried at the Nike Camp (about 15 kilometers before the Three Pagoda Checkpoint.), the rest from the graves of prisoners of war in various camps. The atmosphere in the cemetery was quiet and shady. The interior spaces are beautifully decorated. There was a brass plaque engraved with the name, age and country of the deceased above every tomb. The last line is a mournful mourning. Every year there is a special commemorative day for the deceased people of different nations.
- **Chong-Kai War Cemetery** or called as Khao Pun Allied War Cemetery was a large prisoner of war camp. It is located on the eastern bank of the Kwai Noi River in Nong Ya, about 2 kilometers from Kanchanaburi Town, this cemetery is smaller than at the Don Rak Cemetery, containing the bodies of 1,750 prisoners of war; most of them were British soldiers. The interior is decorated with shady flowers and trees. Traveling to this cemetery by car and may travel by boat along the Kwai Noi River for about 2 kilometers.

- **JEATH War Museum is the** Japan England Australia Thailand Holland. It was built on July 24, 1977 in the area of Wat Chai Chumphon Chana Songkhram or Wat Tai, in Kanchanaburi Town. The building was built as a hut that imitated a prisoner of war camp in the World War II. The museum contains of the collection of paintings and photographs depicting the lives of prisoners of war during World War II. There are also tools Equipment of prisoners of war during World War II such as war weapons, hats, knives, spoons, forks, etc. This museum located only 400 meters from Kanchanaburi Bus Station and is open every day from 8.00 AM to 17.00 PM.
- **Ban Kao National Museum** was established in 1965 to collect the Preserve and display prehistoric artifacts obtained from archaeological excavations at Ban Kao Archaeological Site and other archaeological sites in Kanchanaburi. Due to H. R. Van Hekeren (H.R.Van Heekeren), a Dutch archaeologist who was captured to build the death railway during the World War II, found stone-cracking tools and polished stone axes while working in the Ban Kao Subdistrict after the war was over. He took the stone tools to be studied and analyzed at the Peabody Museum in USA and it has been the start of archaeological excavations by Thai and foreign archaeologists in Ban Kao area in 1956.

The Prehistoric Exploration Group were Thailand-Denmark Archaeological Cooperation Project excavated at Ban Kao Archaeological Site during 1960-1962. The land area was the private land owned by Nai Lue - Nai Bang Luangdang, and the land was found many prehistoric artifacts. Later on, the Fine Arts Department established the National Museum at the site of the excavation which is now called as **Ban Kao National Museum** in Kanchanaburi where the prehistoric antiquities were found in the province. The displayed objects that are important and interesting such as ancient human bones, stone axes, ornaments and pottery obtained from archaeological excavations. The interesting place for another exploration in Kanchanaburi is the **Prasart Muang Singh Historical Park**; the ancient park located on the bank of Kwai Noi River. The park was assumed to be about 800 years old. It's only about 43 kms from town and about 6 kms from Ban Kao National Museum. If you come by a taxi, you should add here after the museum.

The park is the old ruined city built in Khmer or Cambodian architecture. The place was excavated and found prehistoric of human skeleton with metal tools and some instruments.

Prasart Muang Singh was repaired and developed by The Fine Arts Department to be a very beautiful place for visiting. There are signs of QR code of many languages for guiding you inside the archaeological site which is a large layout of the Town Plan and the City Wall which made of laterite. The site of Prasart Muang Singh composes of the following:

- The Historical Site 1; Prasart Muang Singh, the ruins of Khmer Style of Prang, stupa and walls made of laterite.
- The Historical Site2; this site is laterite construction decorated with stucco left only base.
- The Historical Site3; located outside the area, see the ruins of brick and laterite bases.
- The Historical Site4; see the ruins in rectangle-shaped floor; look alike 4 room-building, made of laterite.
- Artifact Gallery; located near the parking lot, see many of architectural parts; like, terracotta stucco, stone and laterite from excavation.
- Prehistoric Human Skeleton Grave; there are four of skeletons found during excavation near Kwai Noi River.
- Guest House in the park for staying overnight.

Discover the end route of the west in Thailand at The Three Pagodas Pass; near the border of Myanmar. This is a historic site since Ayutthaya Period. The Three Pagodas checkpoint is the western end of the Thai border. In the past, it was a channel for the Thai and Burmese army. Tourists can cross the border to visit Phaya Tong Su Market in Myanmar by contacting the office for showing documents at the Sangkhlaburi immigration checkpoint.

The three-pagoda-site was originally just the three piles of stones stacked together, so this place was called the Sacred Three Stones where it was a place for worshiping by Thai people before leaving the Thai border to enter the Burmese border in ancient times. The Chief of Sangkhaburi together with the people in the area built the chedi or pagoda on the piles of the three stones in 1889; each pagoda was approximately 6 meters high, and apart from each other about 5-6 meters. The Fine Arts Department excavated and found the rectangular chedi base with bricks on the south side in 2003, which assumed that the pagoda was built since Ayutthaya Period. Therefore; The Fine Arts Department has announced the registration of the three pagodas as national historic sites in 1955. You can shop for local souvenirs at a local market nearby The Three Pagodas Pass and will notice that mostly people here are Burmese descent; most of them have a yellow herbal powder on their faces, this powder is called "Tanaka"; the popular souvenir for Thai tourists from the herb's property known for skin cosmetics.

If you have a chance to get inside Myanmar, you can visit some temples and local houses nearby. During your trip break or before going back to Bangkok, you should chill out and relax on a raft house restaurant nearby the River Kwai River or enjoy swimming and rafting in the river.

The Hellfire Pass Memorial Museum; the museum built for dedicating to prisoners of war during World War II within the memorial, gathered the pictures telling the story of the misery of the prisoners of war during that time. There are some of the old tools and equipment that built a railway displayed.

This gorge excavation was started in April 1943. The work was delayed, resulting in an accelerated period where workers in each shift had to work up to 18 hours, most of which were manual labor such as extracting mountains by hand which was the most brutal work; the workers had to climb down to extract in the gorge, some of which was 11 meters high and almost no air to breathe.

They had to work in the sweltering heat during March in a shortage of water and food and encountered sickness when the doctors and medical equipment were not enough to treat. Prisoners of war and laborers at the gorge had to work at night with torches and bonfires reflecting the shadows of the prisoners and guards flickering on the walls. This makes it's known as the "Hellfire Pass" in English and the Thai calls "Chong Khao Khad" where the prisoners of war were made to do forced labor for constructing the railway tracks to Burma by the orders from Japanese Troops during World War II. The atmosphere here reminds the visitors of the prisoners' sufferings from the dreadful injuries and diseases from this work condition at that time.

Let's splash in the beautiful **Erawan Waterfall at** the Erawan National Park; a popular destination for all tourists during weekend especially; in summertime. It's the seven-tiered waterfall with a large natural pool for swimming on the second tier and only 65 kms from Kanchanaburi downtown. **The Erawan Waterfall is the waterfall** located in the Erawan National Park at Tha Kradan Subdistrict, in Si Sawat District. Its height above the sea level from 100 to 400 meters, divided into 7 levels; it is a large famous waterfall of Kanchanaburi. The specialty of Erawan Waterfall is that the water is clear and green. You can see more of beautiful waterfalls in Kanchanaburi like the **Sai Yok Yai waterfall and Huay Mae Khamin Waterfall**. One of the famous temples in Kanchanaburi is called **Wat Tham Suea which** is located on the top of the hill with the eye-catching. It is one of the most wonderful tourist attractions in Kanchanaburi.

Wat Tham Phu Wa; a forest temple in the embrace of the mountains where it is quiet, suitable for introspection. It's originally a cave as a chapel, right now it has been restored to be beautiful and magnificent from a sandstone chapel building covering the cave. There are natural beauty of stalagmites and stalactites and the Buddha Relics enshrined inside the cave, Wat **Thipsukontharam** is located in Huai Krachao District, in a large area. The outstanding object here is the huge standing Buddha image for Metta; "Metta" means "Mercy", was built on the occasion of His Majesty King Bhumibol Adulyadej's 84th birthday and on the occasion of at Her Majesty Queen Sirikit His Majesty's 80th birthday in 2012, the Buddha Image stands for being the dependency of the people, built in the style of a 2,000-year-old Buddha image on the Babiyan Mountains that was destroyed by the Taliban and made to reappear in Thailand to bring peace and happiness and to represent stability of Buddhism in Thailand, **Wat Hin Than Lam Phachi** which is located at Ban Hin Than, in Dan Makham Tia District has the most beautiful Ubosoth or the ordination hall in Kanchanaburi where there is a large statue of Somdej Phra Buddhachan Tho Promrangsi(the former abbot of Wat Rakang) enshrined in front of the chapel.

Sampao Kaew; the Chapel of the hundred million, because it cost like 100 million Bahts for construction; which was built flanked by the Ananta Naga Lakshmi Ship**,** the only one in Thailand, located at Wat Hin Than Lam Phachi.

Wat Wang Wiwekaram or commonly known as "Wat Luang Por Uttama", in addition to being an important tourist attraction of Sangkhlaburi District. It is also a temple that is considered very important for the local people and the center of the minds of people of many nationalities living in Sangkhlaburi district for both Thai and Karen (Hilltribe) people, especially for the Thai people of Mon descent. Luang Por Uttama was a famous monk and known as "God of Mon people", Wang Wiwekaram Temple therefore caused by the power of faith towards Luang Por Uttama who lived his monkhood life till he died in this temple. Therefore; a temple become like a representative of Luang Por Uttama when he's gone. It is a sacred place for Mon people in performing rituals according to their traditions and special events such as during the month of February every year; there will be the day for the remembrance of his virtues to the villagers and the Mon people on Luang Por Uttama's birthday include with various activities, religious ritual, ancient Boxing match with rope, local cultural show such as Mon dance Karen dance, and people wear the old style of dress according to the Thai Raman culture. The most popular place in Sanghaburi seems to be at the **Underwater Temple** (Drowning Chapel) at the original Luang Pho Uttama Temple. Some call as the Sunken Ubosoth.

The Sunken Ubosoth was the former Wang Wiwekaram temple. It has become a tourist destination that is considered the Unseen Thailand because it is strange that there are ancient ruins underwater. It is a place that tells stories about the history of Wat Luang Por Uttama and many people call here as "Muang Badan" or the Water world. The **ordination hall has been sunk** under the lagoon of Vajiralongkorn Dam for 27 years, appear the beauty of the old shrine whenever the tide is low, about **March – April.** The Sunken temple was built in 1954 by the former abbot of the temple; Luang Por Utthama and people here. When the dam was finished in 1984, it was flooded from the dam to the temple and the nearby areas. The abbot moved some of the items away to the new temple on the hill and left the ordination hall sunk into the water during the high tide season. You can walk and see inside the hall in March which is the low tide season to see the ruined interior of the wall which is a stunning appearance.

Some of tourists dived under the water for admiring during the high tide period and some of them hire the speed boat to the location of this sunken hall in the dam. This dam is called **Vachiralongkorn Dam** or **Khao Laem Dam**; the first concrete-faced rock-fill dam in Thailand supplies a 300 MW hydroelectric power station with water. It's built in 1979 and started filling with water in 1984. The dam lies across Kwai Noi River located in Thong Pha Phum District in Kanchanaburi. The beautiful climate during winter is at **the longest wooden bridge in Thailand** and the second of the world at **Sang Khra Buri and here is one of** the charming of Kanchanaburi province for admiring the simple living of locals in the morning as a trade route with scenic views of nature surroundings. I think it's the top hit for many photographers and social media. The other popular photo-spot is at **amazing giant Rain Tree** or Samanea saman or "Chamchuri" called as Thai name, approximately 100 years old, spreading its branches with about 25-meter-wide and 20-meter-tall, at Koh Samrong District. If you are fond of posting a beautiful photo, you should add this one on your lists. Trekking on **Chang Phueak Mountain** (during October- February) for 8 kilometers (takes about 6 hrs.) and stay overnight on the mountain at the tent ground. Please contact the Thong Pha Phum National Park for the adventure-activities.

Trek at Lam Khlong Ngu National Park is one of amazing parks of Kanchanaburi at Thong Pha Phum District. The park, caves and waterfall are preserved and protected area of Department of National Parks, Wildlife and Plant Conservation. The cave has the highest monolithic (by nature) in the world. Its height is 62.5 meters.

DAMNOEN SADUAK FLOATING MARKET IN RATCHABURI

Many tourists visit the well-known tour all over the world at Damnoensaduak Floating Market where many of them don't know where it is. Let me introduce Ratchaburi now. **Ratchaburi** is the province with the largest economy in the west of Thailand. (announced in 2019) ranked the 18th in the country. The trading business in agricultural products and agricultural processed products are the main economic structure with the largest fruit and vegetable market in the west which is one of the largest market-centers of Thailand; and has cattle raising; one of the most in the country; such as pigs, dairy cattle, chickens, etc., are abundant in Pak Tho District. and Photharam District. It is the center of energy which full of many large power plants. It has the highest power generation capacity in the country. The other industries such as the automotive industry sugar industry, paper industry, textile industry, and etc. in thousands of factories (2019). The main industrial area is at Ban Pong District. **Ratchaburi** means "The land of King". It's where one of the most famous tourist attractions **"Damnoen Saduak Floating Market"** located.

Damnoensaduak floating market is recognized and listed for a "must" tour in Thailand while many of them haven't known the province it belongs to. Dragon jar is like a symbol for the province and also put in the quote for Ratchaburi Province as "Ratchaburi is the town of dragon-jar". You will see lots of dragon jar for souvenirs in vases, glass, plant pots, and etc. The jars are all local made products and very famous for their unique design of dragon painted. In the olden days; the jars were for keeping the rain water for daily using and still can be seen nowadays; I also have these jars for keeping the water in case when we lack water supply and used for watering the plants in our garden, but some people buy them for home decorations. The design of the dragon jar is also painted on many things like; plant pots, vases and T-shirts souvenirs which are very popular; it looks antique and last long. Ratchaburi is close to Kanchanaburi, Nakorn Pathom, Samutsakorn, Samutsongkram, Petchaburi and some part of Myanmar at the west. The main river pass through the center of the province is The Mae Klong River which flows from Kanchanaburi to the Gulf of Thailand in Samutsongkram Province. The distance from Bangkok directly to the **Damnoensaduak Floating Market is about 100 kms at the western region.**

The Damnoensaduak floating market was named after Damnoensaduak Canal which was a man-made canal in 1904, in the reign of King Rama V. The canal is now the center for all vendors sell their own agricultural products and some handicrafts. This canal was dug from the order of King Rama IV; the purpose was for connecting to Mae Klong and Tha Chin Rivers to be convenient in trade and transportation. It was dug for about 2 years and finished in the reign of King Rama V.

Damnoensaduak Canal was made in straight line of 32 kms. long and become the longest canal in Thailand. There are about 200 canals separated from it.

Most of the local people earn their livings by gardening. Coconut Juice is famous for its sweetness and good smell as well as the natural sugar palm fresh juice and sugar cake made here. All vendors are glad to welcome all the tourists to the market and from their friendly and kind heart make this town attractive all year round.

What shall you do at Damnoensaduak Floating Market?

Must try riding **Sampan Boat**; a small boat of each house, all the locals here have this kind of boat at least one boat for traveling. **I remember** the shocking incident that shocked me while taking my guest on a tour of at the floating market. He was a big man who fell into the canal when he stepped into a small boat and the boat immediately capsized into the canal. But he was finally able to get on the boat and teasing me by inviting me on a boat trip with him; by being the boatman for me, I replied, “I would like to go. But I really can't swim!” But what a surprise! He was able to skillfully paddle among the merchants and reach the **Tha Chin River**; the main river of Ratchaburi. This had become one of his favorites every time he came to Thailand many times. He had to stop by for paddling a Sampan boat for this floating market trip and I was very happy to be his tour guide whenever he came to Thailand. In fact, I'm very happy when my guests get to do what they love to do or try what they should do once; in their lives, in Thailand. I always take into account for Always "Safety comes first" for my clients during travels with me. This man was always very kind and humorous throughout his tour in Thailand with me.

You can also come to the center of the market by land as well and then rent a speed boat for tour around the canal. (in case coming from Kanchanaburi or other provinces nearby) The good time for seeing the beautiful view of plenty of boats is between 8.00-13.00 daily. After the floating market you can visit the Elephant Village.

One of the nice places for visiting in Ratchaburi is the **National Museum in Ratchaburi**; it's the old city hall with pink color buildings, located at the center of the province in the past, which is become the museum nowadays. **Khao Chong Pran** or **Bat Cave is an amazing spot where** millions of bats flying into the sky like a black smoke from the mountain during sunset. **Khao Ngu Stone Park** is a natural where you can trail with nature, it's away from Ratchaburi town about 8 kilometers. You can hike to many beautiful caves, but watch out the big group of monkeys around here.

KHAO YAI NATIONAL PARK

Khao Yai National Park is located in the area of 11 districts in 4 provinces, namely Nakhon Ratchasima Province; Prachinburi Province; Nakhon Nayok Province; and Saraburi Province. It is the first national park in Thailand since 1962. Khao Yai National Park covers an area of 2,215.42 square kilometers; consists of mixed deciduous forest, dry evergreen forest, moist evergreen forest, grassland and second-generation forest, and moist evergreen forest. The mountain is at an altitude of 400-1000 meters above sea level. There are thousands of species of vegetation, more than 200 species of butterflies, more than 300 species of wild birds and about 70 species of mammals, including elephants, tigers, gibbons, deer and wild boars, are found in the vast grasslands. Mostly people come to Khao Yai for seeing the wild elephants in the forests that sometimes appear on the road; they lied on the road and harmed the tourists in the past news.

Travelling to Khao Yai is easy from the Suwannaphum Airport; by taxi or rent a car to go there takes only 2 hours; if you would like to get away from city for seeing the rural areas, I recommend you to tour Khao Yai and Wang Nam Kheiw District in Nakhonratchasima for refreshing and drinking ozone. You will enjoy the nature and local living along the way with a good climate. Khao Yai is a popular place for all tourists; many of resorts or hotels are sometimes fully booked during weekend or public holidays. It's about the same way to reach **Pak Chong**; a district of Nakon ratchasima where you can also get fresh air and picturesque small town. **Wang Nam Kheiw** District also is one of the tourists' destinations in Nakonratchasima for ozone zones of Thailand and it's known for watching the gaurs closely at **Khao Phang Ma Non-Hunting Area**; the top hit **Gaur point** for tourists in cool season. Farm Stays, Homestays and resorts are fully booked during the cool season for this area which is around November-February. You must experience here and enjoy Khao Yai, Wang Nam Khiew and Pak Chong, the top bucket lists of Thailand you should try once. The Express way for Khao Yai will be opened for using by the end of year 2022 and you can reach Khao Yai within an hour. I recommend.

CHA CHOENG SAO: If I don't mention Chachoengsao then this book will be missing the old province, a popular city that Thai people like to visit and very close to Bangkok, only 45 kilometers away from Bangkok's border. Chachoengsao is a province in the eastern part of Thailand. It borders with Bangkok, Pathum Thani, Nakhon Nayok, Prachin Buri, Sa Kaeo, Chanthaburi, Chon Buri, and Samut Prakan.

It has a territory only 12 km from the Gulf of Thailand. The destination for the Thai Buddists from all over the country is **Wat Sothon Wararam Worawihan; which** is a temple where many people come to pray for blessings. Therefore, during the holidays, Saturday - Sunday and public holidays will be crowded with people throughout the day. If one is successful in making a wish; the words are often vowed with boiled eggs or dance dramas, they will come here for paying homage to Luang Por Sothon with things they vowed, boiled eggs are very popular. It is seen normally that people carry a basket of boiled eggs in this temple. **Luang Por Sothon (see photo, the statue on right hand side)** is probably enshrined at Wat Sothon since the beginning of Ayutthaya, in the reign of King Borom Rachathirat II (Chao Sam Phraya) which more than 500-600 years ago, it was a sandstone Buddha image sculpted in the early Ayutthaya art, seated on a four-tiered Buddhist throne, lined with nectar cloth. Therefore; it is assumed that Wat Sothon and Luang Por Sothon should have been located in this area of Ban Sothon for a long time and have undergone renovations in a later period. Originally, this temple was called Sothon. According to the name of Khlong Sothon for a long time. You can look around the Chachoengsao Town for other attractions such as; **Wat Hua Suan** is another place to visit the beautiful stainless Ubosoth, considered one of the Unseen temples. **Saman Rattanaram Temple,** enshrined the largest reclining Phra Pikkanet God image (Ganesha; God of art and success) in Thailand, located on the Bang Pakong River.

Hundred Years House Market or Talad Ban Mai, is another tourist destination where you can touch a classic and old antique market. It is an old market that is over 100 years old, offering a wide variety of delicious food and desserts including the great products of Chachoengsao as well. The province is not so far from the two airports. I love Wat Sothon and the market.

CHONBURI AND SATTAHEEP

Chonburi Province is not known as much as "Pattaya City", although Pattaya is a district belongs to Chonburi. The province was a land that appeared in the history since the Dvaravati, Khmer and Sukhothai periods, but originally it was just an agricultural city with several small fishing communities scattered around this city. It was quite far away from the royal palace of the Ayutthaya period, then Chonburi was designated as a quarter-tier city that time. As Even if it's just a small town but it is rich in resources both on land and in the sea. There has been farming, gardening and fishing since the ancient time. In the past, it's the town where The Chinese came by junk for trading with Siam.

Chonburi Province was the town where people lived since prehistoric times. In 1979, an excavation was conducted at Phanom Di Subdistrict in Phanat Nikhom District; which found the evidences of the ancient prehistoric. The Khok Phanom Dee community could make its assumption that; it was the territory of the 3 prosperous ancient cities namely; Muang Phrarot, Muang Sri Phalo, and Mueang Phaya Rae which were the location of the present Chonburi Province within an area of 4,363 square kilometers. The Neighboring provinces are Chachoengsao, Rayong, Chanthaburi and the Gulf of Thailand. It is now a province at the east coast of Thailand where it's the location of **Laem Chabang Sea Port**; a very important sea port of the east. You can visit here by road, takes about 80 kilometers from Bangkok or about 40 kilometers from Pattaya.

Travelling to Chonburi is normally by car/taxi (takes about 1 hour from the airport, by rail; get off at Chonburi City, by bus; at the Suwannaphum Airport, and by plane to **U-Tapao Airport**.

There are many attractions in Chonburi to visit:

Khao Chi Chan is where The Laser Buddha Mountain image on the cliff built to honor His Majesty King Bhumibol on the occasion of his Golden Jubilee. The place is at Na Chom Thian in Sattaheep district.

Sattaheep District is the Thai Naval Base location in Chonburi Province. It's about 80 kilometers from Chonburi downtown and 30 Kilometers from Pattaya. Please confirm the taxi driver if you supposed to go to Sattaheep not Pattaya, because the fare is very much different.

Many tourist attractions are found in Sattaheep like, the beautiful islands in Sattaheep Bay. If you would like to relax in a peaceful place and swim in a crystal-clear water then stay here because it's not so far from U-Tapao Airport.

Sattaheep Beaches are where there are many interesting places and sea sports like, scuba diving, snorkeling, kayaking, banana boat from these popular islands and beaches such as, **Ko Kham**; a beautiful island with coral range, it's a nice point for snorkeling. You can take a boat to the island at Khao Ma Jor Pier. **Ko Samaesan** is the Thai Island and Sea Nature History Museum. It's nice for diving here. There are so many white sand beaches you can explore; never get tired for exploring when the nature of sea, sand, sun and a good company with you, will make your days terrific in Sattaheep.

Explore the beaches at Sattaheep:

- ❑ Bang Saleh Boathouse.
- ❑ Diving Points at Sattaheep;
- ❑ Sai Keaw Beach,
- ❑ Toey Ngam Beach,
- ❑ Kret Keaw Beach,
- ❑ Nang Rong Beach,
- ❑ Nang Rum Beach,
- ❑ Nam Sai Beach,
- ❑ Bang Sa leh Beach,
- ❑ Sau Beach,
- ❑ Sattaheep Beach,
- ❑ Dong Tan Bay,
- ❑ Ban Ampher Beach and never forget to admire the beautiful viewpoint at Luang Por Dam Temple.
- ❑ **Discover HTMS Chakri Naruebet**; this ship is the smallest functioning aircraft carrier in the world.

- Explore **Nong Nooch Garden Pattaya**; the large tropical garden; about 1700 rais where contained of many botanical gardens and some other things for entertainment.

According to the Sriracha News Center - It was from the case that the Marine Department carried out a project to add sand to the beach in Pattaya, to solve the problem of long-term sea erosion before the beach conditions disappear and also to promote tourism in the future. The project was extended to the **Jomtien beach area and Na Chom Thian beach** as the goal of expanding the beach to be 50-meter-wide; the beaches are occupying the area of 2 local government organizations namely; Pattaya City and Na Jomtien Municipality in a total distance of 3.5 kilometers.

- **Khao Kheow Open Zoo** is located at Bang Phra Subdistrict in Sri Racha District. It is a large open zoo in Chonburi Province; located at the foot of the green hill About 25 kilometers from the city of Sriracha, it is the only forest in Chonburi province. The area of the zoo is more than 5,000 rai, established in 1978 by reviving the deteriorated Khao Khiao forest. There are more than 300 species of animals to see, most of which are located in a spacious area that provides natural conditions that are suitable for the character of animals and allow tourists to walk closely.
- **Bangsean Beach** has always been a paradise for Thai tourists since the past till now. The Thai tourists love to go with family during weekend for lying on the deck chairs for enjoying the beach and seafood.

Bangsaen Beach has a 6 km long beach and very crowded because it's near Bangkok. There's a road that cuts along the beach and lined with restaurants, shops and accommodation all the way. The beach is full of deck chairs for relaxing on the beach under the shade of coconut trees which is suitable for sitting and lying down, eating seafood, grilled chicken, papaya salad, enjoying the breeze, watching the sea view until sunset; I was here once till dawn with a group of friends when I was teenager. Bangsaen beach on holidays is bustling with Thai tourists but not many foreigners. It is a beach where you can swim; with the sand gradually slopes, not dangerous, the water is not so clear but with brown fine sand due to sediment from the mouth of the Bang Pakong River. If compared to Pattaya, Pattaya Beach will be more beautiful than Bangsaen. But during low tide, many crabs and wind crabs can be seen at Bangsaen Beach. Bangsaen Beach activities are like; swim in the sea and there are swimming tubs are available for rent at the beach, banana boats, bicycle for rent, and jetski. It takes about an hour ride from the airport to Bangsaen beach, which is about 100kms, have a nice view and seafood.

PATTAYA CITY

Pattaya City is in Banglamung District of Chonburi but it's considered as special town where the city is self-governing municipal area covers the north, center, south Pattaya Beaches and Jom Tien Beach. It's about 120 kilometers from Bangkok to the east coastal areas of the Gulf of Thailand. You will have fun and enjoy in Pattaya without boredom because Pattaya is the city known among tourists that "No more loneliness". When you reach Pattaya, there's no doubt, for touring **Ko Lan;** the Coral Island, and experience one-night camping in this small island; it's off the coast of Pattaya, in the Gulf of Thailand with clear water and nice atmosphere. Many of the water sport activities are available here.

You will never reach Pattaya if you miss the walking street and red-light district areas in the Pattaya City after sunset, it's really a fantastic night-walk and don't miss the **cabaret shows by "men in women" which is** the best-known shows since the past. I enjoyed everywhere in Pattaya and always had a great time here; although the road was not in good condition like nowadays, I loved to drive here and took my clients to see Pattaya even only one day trip. Pattaya is a wonderful entertainment city where you should not miss.

Right now; the beautiful artwork of **The Sanctuary of Truth** or **Prasart Satchatham building is seemed to be hit among all tourists**; it's the group of wood carving buildings built in the ancient Thai architecture style located by the sea. The architectural style of the Sanctuary of Truth was built in a tetrahedron (Jaturamuk as Maha Viharn), using the hardwood type like teak, Takhianthong, and red woods for the buildings that has 170 pillars which decorated with a roof in the shape of a junk boat; of 100 meters wide, 100 meters long, and 100 meters high. Inside the Viharn, contained of the wood carving sculpture with philosophical content, simulation of important figures.

The Sanctuary of Truth is the largest wooden castle in Thailand located at Laem Ratchawet at Na Kluea Subdistrict, made by Mr. Lek Wiriyaphan, a businessman who loved Thai architecture and Buddhism. He was also the owner of the Erawan Museum and the Ancient City. The villagers call this castle generally "ancient palace" or "wood castle". Inside the castle has hidden philosophical content and cultural art which is the human heritage reflects the importance of religion which is a support for the world.

- **Jomtien Beach** with a new look make you feel like you're in Miami Beach, no canvas beds but enjoy more along with street food for tourists to choose. Making many people want to visit, 4 kms from the south Pattaya.
- **The Suan Suea or Tiger Park Pattaya** at Banglamoong is lovely for getting closer to tigers and photos with them. If you miss a floating market trip in Bangkok, you can experience the Sampan Boat for looking around at **The Four -Region Floating Market in Pattaya**; it's the simulation of the traditional floating market and the Thai life styles from the four regions of Thailand; like, culture shows, houses, shops, food and local products of the regions.

THE TOP 29 ISLANDS IN THAILAND

"ISLAND" IS CALLED "KO" OR "KOH" IN THAI; for example, we call Ko Phuket, Ko Samui etc. Thailand is one of the Southeast Asia countries on the mainland of Indochina Peninsula. The country connects The Gulf of Thailand at the south and The Andaman Sea at the west. The total length of Thai coast is 3,148 kilometers. There are many beautiful beaches and islands for exploring in Thailand. The best time to tour at Andaman coast; Phuket, Krabi, Satoon, Ranong, Trang and Phang Nga, is in Jan-Apr or Nov-Dec. The good time for the south sea by the Gulf of Thailand coast; Suratthani, Chumpon, Nakonsithammarat, Songkla, Pattani, Narathiwat and Pattalung, is about Apr-Oct. The best time for tours at the eastern and western coast of the Gulf of Thailand; Trat, Chonburi, Rayong, Pattaya, Chantaburi, Prachup, Hua Hin, and Cha Am is about in Jan-Apr and Nov-Dec.

1. PHUKET

Phuket is the biggest island in Thailand located in Andaman Sea, travel about 900 kilometers from Bangkok. There are 39 islands of Phuket Province. It was assumed found since 2nd Century from the archaeological evidences such as ancient tools and weapons showing that there's humans lived at least for 3000 years ago. Mr. Claudius Ptolemy; a navigator mentioned in his records about this land; it's the long cape, called Takola Cape, from Phan Gna Province, but due to the movement of the fault of a large crust known as Klong Marui Fault; which stretches from Surathani and Phang Nga down to the east of Phuket.

The wind waves eroded the soil land to the sea and cut the Takola Cape from the mainland to become a narrow channel between Phuket and Phang Nga. It's called Pak Phra Straits; where the deepest part of the sea here is 8-9 meters nowadays.

Phuket is called from the foreigners and ancient people in the past; as Takola, Jungceylon, Manikram, Phuket, Thalang and Thung Kha.

Phuket is the center destination of Andaman Sea for tourists from all over the world. There are many hotels, resorts, guest houses, houses for rent with facilities. All water sports are available almost everywhere in Phuket; scuba diving, snorkeling, swimming, fishing, surfing and nature trails. There are about 39 islands belong to the Phuket Island Groups such as; Ko Racha Yai, Ko Hey, Ko Kaew, Ko Bon, Ko Ma Prow, Ko Rang Yai, Ko Rang Noi and Ko Mai Ton; which are also tourist attractions during visiting Phuket Province.

Travel to Phuket can be done by plane, rail and road. The government has planned to make Phuket as "The World Tourism Hub" by including modern of International Health/Medical Plaza, Premium Long - Term Care, Hospice Homes, and a Rehabilitation Center.

2. KO SAMUI

The island was known since Ayutthaya period. It's now a district belongs to Suratthani Province, locates in the Gulf of Thailand by the east, away from Suratthani about 84 kms, but from Donsak Pier about 27 kms. It connects Ko Phagnan at the north, the Gulf of Thailand at the east, the sea at Khanom District at the south and Donsak at the west. Travel by plane, by road and continue with ferry at Donsak Pier, express boat and night boat from Ban Don takes about 7-8 hours.

3. PHA GNAN

It's a district belongs to Suratthani Province, away from Suratthani about 100 kilometers. King Rama V visited the island and gave names for the waterfalls here; Tharnsadet, Tharnprapas and Pravej Waterfalls since 1888. It is a beautiful island at the southwest of Thailand, well known for Full Moon Party at Rin Beach.

4. KO TAO

The island was named "Tao"; which means "Turtle", because there were many turtles found in this island. Ko Tao was an abandoned island and it's a prison for political prisoners in the past. It was opened and allowed residents in 1947. The island is unique beautiful beaches and crystal-clear sea water. It's known among tourists for scuba diving points; which are Kong Hin Chumpon, Hinbai and Kong Hin Toongku, belongs to Suratthani and is about 45 Kms. from Pha Gnan Island. Travel here can be done by planes, trains, buses, and cars to Suratthani and connect ferry boats here.

5. KO NANG YUAN

Ko Nang Yuan is about 500 meters next to Ko Tao. You can go from Ko Tao by speed boat. There are three small islands connected by sand beaches when the sea opens, it's where you can walk among the islands of Ko Nang Yuan. It's a nice island for snorkeling.

6. ANGTHONG

The Angthong Islands or Mu Ko Angthong are groups of islands of Angthong National Marine Park of Thailand. It belongs to Suratthani; away from Ko Samui and Pha Gnan about 20 Kms. The islands are about 42 islands which are mostly lime stone hills with 10-400-meter-high and formed in different shapes to become caves and cliffs. Travel to the **Angthong Islands** by ferry boats at Nathon and Bophut Piers in Ko Samui. You can stay at Ko Wuo Talab, one of the Angthong Islands or connect the National Park Office for accommodation. **Activities at Mu Ko Angthong**; Nature walkway, Cave/geological studies, Plant viewing, Boat trip, Boating, and Snorkeling from December 16 to October 30 of every year. There are important islands such as Koh Phaluai, Koh Wua Jiw, Koh Wua Ta Lap, Koh Mae Ko, Koh Sam Sao, Koh Phai Luak, Koh Kha, Koh Hin Dub, Koh Phi, Koh Wua Kantang, Koh Pa Yat, Koh Wua Te, Koh Nai Phut, Koh Chang Shabby, Koh Hanuman, Koh Tai. Plao, Koh Hua Klong and Koh Khon Ban, etc. The condition of most of the islands is limestone hills.

7. KO PHALUAI

The island belongs to the Group of the Angthong Islands. It's known as a "Virgin" island with green energy where you can still touch the nature with clean surroundings and fresh air. Travel here by fisherman boats at Donsak, Suratthani and can stay at homestay here.

8. TAPU OR JAMES BOND ISLAND

"Tapu" means "Metal Spike" was the name called the island; which is a tall islet, locates near Khao Phing Kan; the limestone karst islands of the Ao Phang Nga National Park in Phang Gna Province. It's famous from Jame Bond Movie in 1974; "The Man with the Golden Gun" series, and becomes the landmark of Phang Nga province which seems to be well known all over the world. Travel here from the tour boats at Surakul Pier.

9. LANTA ISLANDS NATIONAL PARK

Lanta islands is a big group of islands and become a district of Krabi Province; consist of many islands, but the biggest is Ko Lanta Yai; where many people live, the rest which are attractions; such as, Ko Rok Nai, Ko Rok Nok, Ko Ta La Beng and Ko Gnai. The fishermen villages have been living here and keeping old traditions for more than hundred years. Travel here from Bangkok are by planes, buses, cars and connect boats to the island at Chao Fa and Saladan Piers about 2 hrs. Let's see dolphins swim during cool season; January-February!

10. PHI PHI DON & PHI PHI LEY

Phi Phi Islands are part of Had Nopparath Thara National Park; the distance is about 40 kms from Krabi Province. The island was called by locals "Pulao Phiarphi" which means the kind of sea plants and finally called Phi Phi. The groups of islands are Phi Phi Don, Phi Phi Ley and some small islands. The big ones are Phi Phi Don and Ley. The Phi Phi Don Island is a large center with many hotels, resorts with fully facilities and picturesque white sand beaches. It's great for scuba diving and swimming.

11. KO HONG ISLAND IN KRABI PROVINCE

Ko Hong or called as Ko Lao Bireh locates in the Tharn Bok Khoranee National Park; consist of many islands. The beautiful beaches here are curved bay with lime stone hill and a nature trail on the island. Travel here at Thab Kaek Resort.

12. KO HONG IN PHANG GNA PROVINCE

Ko Hong is a large island and can pass through its caves or tidal lagoon which is about 2-10-meter-wide and 150-meter depth. It locates in Ao Phang Gna National Marine Park. Most of tourists explore by kayaking through its caves during an appropriate level of tides. Please always check. Ko Hong is near Pan Yi, Ta Poo Islands. Travel from Tah Dan Pier in **Ta Kua Thung District.**

13. KO KRADAN

Ko Kradan has the most beautiful beach in Trang province. The island is about 10 Kms. from the southeast coast of Thailand. The main parts of island belong to Hat Chao Mai National Marine Park, with 2 Kms. Long beach. The island is very well known to the world-famous underwater weddings, which is held during February every year. It was recorded in the Guinness Book of World Records as the largest underwater wedding in the world. Travel here by a boat from Pak Meng Pier about 30 minutes.

14. KO PAN YI

Ko Pan Yi was found about 200 years ago by Indonesian. It's known as the amazing fishermen Village in the sea; about 200 homes, of Phang Nga Province. The island has been very popular and nice to explore. It's mostly for lunch stop for package tours. One of the major attractions is an amazing football field on the sea here. Travel here by a boat at Thadan Sullakakon Pier.

15. KO SIMILAN

"Similan" means "Nine", the islands are 9 islands in Similan Islands Group of National Marine Park in Phang Gna.It's about 70 kms.from Thablamu Pier in Phan Gna and 90 kms. from the pier of Patong beach in Phuket. It's called as "Heaven of Andaman Sea" where there are many corals, rare fish. The best time to come here is in Nov-Apr.

16. KO SURIN ISLANDS

Ko Surin Islands are Surin Islands National Marine Park in Phang Nga Province. It borders Myanmar in Andaman Sea and away from the western coast about 70 Kilometers. Ko Surin Group is 5 islands and has a stunning seaview with coral reefs, forests and white sand beaches. Travel here from Kuraburi Pier about 1.5 hours. You can do "One day trip" or stay overnight at Ao Chong Kard" of Ko Surin Nua.

urin Island

17. KO KAI

Ko Kai is one of 4 island trips for tourist attractions; Ko Porda, Ko Thub, Ko Mor and Ko Kai. “Kai” means “Hen”; some said it looks like hen’s head. The tourists swim and enjoy at Porda Island where there are resorts and great white sand beach. The four islands are popular in the sea of Krabi.

18. KO PHAYAM

Ko Phayam is a beautiful island in Ranong Province which is about 600 kms from Bangkok. Travel to Ranong can be done by buses, cars, rails and by planes. You can ride the boat from Paknam Pier to Ko Phayam. It’s the island with a wide beach. There are bungalows and resorts around the island.

19. KO LI PE

Start your trip at Pakbara Pier in Satoon Province for about 67 kms to Ko Li Pe. The island is near the border to Malaysia. It's a part of Talutao National Marine Park. It's famous for scuba diving and beautiful white sand beach. You can also enjoy Walking Street here. The popular beach is called Pattaya Beach where you can find many hotels, restaurant and Walking Street in the late afternoon. Travel to Ko Li Pe with exploring other interesting small islands along the way like; Ko Khai, Ko Hin Gnam, snorkeling at Jabang Point to see corals, Ko Ravee for enjoying the clear water, Ko Phueng, and also can snorkeling at Ko Hinson.

20. KO TALUTAO

Ko Talutao was the prison in 1936 for serious prisoners. It's the biggest island of Talutao National Marine Park; there are 51 islands grouped in Andaman Sea, locates in Satoon Province near Langkawi Island of Malaysia. Travel here by a boat from Pakbara Pier in Satoon. The activities are: Nature Trail, Hiking Trail, Waterfall, Cave Tour/Geological Study, History/Culture, Plant View, Bird Watching/Butterfly Watching/Animal Watching, Mountain Bike, Boating, Snorkeling, and scuba diving. Open tourist season from November 16 - May 15 of every year.

21. KO CHANG

Ko Chang **is in Trat province; it's** the largest island in The Gulf of Thailand and the 2nd largest island; next from Phuket. "Chang" means Elephant. The island named from its size because normally Thai compares big things or places to elephant, the huge animal.

Ko Chang is full of resorts and hotels which are more comfortable than other islands but you can also have time to explore many beautiful islands around; Trat is called "The province of Islands"; there are 66 islands here.

Ferry-Piers to Ko Chang are at Ao Thammachart Pier and Center Point Pier at Laem Ngop. It takes about 45 minutes to one-hour ride but you can enjoy nice view from the deck.

22. KO KUT

The island is 4th largest in Thailand and located at the end of the eastern sea in Trat. You can travel from Laem Sork Pier in Trat or planes to Soneva Kiri Airport or Ko Mai Si from Suwannaphum Airport. The best time for this island is in Oct-May.

**The minibus for Trat to Ko Kut is available at Suwannaphum International Airport at the 1st floor, gate no. 8, the fare of the trip includes ferry trip to the island.

You can enjoy all islands during staying somewhere in Trat but recommend for snorkelling around the coral reefs at **Ko Koot** in cystal clear sea water and enjoy beautiful natural creations. There are resorts and hotels in Ko Kut for anyone who prefers peace and less crowded than Ko Chang.

23. KO MAK

Ko Mak is an island locates between Ko Chang and Ko Kut. It's about 39 kilometers from the shore; having the length of beach about 27 kilometers. There are coral reefs found perfectly in the island area. Many hotels, a temple, market and a health center are here. You can also walk to Ko Kham from here. Koh Mak has been under the development by the Tourism Authority of Thailand and DASTA; the Special Area Development Administration for Sustainable Tourism, to be a low-carbon destination. The activities in Ko Mak are mainly cycling, kayaking, and sailing. It's a good place for family tourists to enjoy the richness of nature.

24. KO LAN

Ko Lan is a popular island for those who visit **Pattaya City in Chonburi** Province. It's only 7.5 kms from Pattaya beach, located in the Gulf of Thailand, having Ko Sak and Ko Krok is in group of islands. Ko Lan was originally a subdistrict and inhabitaed for a long time by farming and fishing before; but because of being robbed by the pirates and Cholera disease during the World War II and in addition to inconvenient transportation here; therefore, Ko Lan was dissolved and merged to Nakrua Subdistrict and become part of Pattaya City in 1978. You can come here by speed boat or ferry boat at Laem Balihay Pier (7 am-18.00pm). If you prefer to stay here, the accommodations are available. People enjoy Ko Lan at Ta Waen Beach, Sang wan Beach, Thong Lang Beach, Ta Yai Beach, Samae Beach, Tien Beach, Nuan Beach, Khao Nom View Point and Kang Han Lom View Point.

25. KO KHAM

This is an island of crystal-clear water and a white sand beach which is well known for Underwater Park; a beautiful sea of Sattaheep in Chonburi Province. It's popular beach and sea near Bangkok. (2 hours by car)

26. KO SAMAE SAN

The island is for one day trip in Sattaheep. There are activities, such as, snorkeling, kayaking, biking and walking along nature trail. The last boat for return to the land is at 16.00 PM.

27. KO SAMET

The island is upper part of the gulf of Thailand, locates at Ban Phe in Rayong Province. The area of island is full of jungle and mountains. There are many beautiful bays and beaches with hotels and resorts in the island.

28. KO THALU

Ko Thalu is a big island in Bang Saphan Noi District Prachuap Khiri Khan Province. This area is caused by erosion of waves and winds for a long time, causing a hole to penetrate able to walk through but most of the beaches are rocky beaches. It is a place of snorkeling in shallow water. The northern tip of the island has a red sheer cliff with a large hole that can penetrate to the other side, hence; to be named as "Koh Talu". The island has beautiful beaches, clear waters, white sandy beaches besides; around the island have many complete and beautiful coral reefs. The water is so clear that you can see it with the naked eye. Ko Thalu is the first sea for snorkeling before going to the south. It's a wonderful island of the Gulf of Thailand, the distance from Bangkok to Prachub Khiri Khan is about 400 kms. Travel to the island from Had Laem Son Pier for 30 minutes by speed boat.

29. KO LANKA JEW

Ko Lanka Jew is a bird's nest concession island, part of Mu Ko Chumporn National Marine Park in Chumporn Province. The coastal coral reefs appearing on the western side of the island are still in very good condition. It's a restricted area but you can visit for day trip 8.00-17.00.

The Southern region is a region located on the Malay Peninsula flanked by the Gulf of Thailand on the east coast and the Andaman Sea on the west coast It has a total area of 70,715 square kilometers. The length from north to south is about 750 kilometers. All provinces of the region have coastal areas except Yala and Phatthalung provinces. The southern region is a tropical monsoon climate where the terrain of the south looks like a long peninsula with the sea flanking both the western and the eastern side, this makes it rain all year round and is the region with the most rainfall. The southern provinces are mainly full of attractions like islands, beaches, and many old temples. The highest temperature was in Trang Province at 39.7 degrees Celsius and the lowest temperature was in Chumphon Province of 12.12 degrees Celsius.

SAMPLE ITINERARY IN BANGKOK

First Day

9.00 Wat Trimit then go to Wat Pho

12.00 Lunch at Tha Maharaj

13.00 The Grand Palace and Wat Phrakaew

15.00 Ride an Express Boat to Wat Arun

18.00 Back to Tha Phra Chan for dinner

20.00 Go to nightlife at Khaosan Road

Second Day

7.00 Damnoen Saduak Floating Market

13.00 Nakonpathom for The large Pagoda and Sanam Chan Palace

19.00 Dinner Cruise at the River City

Third Day

9.00 The Marble Temple and Ratchadamnoen Avenue for Wat Inthraram, Wat Saket, Wat Ratchanaddaram

12.00 Lunch near the Giant Swing areas

13.00 Admire Wat Suthat near the Giant Swing, if you stay here until sunset, you can have a nice dinner along Mahachai Road for Pad Thai at Thip Samai or Crab meat stuffed with eggs at Jay Phai's. Or go to Siam Square (at BTS Siam Station) for snacks and visit Lumpini Park, then have a streetfood on Silom and see Patpong.

Fourth Day

8.00 Kanchanaburi or Ayutthaya for one day trip

Relax nearby hotel

Fifth Day

9.00 Sathon Pier and have a boat ride for Talat Noi, Flower Market, Wat Rakang, Kudichin Community and Wat Kalayanamit and hop on the boat to Nonthaburi

13.00 Lunch at Nonthaburi Pier and walk around to see the former Nonthaburi Provincial Hall

14.00 Explore Ko Kret

18.00 Have a dinner at one of a restaurant near the Impact Muang Thong Thani or Soi Chaeng Wattana 37 of Pakkret Road; nearby Sukhothai Thammathirat University areas. (Many of international restaurants)

20.00 Night life at a rooftop bar at Sathon Road

Sixth Day

9.00 Bangkok Museum and go to Victory Monument

12.00 Lunch at Or Tor Kor Market (if it's Sat-Sun, you can go to Jatujak Market) or go to Pratunam Market

18.00 You can go to have a dinner at The Central Ladprow Department Store which is close to Jatujak or if going to Pratunam market then go to the Central World to see Ratchaprasong Intersection or Chidlom.

What is your Itinerary in Bangkok?

ABOUT AUTHOR

Name: Varani Bumrungluck
Born: 4th Jan, 1958 in Thailand
A.B. English from Far Eastern University
Tourist Guide License No. 11-76006 since 1985
Award: Best Sales Manager Award of Toyota's Dealer received from Toyota Motor (Thailand) Co., Ltd. in 2006.

The travel guide book **"WELCOME TO BANGKOK, Krungthep Mahanakorn"** is a guidebook/handbook for traveling to Bangkok and its vicinity as well as my experiences with my clients to be as your guidelines. I have also added 29 islands in Thailand for your information in case you have a plan for a long vacation. I have released the first book, "Top Bucket Lists Thailand", which is a summary of the central provinces and northern regions such as Chiang Mai, Chiang Rai and various islands to provide suitable information for tourists so that you can prepare for the long weekend or for ticking a place you might not want to miss.

I would like to thank you for your support of all the books that I have released under my pen name Supennee K.B. and Penny V.B., such as; sales planners, diaries, children's books, and low content books. Please feel free to comment or give me advice through my email address. Or if you need some advice for your trip, I'm also pleased to do.

Khob Khun Kha.

varaniweb@gmail.com
http://www.facebook.com/varani.bumrungluck